Geo. E. Spencer

**Report of the Joint Committee of the General Assembly of Alabama**

In Regard to the Alleged Election of Geo. E. Spencer

Geo. E. Spencer

**Report of the Joint Committee of the General Assembly of Alabama**
*In Regard to the Alleged Election of Geo. E. Spencer*

ISBN/EAN: 9783337163242

Printed in Europe, USA, Canada, Australia, Japan

Cover: Foto ©Suzi / pixelio.de

More available books at **www.hansebooks.com**

# REPORT

OF THE

# JOINT COMMITTEE

OF THE

## GENERAL ASSEMBLY OF ALABAMA,

IN REGARD TO THE ALLEGED

## ELECTION OF GEO. E. SPENCER,

### AS U. S. SENATOR,

TOGETHER WITH

## MEMORIAL AND EVIDENCE.

MONTGOMERY, ALA.:
W. W. SCREWS, STATE PRINTER.

1875.

# REPORT.

*To the General Assembly of Alabama:*

The Joint Committee to whom was referred an inquiry into the facts relating to the alleged election of George E. Spencer as a Senator of the United States from Alabama, and the means by which such election was procured and his credentials as a Senator were obtained, respectfully submit the following report. A statement of the proceedings of the committee, and the depositions of all the witnesses who were examined by the committee are herewith submitted:

The committee, through its chairman, informed Mr. Spencer by letter and by telegraph of the time and place of the opening of the investigation, and invited him to attend in person or by his agents. He did not see proper to avail himself of the opportunity.

The resolutions of the General Assembly of Alabama, under which your committee was required to act are as follows:

"WHEREAS, in the opinion of the General Assembly of Alabama, Hon. George E. Spencer does not rightfully occupy a seat in the Senate of the United States, as a Senator from Alabama.

*Be it resolved by the House of Representatives,* (the Senate concurring,) that a joint committee to consist of two Senators and three members of the House of Representatives, be appointed to investigate, examine and report to the two Houses of the General Assembly the facts relating to his alleged election as Senator, and the means by which such election was procured, and his credentials as a Senator were obtained.

*Resolved 2.* That said committee, or a majority of them, may sit during the session of the General Assembly and during the recess at any place in this State, and shall have authority to send for persons and papers, and to call witnesses before them to be examined on oath, and to employ a clerk to keep the record and proceeding of the committee.

*Resolved 3.* That said committee report with all convenient speed a memoral to be addressed by the General Assembly to the Senate of the United States touching the claims of George E. Spencer to a seat in that body as a Senator from Alabama, and shall report to the two Houses ₁the evidence taken under these resolutions.

The first branch of the inquiry submitted to the committee, as to the facts relating to his alleged election, is answered by the records of the proceedings of the two bodies which met in Montgomery on the 18th November, 1872, one at the capitol and the other at the United States court room, each claiming to be the General Assembly of Alabama. Said proceedings appear in the Journals of the Senate and House of Representatives of the General Assembly of Alabama of the session of November, 1873.

Your committee does not consider it necessary to review the action of said bodies further than the same relates to other matters, disclosed in the evidence herewith submitted.

The Senate of the United States has voted upon two propositions in connection with the alleged right of Mr. Spencer to a seat in that body.

1st. That a certificate of election issued to him by the Governor of Alabama, under the great seal of the State, conformably to the requirements of the laws of the United States, entitled him *prima facie* to a seat in the Senate, but that this right is subject to be contested.

2d. That Mr. F. W. Sykes was not duly elected to the seat in the Senate thus held by Mr. Spencer.

Your committee does not deem it necessary at this time to question the decisions resulting from these votes, in order to ascertain the merits of Mr. Spencer's claim to a seat in the Senate, but it is respectfully insisted that, under the constitution and laws of Alabama, a lawful general assembly consists, in the first instance, of those who hold certificates of election issued by the Secretary of State, upon returns made to him by the county and district supervisors of elections, as the case may be.

It certainly is true in our American system of State governments, each acting under the powers asserted by it in its own constitution, and conceded to it by its sister States, and by the Federal government, that when a house of a legislature, admitted to be a lawful body, has made a decision that is final as to its membership, the Senate of the United States cannot reverse or disregard that decision. The report of the majority of the committee on privileges and elections of the Senate of the United States in Mr. Sykes' case is conclusive on this point.

That committee say: "In the opinion of your committee it is not competent for the Senate to inquire as to the right of individual members to sit in a legislature which is conceded to have a quorum, in both houses, of legally elected members." Any final decision made by the respective houses of the consolidated legislature, as to the election of persons claiming seats therein, and if made in accordance with law, must be taken as final and conclusive on every other tribunal. The question submitted to the Senate of the United States by the report of the majority of said committee, is thus stated by it : "That Mr. Sykes makes no case entitling him to the seat now occupied by Mr. Spencer."

The minority of the committee submitted with their report the following resolution :

*Resolved*, That Francis W. Sykes, having been duly and legally elected a Senator from the State of Alabama for the constitutional term commencing March 4th, 1873, is entitled to the seat in this body now held by the Hon. George E. Spencer."

In the Senate of the United States the contest was alone between Mr. Sykes and Mr. Spencer. Both reports relate to the right of Mr. Sykes to a seat in the Senate, and the action of the Senate, following this question, only decided that Mr. Spencer's right, on his mere credentials was better than Mr. Sykes' right to the seat. This decision is not irrevocable, but, treating it as such for the present, it does not cover the question now presented by the States. As between the people of the State of Alabama, the real constituent, and Mr. Spencer, the incumbent of the office of Senator, *it is still an open question whether he is rightfully and lawfully entitled to that office.* The Senate has only decided that, *prima facie*, he is entitled to occupy by the seat, because no one has appeared and asserted a claim to the seat he holds who has a better right to it.

In the opinion of your committee, the General Assembly of Alabama should ask the Senate of the United States to reconsider some of the grounds apparently taken in the vote by which the resolution accompanying the report of the majority of the Committee on Privileges and Elections in the Sykes-Spencer contest was adopted; and especially that part of the report which seems to assert the proposition that the Senate can rightfully assume that certain individuals, who hold certificates of election, are not members of the houses of the General Assembly, because they were not elected, without an opportunity having been afforded to them, either by the Senate of the United States or by the houses to which they were accredited, to establish the fact of their election.

In arriving at the conclusion that Mr. Sykes was not entitled to the seat occupied by Mr. Spencer, the committee of the U. S. Senate deny that a Legeslature can be lawfully composed of persons holding certificates of election, unless a quorum is present in each house, of persons actually elected, and rest the legality of the body that elected Mr. Spencer upon the fact, as asserted, *that in each house there was a quorum of members actually elected by the people, at the time of his election.*

In their report the committee say, "Therefore, in determining as to the right of Spencer or Sykes to this seat, the Senate is compelled to choose between the body in fact elected, organized, acting and recognized by the executive department as the Legislature, and another body, organized in form, but without election, and without a recognition on the part of the executive of the State at the time they pretended to elect Sykes."

That committee further say: " *The persons in the two bodies, claiming to be the Senate and House of Representatives, who voted for Spencer, constituted a quorum of both houses of the members actually elected.*" It is also stated in the report that these matters were conceded as facts on the Sykes-Spencer contest. They are not facts, and the State has never conceded them. The committee in its report does not deal with them as ascertained facts. The committee states the number of persons in the two houses that elected Spencer who were actually elected, but who had no certificates of election, at the uncertain number of *eight* or *nine*. On the theory of the majority of that committee, it required *nine such persons* to complete a quorum—six in the House and three in the Senate. There were only two Senators who were afterwards declared elected, (Messrs. Dereen and Black,) who were seated in the Court-house Senate without certificates of election. If it was not true, then, that the persons who voted for Spencer constituted a quorum of both houses of the members " *actually elected*," Spencer was not elected by a lawful body, according to the principle stated by the committee of the Senate.

Your committee assert that there was not such a quorum in the Senate at the United States Court-rooms when Mr. Spencer was voted for. Nineteen persons were present in said Senate, and all voted for Mr. Spencer. Of these, three were not, in fact, elected, to-wit: BAKER, CHISHOLM, and MILLER.

Neither did either of these persons hold certificates of election. So that, of the persons actually elected to the Senate of Alabama, or holding certificates of election, only sixteen were present when said pretended election took place.

Baker and Chisholm were not recognized in the reorganization of the Legislature under the plan of the Attorney General of the United States, as having ever been members of the Senate.

They never attempted to assert a right to a seat in the reorganized Senate, and there is nothing in the archives of the State to show that they had ever been elected. From the beginning their election was not seriously asserted by any person. Several witnesses testify that they were brought to Montgomery for the purpose of occupying seats to which all knew they had no just claim, Chisholm being relieved from duty in the custom house for the occasion, and Baker paid for his services.

At the time of Mr. Spencer's alleged election, Mr. Martin of the senatorial district composed of the counties of Butler and Conecuh, and part of Escambia, held a certificate of election issued by the Secretary of State, and was seated in the Senate at the Capitol. Mr. Miller claiming to be Senator from the same district, but having no certificate of election, was seated in the Senate at the Court-house—his presence there being necessary to a quorum of members in that body. No contest had then been instituted by Mr. Miller. Upon the reorganization of the Legislature under the plan of the Attorney General, Mr. Miller did contest Mr. Martin's seat, and the ultimate decision of that contest by the Senate of the State settles finally the question as to which of the claimants was *actually elected* from that district to the Senate of the State.

It will be seen from an examination of the proceedings of the Senate in that matter, that Mr. Martin held the certificate of election, duly issued according to law, and that he was also actually elected to the office. The reports of the majority and minority of the committee show this fact in the most unquestionable way.

Since the entire question of the legality of the body that elected Mr. Spencer to the Senate, according to the views of the majority of the committee of the Senate of the United States on Privileges and Elections, depends on the fact whether Martin or Miller was elected, it is proper, in the opinion of your committee, to present in this report the history of the action of the Senate on this question, and, in its appropriate place, a review of the evidence, herewith submitted, which shows the conduct of Mr. Spencer in attempting to procure a decision of the contest in favor of Mr. Miller—conduct in the highest degree reprehensible, involving fraud, force, violation of honorable pledges, and bribery.

On the 23d April, 1873, sixteen Senators presented a protest to the Senate of Alabama, which has been proven before your committee, to set forth the full and true state of facts relating to the Miller-Martin contest, which is as follows:

"Mr. Parks presented the following protest, which was ordered to be spread upon the journal:

" The undersigned, members of the Senate of Alabama, dissent from the proceedings in the Senate, upon the 30th and 31st days of January, 1873, in the matter of the contest between William Miller, jr., and Edmund W. Martin, for the seat in this Senate from the 31st senatorial district, and protest against the acts and rulings of the President of the Senate, upon the motions and resolutions before the Senate, by virtue of which the said Wiliam Miller, jr., has taken, and now occupies, a seat in this body as Senator from said district.

"The journal shows that the committee to which the said contest had been referred, to take testimony and report thereon, presented a divided report. One signed by Senator Pennington, chairman, reported that said Miller is entitled to the said seat; the other, signed by Senators Parks and Edwards, of the same committee, reported the following resolution:

" *Resolved*, That Edmund W. Martin, the present sitting member, is legally and constitutionally elected for the 31st senatorial district, and is entitled to his seat as a member of this body for the term prescribed by law.

"Upon the coming in of said reports, the Senator from Wilcox county moved—which was seconded by a Senator—that the resolution thus reported by Senators Parks and Edwards, of said committee, be adopted as the resolution of the Senate. Pending that motion, the Senator from Dallas moved —which was also seconded—as a substitute therefor, that the report presented by the chairman of that committee be adopted.

" After discussion by the Senate, the President proceeded to take the sense of this Senate upon the question then pending. The vote was taken by call of ayes and noes, and resulted in 16 ayes to 14 noes.

"The President announced that the result of the vote was that Mr. Miller was entitled to be seated as Senator from the 31st senatorial district.

"The Senator from Shelby, upon the call of his name, voted nay, but within the time allowed by rule, changed his vote to aye, in order to be entitled to move a reconsideration of the vote ; and upon the announcement of the vote by the President, did move to reconsider the vote just then taken by the Senate. This occurred on January 30, 1873. The President intimated that the motion to reconsider was out of order, and would not be allowed.

"Pending this question, the Senate adjourned till the 31st January, 1873, the Senator from Shelby retaining the floor.

"On the morning of said 31st day of January, after further remarks by the Senator from Shelby, the President ruled that the said motion to reconsider the vote taken by the Senate as above stated, was out of order, and was not allowed. (The Senator from Shelby immediately demanded an appeal to the Senate from the decision of the chair upon the propriety and legality of his motion. The President decided that an appeal did not lie to the Senate from his said decision, and refused to permit any question to the Senate, whereby his said decision could be reviewed by the Senate.) The Senator from Shelby thereupon in open Senate, from his place therein, protested against the said decisions and rulings of the chair, and stated that as to proceed further would probably inaugurate violence and revolution, and as he saw no peaceful remedy provided by the law, he submitted, but with no concession as to the rights he claimed as a member of this Senate.

"During the same session of the Senate the Senator from Pike called the attention of the Senate and the President to the State of the question pending before the Senate, that the vote which had been taken upon the motion of the Senator from Dallas, had placed his substitute (to-wit, that the report made by the chairman of the committee be adopted,) before the Senate, in the place and stead of the motion offered by

the Senator from Wilcox, and that this substituted motion
should now be put to the Senate for a direct and final vote
thereon, and moved—which was seconded—that the vote of
the Senate be taken upon said substituted motion. The President ruled that the Senator from Pike was out of order, and
that his said motion was out of order, and refused to put his
said motion, and refused to put the substitute offered by the
Senator from Dallas to any vote other than had already been
taken by the Senate.

" From this ruling and decision of the President of the Senate, the Senator from Pike demanded an appeal to the Senate,
and claimed such decision by the Senate itself upon the rulings of its presiding officer, as a matter of right, belonging to
him as a Senator, representing a portion of the people of this
State. The President of the Senate ruled, and so decided,
that no appeal to the Senate lay from his said decision, and
refused to put such question of appeal himself, and refused
to permit any appeal from his said decision to be put to the
Senate by the Senator himself, or by any officer of the Senate,
whereby his said decision might or could be reviewed by the
Senate.

"The Senator from Pike thereupon, from his place, in open
session of the Senate, after prolonged and determined resist-
ance, protested against the said decisions and rulings of the
chair, and desisted from further pressing the assertion of his
rights as Senator, only because prevailed on by his fellow
Senators that all peaceable remedies were exhausted, and to
assert his rights would require violent and revolutionary measures; and thereupon the Lieutenant Governor, from the chair
of the Senate, as President thereof, declared William Miller
to be entitled to be seated in this Senate, as Senator from the
31st senatorial district, and directed him to be sworn in as
such Senator.

"Other Senators from their places in the Senate, likewise
gave notice that they coincided in the views of the Senators
from Shelby and Pike, and united with them in protesting
against the rulings and decisions of the President in the
premises, and against which they protested.

"Wherefore, the undersigned Senators from the districts set opposite their names, for themselves individually, and in behalf of the people, citizens of Alabama, of their said districts, whom they represent, do solemnly make and enter upon the journal of the Senate, this their protests against the said acts and doings of the said Lieutenant Governor, as President of the Senate, by him done in the presence of the Senate, and while presiding therein;

"Because the said Lieutenant Governor, as President of the Senate, announced as the result of the vote of the Senate upon the motion of the Senator from Dallas, that Mr. Miller was entitled to be seated as the Senator from the 31st senatorial district of Alabama, when the true result was that said motion was substituted for the motion of the Senator from Wilcox, and should have been then put to the vote of the Senate for its final decision;

"Because, in overruling the motion of the Senator from Shelby for a reconsideration of the vote upon the motion of the Senator from Dallas, and refusing to put the same, he violated the rules of order and parliamentary practice, which by law and custom govern the proceedings of the Senate and protect the rights of individual members and of the minority, and denied to that Senator his rights as a member of this body, secured to him by its rules;

"Because, in refusing to allow and put an appeal to the Senate, whereby the sense of the Senate could be taken upon the propriety of his ruling upon the former motion to reconsider the vote upon the motion of the Senator from Dallas, the Lieutenant Governor, as President of the Senate, not only deprived the Senator from Shelby of rights which belonged to him as Senator, but endangered the peace of the community, and assumed to himself dangerous, arbitrary and despotic power, whereby the liberty and security of the citizen are put in jeopardy.

"We protest for the same reasons against the course pursued by the President of the Senate toward the Senator from Pike, whereby the dignity of the Senate is invaded, and the rights of Senators and of their constituents, the good people of Alabama, are denied.

"We further protest against these proceedings by and on the part of the President of the Senate, because, thereby, by his rulings and decisions, and not by the vote of the Senate, to whom alone such right and power constitutionally belong, one claimant to the seat in this body from the 31st senatorial district has been displaced, though he holds the legal certificate thereto, and another has been seated in his place, without the judgment and sanction of the Senate legally and constitutionally expressed.

"We cannot but regard these acts and rulings and decisions of the Lieutenant-Governor, who, by the law of the land, is simply the presiding officer of the Senate, but not a component part thereof, and not entitled to participate in its deliberations, or to vote therein, except when its own judgment is so evenly balanced that it can make no expression of its will, as destructive of the integrity of the government, and of the right and freedom of the citizen.

R. W. COBB,
*Senator 8th District.*

WM. H. PARKS,
*Senator 32d District.*

DANIEL COLEMAN,
*Senator 1st District.*

J. D. DRIESBACH,
*Senator 29th District.*

R. H. ERVIN,
*Senator 30th District.*

J. M. CARMICHAEL,
*Senator 33d District.*

G. W. HEWITT,
*Senator 7th District.*

S. WALTON,
*Senator 27th District.*

W. H. EDWARDS,
*Senator 3d District.*

J. J. ROBINSON,
*Senator 11th District.*

J. M. MARTIN,
*Senator 9th District.*

A. SNODGRASS,
> *Senator 5th District.*

A. CUNNINGHAM,
> *Senator 10th District.*

THOMAS BUTLER COOPER,
> *Senator 6th District.*

P. HAMILTON,
> *Senator 28th District.*

JOHN A. TERRELL,
> *Senator 12th District."*

The testimony of Hon. Lewis E. Parsons and other experienced parliamentarians, shows that this action of Lt. Gov. McKinstry, who was presiding in the Senate, was entirely without precedent, and a gross violation of the rights of the Senate.

At a succeeding session of the Senate, it proceeded to dispose of this contest, by taking up the question in the stage in which it had been left, at a preceding session and by a final vote decided it in favor of Mr. Martin.

An examination of the majority and minority reports of the select committee on the Miller-Martin contest, copies of which are herewith submitted, shows that Martin received a large majority of the legal votes actually cast; but, in one county the vote for Martin was deposited in separate boxes, while that for Miller was deposited in the same boxes in which the ballots for other officers were deposited. This occurred by reason of the fact that the Senatorial district was composed in parts of new counties, and the boundaries of the Senatorial districts remained as they had been, and so divided the new counties.

Gov. William H. Smith, the first Republican Governor of Alabama, in a proclamation of October 20th, 1870, advised the voters in the parts of new counties, thus included in said senatorial districts, to deposit their votes in separate boxes, so that the ballots for Senator could be sent for inspection to the supervisors of elections in the county designated by law as the counties to which returns of Senatorial elections should be made, without any interference with the ballots cast in other local elections.

It admits of no reasonable doubt that the advice thus given the people by Gov. Smith was correct. Those who voted for Martin followed these directions. It was upon this transparent pretext alone, that it was claimed that 453 votes, honestly and lawfully cast for Martin should be rejected, and that Milller should be therefore declared elected.

The Senate of the United States has given to the fact of an actual election by the people so much weight in determining even the lawfulness of a General Assembly, that your committee cannot suppose it will even sanction, and certainly will never order the expulsion of a member of a State Senate, by rejecting 453 votes cast for him, for no better reason than because the managers of the election gave honest heed and respect to a proclamation of the Governor, that the votes for Senator should be deposited in a separate box.

If the Senate of the United States could have the legal right to reverse the decision of a State Senate as to the right of a person to a seat therein, your committee are satisfied that after the most scrutinizing examination and unfriendly criticism of its action, the Senate of the United States must sustain and approve the final decision of the Senate of Alabama, in declining to seat Mr. Miller in the place of Mr. Martin—a decision made in strict compliance with parliamentary law and in the honest support of the rights of the people.

Mr. Miller never for one moment, held his seat in the Senate of Alabama by the consent of that body, nor by any other authority, judicial or ministerial, known to the laws of Alabama, and never had a right to hold such seat, not having received the vote of the people so to entitle him, and having no certificate of election.

The branch of the inquiry under consideration will be further examined in discussing the evidence taken by the committee, and we now proceed to examine the other branch of the inquiry that relates to the means by which Mr. Spencer's pretended election was procured, and his credentials as a Senator were obtained.

A large number of witnesses have been examined, but some have not been examined who know important facts touching these inquiries.

Your committee preferred to confine the examination, as far as practicable, to those witnesses who are of the same policical party with Mr. Spencer. More than three-fourths of the witnesses are Republicans in their party relations.

In 1872 the legislature was to be chosen that would elect a United States Senator. It was a doubtful matter whether the State would vote Democratic, as it had done two years previous, or Republican, as it had done four years before that time. A canvass for Senator was instituted in the Republican party, in which Mr. Spencer was an active candidate. His relations with the Executive Committee of the National Republican party gave him influence and money, and his position as a Senator gave him a charge of official patronage, of which he had scured almost the entire control in Alabama. He had succeeded in breaking down the influence of Senator Warner, to a great extent, while they were colleagues, and had the possession of the entire field. His letter to Mr. Putnam, then postmaster at Mobile, dated August 12th, 1871, shows that even then he so far counted upon his power as that he boasted that he had already gotten President Grant alarmed, and that he would soon do what Spencer and his friends wanted him to do.

"NEW YORK, August 12, 1871.

" *My Dear Putnam:* I have been travelling for the past two weeks and have just returned, and have just received and read your letters. I will promptly attend to all you wish. I wish you would pay for me, to the *Herald* Company, $100—immediately. I will send you the money on the 25th, by express. I can not sooner, as I have been to some heavy expenses recently. The *Herald* is splendid, and just what we have needed. We must keep it alive, and will in a short time break down the opposition. Grant is already scared, and will soon do what we want. Keep the paper *red hot.* We must carry the war into Africa, and we will succeed. Send the paper to all the leading Republicans in the State. If the Warner paper attacks me, give them the devil in return. My record, both public and private, will bear investigation. Tell Dr. Foster not to be alarmed, that I have not time to write him, but that I will stand by him. I have been working for a month on a matter, and shall succeed, that will make us a power in Alabama, and worth all the Federal patronage in a dozen States, and when accomplished they dare not deny us the patronage. Write me often, and keep me fully posted. I shall go to Washington this week, and will then attend to everything. Pay the *Herald* the $100, and I will surely send it to you on the 25th.

"In great haste, your friend,

"GEO. E. SPENCER."

This letter also discloses the fact that Mr. Spencer, who was then in the Senate, was using the power of his official station to get control of the Federal patronage in Alabama, and was using it as a perquisite of his office. This and other evidence in the case also establishes that Mr. Spencer's opposition to Gen Warner, a Republican Senator, was attributable to his determination to have exclusive control of the patronage in Alabama, and that he intended to use it, and did use it almost entirely, for his personal and pecuniary advantage.

In 1872, Mr. Spencer employed William V. Turner, a colored ex-member of the Legislature from Elmore county, to assist in procuring the nomination of candidates by county conventions in several counties for the Legislature, who would give pledges to support him for the U. S. Senate.

Turner had full authority from Spencer to promise these men Federal offices in consideration of their support. He made the promises and secured the nomination of the persons, who thus exchanged pledges with him.

Turner was paid money by Mr. Spencer for this service and was also promised by him any position that could be secured by his influence in the United States service, for securing those votes for him as United States Senator.

During the canvass of 1872, Turner was appointed, through

3

Spencer's influence, special inspector of customs at Moblle, to enable him to support himself while in the canvass.

He rendered no service in the custom-house, being constantly employed in the canvass. He received four dollars a day, and signed his vouchers and sent them to Mobile. He was not there during his term of office, except when he was sworn in.

This office continued until Spencer was elected to the Senate. During the two months Turner received $248.

In support of his statements Turner produces a letter from Mr. Spencer in the following words:

WASHINGTON, September 14, 1872.

MY DEAR SIR: Your confirmation as inspector of customs was forwarded to Collector Miller yesterday, at $4 per diem pay. Go at once to Mobile, be sworn in, and apply for leave of absence until after the election, which Collector Miller will arrange for you. Show him this letter; he will understand it.

In haste, truly yours.

GEO. E. SPENCER.

Hon. W. V. TURNER, Wetumpka, Ala.

Further important support is given to Turner's statements by the letters of Spencer attached to his deposition, dated respectively September 4th, 1872, October 19th, 1872, December 16, 1872, and October 7th, 1874.

The last letter shows that an intimate friendship was maintained between Turner and Spencer until late in 1874, and that Spencer was then using him as a stump-speaker in his interest in Alabama.

In October, 1872, Spencer also had Robert Barber in his service, attempting to procure his election to the United States Senate, and to defeat other Republican aspirants.

Mr. Barber was Clerk of the House of Representatives at the Court-house, and afterwards of the consolidated Legislature at the Capitol.

He was promised a Federal office by Spencer, in consideration of the assistance he should give Spencer in procuring his election to the Senate. Two letters from Spencer to Barber, dated respectively 16th and 20th of October, 1872, are important supports to his statements.

Spencer having heard that ex-Gov. Parsons, a Republican, was a candidate in Talladega county for the Legislature, and would also be a candidate for the U. S. Senate, sent Barber to a Mr. Wood, a Republican, to procure him to offer as an independent candidate to defeat Parsons, and to inform him that he would see that all the expenses of the canvass would be met.

H. Ray Mayer and P. G. Clark were sent to Dallas county to defeat Alexander White, who was a candidate for the Legislature, by electing Beach, then a deputy collector of internal revenue under Widmer, because White was supposed to be in Parsons' interest.

The better to succeed, Beach was to be a secret candidate, and White's name was to be left off the tickets, which were to be printed in Washington. The tickets were so printed, and White's name was left off almost one-half of them. White discovered the fraud in time to have his name printed in the blanks, and defeated Spencer's plan. With shameless falsehood Spencer charged, in one of the letters to Barber, that Gov. Parsons had gone to New York to obtain money to secure his election to the Senate by the Legislature. Gov. Parsons, unconscious of the libel, voted for Spencer in the Court-house Legislature!

Spencer gave D. C. Whiting $300 which he took to Lowndes county "to defray expenses" of a crowd that went there with Barber to beat Stanwood and a colored man who were known opponents of Spencer, and to put in Hunter and two colored men who were favorable to Spencer. This plan succeeded.

After Spencer's election, Hunter was promised Consul to Alexandria, Egypt. Spencer failed to keep his promise, and Hunter quit him in disgust.

Hunter says, "After the reorganization, and a day or two before the day upon which I attempted to bring on an election for United States Senator in the consolidated or reorganized legislature, D. C. Whiting showed me a telegram from

Spencer, who was then in Washington, in these words: 'Shall I have Hunter appointed now, or wait until the legislature adjourns? I think the latter plan preferable. Signed, Geo. E. Spencer.' The appointment referred to was the consulate to Alexandria, which had been filled by a Utica, New York, man, two weeks previous to the date of the dispatch, and published in the Associated Press dispatches, and of which Spencer was fully aware."

The intention of Mr. Spencer to procure a seat in the Senate at every hazard, is sufficiently proven by the frauds and contrivances to which he resorted to defeat the election of such Republicans as he could not suborn to his purposes.

But his evil machinations took a much wider sweep and a most dangerous form when he conspired to use the military power of the United States to deter men from voting in the State elections. His letter to Robert Barber dated October 22, 1872, admits of no other possible explanation than that given by Barber in his answer to the following question:

"2. I notice in the letter of October 22, 1872, the expression—'I wish Randolph, deputy U. S. Marshal, would use the company at Opelika in making arrests in Tallapoosa, Randolph and Cleburne, as ——— suggests;' please explain the meaning of this."

"A. I received a letter from Randolph county before the date of these letters, (6th and 22d of October, 1872,) suggesting that if troops should be sent into the counties named, enough voters would be run out of them, through fear of arrest, to secure the election of Republican representatives from these counties, and the letter of October 22d was in reply to a letter written to Spencer conveying to him this information."

In the same letter in which he expresses this wish, he tells Barber that he had just returned from Louisville, where he had been to see Gen. Terry about troops for Alabama. He says:

"I have had a company of cavalry sent to Livingston, a

detachment to Pickens county, a company of infantry to Eutaw, a company to Demopolis, and a company to Seale station, Russell county; also, a squadron of cavalry to report to Marshal Thomas at Huntsville."

No doubt can remain that this army of troops was sent by him to Alabama for the sole purpose of doing that in many counties, that he desired deputy marshal Randolph to do in Tallapoosa, Randolph and Cleburne. His object was to terrify the people.

Several of the leading politicians of the Republican party of Alabama have been examined as witnesses in this cause, and with one accord they swear that this demand for troops was not made at the instance of that party.

It was a personal enterprise of Mr. Spencer to secure the power to force himself into the Senate against the wishes even of the better men of his own party.

General Healy, the U. S. Marshal for the middle and southern districts of Alabama, proves that no troops were used or needed after May, 1872, in making arrests or enforcing obedience to law in those districts, and Mr. Spencer had no control of Randolph or any other deputy marshal acting under him.

Judge Bruce, Governor Smith, Governor Parsons, and others, fully sustain and corroborate these statements.

The testimony of Perrin and Squires, and other witnesses, touching the use of troops in other counties of the State, by the direction of Spencer and his agents, is strictly in accordance with Spencer's confessions in his letters to Barber. On this point, the evidence comes from various quarters and is all in harmony.

It proves that Spencer devised and executed a general plan to use United States troops to organize the people of his own party into national guards for his support to crush out opposition in the Republican ranks, and to oppress and worry the opposing party until they should be afraid to oppose him. He knew that his own party would not support him if they were left free to express their own wishes.

After all, the election in November, 1872, was very close between the political parties, and the seat in the Senate of the United States became an object of extreme solicitude.

Almost every witness who had good opportunities to know the feeling in the Republican party declares that Spencer was not choice of his party for the Senate.

They declare further that his election to the Senate became a political necessity, to prevent him from dividing his party by seceding, with a following of his personal retainers, from the Assembly at the Court House, and going to the Assembly at the Capitol. His desertion of his party was looked for at any moment, that the Democratic party might make a bid for him.

These facts are referred to because they reflect light upon the means by which he attached to his fortunes and controlled the persons who supported his demand for a re-election to the Senate.

These means your committee declares upon the evidence were utterly corrupt.

In a large number of instances, the persons who rendered to Spencer the most active and important services were rewarded with federal offices and employment through his assistance, as a Senator of the United States, as a compensation for such services.

These offices and employments were promised before the services were rendered, or whilst they were being rendered. Some such promises were made that were never redeemed.

Promises were made by Spencer in person to members of the Legislature and others, and Hinds, Barber, Turner, H. Ray Mayer, Philip King and others had full authority from Spencer to make any promises of federal offices that were required to secure the influence of any persons in his behalf.

These agents of Spencer made promises to any persons who could be influenced by them, and made direct bargains with them for their assistance, for which they in turn were to be paid with federal offices and employments.

The evidence of Turner, and other witnesses, shows that by direct authority from Mr. Spencer promises were made to members of the Court House Legislature of appointments to federal offices in consideration of the support of Mr. Spencer for a seat in the United States Senate, and witnesses M. D. Brainard and others testify that a large number of the members of that body did afterwards receive such appointments, as the following numeration will show:

Senator J. Black was appointed deputy collector of internal revenue under Lou H. Mayer.

Senator J. W. Dereen was made postmaster at Demopolis.

Senator George M. Duskin was made United States District Attorney at Mobile.

Senator J. C. Goodloe was appointed Collector of Customs at Mobile.

To carry out an agreement of Spencer's, made with Barber, to secure his influence in his election as Senator, Spencer procured a position for Barber in the Custom House at Mobile, which paid him a considerable sum of money monthly.

Goodloe wrote to Barber and asked him to send on to him his application for the place, under the civil-service regulations, and told him that no duty would be required of him, and that when his monthly pay should fall due he (Goodloe) would send him blank drafts or receipts, which he could sign and forward to him, so that he would be saved the trouble even of visiting Mobile to get his pay; so that Goodloe not only procured office for himself, but assisted Spencer in paying a debt to Barber with an office, whereby the United States was grossly defrauded. And so it has been in reference to several sinecure positions which Goodloe has aided Spencer's followers to get.

William Miller, jr., who had the contest with Martin for a seat in the Senate, received the office of postmaster, and was made deputy collector of internal revenue. His brother, an unnaturalized foreigner, and just arrived at age, was appointed to the important office of deputy collector of customs at Mobile, as stated by Mr. Southworth.

J. L. Pennington, Senator, was made Governor of Dakota Territory.

A. P. Wilson, Senator, was made postmaster at Montgomery.

W. R. Chisholm, Senator, was Inspector of Customs at Mobile when he was sent for to come to Montgomery, to take a seat in the Court House Senate. He was suspended from his office until after the Miller-Martin contest was ended; he was then reinstated and drew his pay for the whole period of his suspension.

R. P. Baker, Senator, occupied nearly the same position as Chisholm, having no real claim to a seat, and was afterwards appointed United States marshal for the Northern District of Alabama.

John Lamb, Representative, received an appointment in the Custom House at Mobile.

Thomas J. Clark, Representative, was afterwards appointed to a place in the police of Washington City.

P. G. Clarke, of the House, was afterwards appointed United States mail agent.

Henry Cochran was promised the office of postmaster, after he was elected to the House of Representatives, voted for Spencer, and was afterwards appointed postmaster at Selma.

C. H. Davis, of the House, was appointed postmaster at Union Springs.

Green S. W. Lewis, of the House, received the appointment of mail agent.

J. M. Levey, of the House, received the appointment of United States gauger at Montgomery.

C. W. Dustan, of the House, received an appointment in the Custom House in Mobile.

N. S. McAfee, of the House, received the appointment of United States District Attorney for the Middle and Northern Districts of Alabama.

George Patterson, of the House, was appointed United States mail agent.

B. R. Thomas, of the House, received the appointment of deputy collector of internal revenue for the second district, and afterwards revenue agent.

J. H. Goldsby, of the House, was appointed route agent of the Postoffice Department.

Thomas D. McCaskie, of the House, was appointed weigher and gauger in the Custom House.

Other members of the Court House Legislature have since received appointments to important federal offices, but your committee are not satisfied that they were conferred under any direct bargain with Mr. Spencer.

Other persons who were assisting Spencer in his election, and aiding in the many unworthy schemes by which he secured the vote of the Court House Legislature, and afterwards the fraudulent disposition of the Miller-Martin contest, were also rewarded with appointments to federal offices through his influence. Amongst these were:

P. D. Barker who was appointed internal revenue collector for 2d district, and J. C. Hendrix who was made an assistant in Barker's office. Barker was also appointed Superintendent of Education in Dallas county, while holding his collectorship

Lou. H. Mayer, was appointed collector of internal revenue for 1st district.

Meyer Goldsmith, was reappointed auditor and deputy collector under J. C. Goodloe.

D. C. Whiting was appointed appraiser of merchandise in the custom house, and drew his pay, rendering no service.

James Samuell, appointed receiver at the land office at Mobile; Peyton Finley receiver of the land office at Montgomery; Jerome J. Hinds, marshal of the Middle and Southern Districts of Alabama.

J. J. Osborne, deputy collector of the 1st district of Alabama.

H. A. Candee, deputy collector.

H. J. Europe, deputy collector.

Phillip King, deputy collector.

M. G. Candee, deputy collector.

M. C. Osborne, special clerk of the Supervisor.

R. A. Moseley, postmaster at Talladega.

R. M. Reynolds, collector of the port at Mobile.

The witnesses generally concur in the statement that Mr.

4

Spencer controlled the government patronage in Alabama almost exclusively.

The principal agents and managers of Mr. Spencer, as shown by the testimony of Barber, Brainard and others, were J. J. Hinds, D. C. Whiting, H. Ray Mayer, and Lou Mayer, and Robt. Barber. To these he confided more authority to make pledges for him and to arrange to place his other retainers in the subordinate offices, than to any other persons.

He demanded the right to designate every subordinate officer and employee in the Custom House, Postoffices, Internal Revenue offices, and other places to which appointments had been made under the influence of his patronage, and on several occasions assigned to Hinds and H. Ray Mayer, the duty of selecting such employees, and required obedience to their orders.

These persons were associated with Spencer in the most intimate manner, and conducted for him, chiefly, all the plans by which others were corrupted to do his will and keep him in the Senate.

Hinds has been living with Spencer almost constantly since he came to Alabama, and H. Ray Mayer was a large part of the time in his company, until he was appointed to a Consulship in the Dominion of Canada.

Lou H. Mayer boasts of intimate friendship with Spencer and "congeniality of feelings and sentiments."

That George E. Spencer used money corruptly, and in considerable sums, to procure his election to the Senate by the Court House Legislature, and to influence the Martin-Miller contest, and to defeat the election of a Senator by the General Assembly at the Capitol, is established by the evidence of many witnesses, corroborated by evidence of written instruments, and by the opinions and convictions of those of his party, who were present in Montgomery, and had good opportunity to understand his proceedings and those of his friends.

A full discussion of all the evidence herewith submitted, that is relevant to this proposition, would unnecessarily enlarge this report.

The money that he thus used was drawn mainly from four sources.

1. The Post-office at Mobile.
2. The office of Internal Revenue at Mobile.
3. The office of Internal Revenue at Montgomery.
4. The Treasury of the National Republican Executive Committee, or the State Republican Executive Committee.

The testimony of Mr. Mitchell, and the accounts furnished by Mr. Campbell, showing the cash dealings of Spencer, Hinds and Whiting, with the First National Bank at Montgomery from the 26th of October, 1872, to 5th of December, 1872, and Hinds dealings from the 10th of December, 1872, to the 14th of February, 1873, prove a common purpose existing between them in the use, or intention to use, a sum amounting in the aggregate to $29,128 00.

Hinds and Spencer opened their accounts in said Bank on the same day, 19th November, which was the day after the Court House Legislature assembled, and they and Whiting drew out their balances on the same day—the 5th of December—which was the day after Spencer's election.

During this time, Whiting a very poor man, had used $2,493 75, Hinds had used $2,750 34, and Spencer had used $2,000 00. After this and up to the 14th of February, 1873, Hinds used $9,450 34.

None of these persons had any visible business in Montgomery that required the use of large sums of money. The sums checked out by them were mostly round sums, except the balances, and were from $50 up to $1,000 00. They each knew the state of the others accounts on the books of the bank, and examined them at pleasure, each exhibiting solicitude to know how the accounts of the others stood.

Hinds' account was again balanced on December 23, 1872, and was opened again on the 17th of January, 1873. It closed on the 14th of February, 1873, with a check for $109.

About the middle of January, 1873, when the Martin-Miller contest was approaching a termination, Hinds reappeared in Montgomery, and told Mr. Mitchell, who was cashier of the National Bank, that he wanted a thousand or more dollars, that he could not tell exactly when he would need it, it might be the next day or during the week, but when he did want it he must have it. He drew two drafts on persons in Washington (one of them being Spencer,) for $1,000 each, and Mr. Mitchell let him have the money on them.

Hinds insisted that the names of the parties upon whom these drafts were drawn should not appear upon the books of the bank, and Mr. Mitchell consented. He also had a dispatch sent from a way station on the railroad advising parties of the drafts, fearing that the names might be known if sent through the Montgomery office.

This furtive conduct is not consistent with ordinary fair dealing with one's own money or credit, and when it is associated with the other facts which show its purpose, no rational doubt remains that this money was procured for the purpose of being used to corrupt members of the General Assembly.

John J. Moulton of Mobile, then postmaster, was one of the persons who furnished to Spencer and Hinds a large part of the money they expended in bribing members of the General Assembly.

He had been put in the post-office at Mobile by Spencer's influence, to take the place of Mr. Putnam, whom Spencer had caused to be removed because he refused to pay tribute to Spencer on the demand of H. Ray Mayer. When Moulton was appointed to office, Spencer knew that he was very much embarrassed in his monetary affairs, and that he had once made a deficit in his accounts, as money-order clerk under Putnam, which he afterwards made good.

A few days before Spencer's election in 1872, Moulton was at Montgomery, and saw Spencer. He was active in his support of Spencer for the Senate. Moulton then asked of Spencer the repayment of $10,000.

He says, " for eighteen months before this, drafts had been drawn upon me by different persons for political purposes, at Spencer's instance, and in this way I had advanced a large amount of money, in which I was assured I would be protected by Spencer. It was in this way that the sum had accumulated that I told Spencer must be refunded to me. The amount I had advanced exceeded $10,000."

Q. Did he ever deny to you his liability to refund this money to you?

A. He did not.

Q. Were any of these drafts drawn by Whiting or Hinds?

A. They were.

Q. In the latter part of 1872 did you tell Spencer you were broke?

A. I think I told him I was bankrupt.

Q. Did you tell him, or give him to understand, that the heavy drafts made upon you was the cause of it?

A. Spencer knew it, and always recognized it in his conversations with me.

In this conversation Moulton told Spencer that he was discouraged, and would resign unless the money was paid. Spencer said, "Don't do it." Moulton said he would be compelled to do so. Spencer replied, "Don't do it; I'll stand by you. I can make it all right in Washington." "He (Spencer) told me to wait until he was elected to the Senate, and he would have $10,000 left, he thought, and I should have every dollar of it." He furthermore said to Moulton, "Don't resign; I will stand by you till hell freezes over."

Spencer had received from Moulton, about 24th November, 1872, about $5,000 of the sum that had produced such distress to Moulton.

Moulton had used post-office funds to get drafts from T. P. Miller & Co., which were used for Spencer, and he knew this; and Moulton and Lou H. Meyer had used post-office money with Moses S. Foote to get money for Spencer's benefit, and upon his written authority.

He knew that Moulton was in great danger, and attempted to soothe him with promises of ten thousand dollars as soon as he should be elected to the Senate, and with assurances of his power to protect him at Washington with the government.

On the day of Spencer's election Moulton returned to Montgomery and asked Spencer to keep his promise. Spencer paid him $2,250, in a draft on the National Commercial Bank at Mobile, drawn on the 4th December, 1872, by E. R. Mitchell, Cashier. The original draft is in evidence.

After this, Moulton visited Spencer in Washington. Spencer had taken over $11,000 00 with him to Washington, but Moulton did not know it. He suspected it; and this, in part, caused his visit to Washington.

The Attorney General's proposition for a compromise was made on the 11th December, 1872, and it was then evident that Spencer could not hold his seat, if the said proposition should be accepted, unless he could turn Mr. Martin out of the State Senate.

On Tuesday, the 17th December, 1872, the two legislatures met in the Capitol.

About that time Spencer telegraphed Moulton at Mobile, in cypher, to meet Hinds in Montgomery on the next Friday, and bring funds.

Moulton went, and took with him a letter of credit of Thos. P. Miller & Co., dated 19th December, 1872, to Farley, Smith & Co. of Montgomery, for $2.500, and on the 21st December drew for the full amount. On that day Hinds deposited $2,000 in the First National Bank at Montgomery. Hinds gave Moulton a receipt, dated 21st December, Montgomery, for $1,880 on account of Spencer. Moulton also paid for him $500 for Senator Glass, $100 for a Democratic member of the House, besides other sums, and gave him a draft on Bingham, State Treasurer, for $250.

Spencer knew that Moulton had no other means to raise this money than from the post-office, and Mr. Eagan testifies that the $2,500 was post-office funds, cash taken out of the drawer for political purposes, and deposited with Miller & Co. to protect their acceptances.

When Petherbridge, the post-office detective, came down on Moulton, about the 10th January, 1873, he (Moulton) drew on Spencer for $5,000. The draft was dishonored, and the victim of his criminal cruelty and subornation was handed over to the law.

Moulton's wife and friends had to impoverish themselves to save him. Lou H. Meyer, though a person in straightened circumstances, paid $1,000 of the money; but this was done most likely to save himself from the consequences of his complicity in the use of post-office money and stamps, and certified pay-rolls, (not due by a month,) used by him and Moulton to secure money to purchase supporters for Spencer in his election.

Moses S. Foote's testimony shows that Moulton, on the 21st October, 1872, deposited in his bank $1,240 00 of post-office money, in the name of "W. H. Lewis, agent," as collateral to a bill for $2,000 at sixty days, which he discounted for Moulton and Lou H Meyer.

This paper was extended at maturity.

Foote states that Moulton and Meyer both informed him that the reason for asking the extension was "that Spencer had gone back on them, he having told them that $2,500 was set apart for political purposes, to carry the State, by the Republican National Executive Committee, and that they had been authorized in anticipation of this amount to make the loan, or any money arrangements necessary, and that Spencer had not provided the means promised, and they therefore asked for further time." Meyer stated at the same time, complaining of Spencer, "that he (Spencer) knew that Moulton had used post-office money, and he (Meyer) had pledged his wife's jewels, and all the money he could get, as well as *Revenue Money* to pay these accommodations."

Meyer pledged pay-rolls of his subordinates in the assessor's office, certified by John T. Foster, Revenue Collector, a month before they were due, as collateral for loans, and offered to pledge *postage stamps* for other loans.

When Foote inquired of Foster about this *irregularity*, and asked him what would be the consequences if some of Meyer's subordinates should die before the end of the month, he replied that "he and Meyer would have to make it up," "that they were riding him to death in this Spencer matter, and that he was tired of it and did not intend to submit to it."

When Moulton and Meyer came in company to Foote to get the $2,000 accommodation, Moulton took a letter from his pocket in Meyer's presence, which he said was from Spencer, authorizing him to make money transactions and pledging to them the $2,500.

On being admonished by Foote that the pledging of certified pay-rolls before they were due was unlawful, Meyer replied "I know what I am doing and have the approval of the department, and will be protected." During these transactions Meyer said to Foote—"That if Grant carried the State, Spencer would be elected to the United States Senate, and he would then, through Spencer, be appointed Collector of Internal Revenue at Mobile, over Dr. Foster, when the office of Collector and Assessor of Internal Revenue would be consolidated." Moulton also told Foote that. Meyer would get this office, and Meyer got it.

Meyer says Spencer got him the appointment of Revenue Assessor in 1871. "I have always regarded him as one of the best friends in the world. I would do as much for him as any man in the world," and that he went to Montgomery to assist in Spencer's election.

After proving that Widmer was one of the best officers in the country "and a correct man," Meyer was asked this question : "If Widmer were to tell you on his dying bed that he had loaned Spencer $5,000 and Spencer were to tell you that he had not, which of them would you believe?" He answered I would believe Mr. Spencer."

Such faith in Spencer in 1875, after the confessions of Meyer made to Foote in 1872, furnishes a strong support to Meyer's other statement that the ground of their long intimacy was "congeniality of sentiment and feeling." This can scarcely be doubted. The bill discounted for Moulton and Meyer by Foote, on 31st October, 1872, matured on 30th December, 1872.

Foote states that this bill was extended.

Mayer attempts to prove that he saw Spencer hand Moulton $2,250 00 in money, on 4th December, 1872, but Mr. Mitchell's evidence shows that this sum paid on that day was in a check on Mobile, and the original check is produced in evidence. This check went to replace money taken from the cash drawer of the post-office by Moulton and deposited with Miller & Co.

Another part of the money used by Spencer, Hinds and

Whiting was obtained from Francis Widmer, Collector of Internal Revenue for the 2d District of Alabama.

In September, 1873, Widmer, Internal Revenue Collector at Montgomery, was arrested at the instance of the United States government for embezzlement in his office. His sureties on his bond made some examination into his affairs. He told Mr. Woolfe, one of the sureties, that he was afraid that Beach, one of his deputy collectors, (the same person with whom Spencer had attempted to defeat Alexander White, in Dallas County,) had been guilty of a default to the amount of $6,000, "that his own accounts were short only about three or four thousand dollars; that the amount he was short was due him by very influential parties, who would be able to pay as soon as he called upon them." "He refused at the time to give me the names of the parties who owed him. I offered him my assistance in attending to some business in Selma, and garnisheed several parties who were bondsmen for Beach. Upon my return from Selma, or a short time thereafter, Widmer showed me three notes on parties who were owing him money; he stated that with these three notes, and the amounts for which the parties in Selma were garnisheed, he could make good his accounts." There was one note on J. J. Hinds for $2,500 with a credit on the back of it for $900." "There was another note made by Hinds and Spencer, either payable to Hinds and endorsed by Spencer, or payable to Spencer and endorsed by Hinds for $1,800 I think; I am not certain as to the amount. The third note was Strassburger's." "He said they were for money loaned. That, occupying his position, he was compelled to do more for them than for other persons;" "I saw the notes and have no doubt about their being genuine documents." "He (Widmer) said he had called upon the parties for the money, and at that time he had no response, but expected to get the money."

The yellow fever broke out in Montgomery on 24th September, 1873, and was a fearful epidemic; Widmer died of it on the 14th October—he had no wife, and was alone in the world, only attended occasionally by his white friends, but constantly by his colored servant Jackson Morgan, a man of good character, and of more than ordinary intelligence. Morgan performed the last offices for Widmer, and prepared his body for burial.

He had seen the notes on Spencer and Hinds; had heard Widmer after his arrest, and during his illness, say they owed him enough to settle his accounts, and complained that they had not relieved his troubles. He saw Widmer put the notes in his inner safe, and put the key in his pocket. This was when the U. S. detective was about.

Immediately after Widmer's death, Morgan took the key out of Widmer's pocket and gave it to Fritz, a bailiff or tip-staff of the United States district court, who, with his wife, lived in the house where Widmer kept his office and apartments.

Soon after Widmer's death Fritz told Mr. Hatchett, Widmer's administrator, and Judge Rice, the attorney of Widmer's securities, and Mr. Faber and Mr. Goetter, two of his sureties, that he had the notes on Spencer and Hinds, and one on Strassburger. To some of them he set up a claim to these notes, as having been given by Widmer to his wife.

Fritz confesses to having seen Hinds in Montgomery about a week after Widmer's death. This was in the worst time of the yellow fever epidemic, when the city was almost depopulated. Hinds then lived at Decatur, Ala. After this, when Hatchett sued Fritz for these notes, he swore he had never seen them!

Widmer, shortly before his death, told Wade McBryde— "My head has been cut off; but mine is not the last one that is going to come off. These damned theives have got money from me and at the proper time I will expose them all, from Senator down." He adds: "Widmer was a republican."

Your committee can not resist the conclusion that Hinds got those notes when he braved the yellow fever to visit Montgomery, soon after Widmer's death, without having any other object in coming. Widmer had no visible property, from 1865 up to the time of his death. He had kept, in partnership with others, a small lager beer saloon at the time he was appoited a collector of internal revenue, which was done through Spencer's influence. He then gave up his saloon.

The note of Spencer for $1,800, and of Hinds for a balance of $1,600, corresponded nearly with the amount to the credit of Whiting from October 26, 1872, to December 5th, in the First National Bank of Montgomery, viz: $3,493.75.

This was covered with a very thin disguise on the 5th December, 1872, when, on the same day, he deposited $1,000 and drew it out in a single check for $1,000. This was scarcely a business transaction ; it was more probably a manœuvre to cover the fact that he had gotten his former deposits from some improper source.

The question of the precise manner in which Mr. Spencer used the money he had thus procured, in securing his election, or the persons to whom he paid it, is naturally involved in some obscurity and doubt; because it is not to be expected that persons engaged in the schemes of bribery will leave behind them any evidences of their guilt which they can possibly obliterate. In all courts, and in the most solemn issues, the rule is accepted that where a conspiracy is established by the evidence, the statements and confessions of one conspirator, made at the time the offense is being committed, or while preparations are being made to consummate it, are evidence against the co-conspirators. This rule authorizes your committee to consider the statements and acts of various persons as evidence against Spencer.

His participation in these crimes was intended to be concealed, but the devices have failed of their purpose. He has betrayed himself in many ways, and especially through his co-conspirators. The corruption of members of the legislature by promises of Federal offices, and the abuse of his senatorial influence and powers by promises and bargains in reference to other offices, has been directly shown by many witnesses.

This adds much to the credibility of the other proposition, that Spencer used money also to purchase the votes of members of the Court-house Legislature. A Senator who would prostitute his high office to the purpose of securing a re-election by promises of Federal offices and employment, would not probably hesitate to use money to the same end. Moulton testifies that this was the purpose for which money was demanded of him. That he furnished Hinds $500 to pay Senator Glass, $100 to pay a Democratic member of the House to absent himself from the Assembly at the Capitol, and other sums to be paid to other members.

When it was supposed that Jones (Senator from Lowndes) would abandon the Court-house body and repair, with his followers, to the Capitol, Spencer, through his managers, authorized Barber to offer Jones $2,500 to prevent his leaving the Court-house body.

A guard watched the suspected members from Lowndes all the night of the 3d of December, 1872. A pedestrian was sent on foot, by night, to Lowndes county, and paid $50, to bring L. Bryan to Montgomery to control the supposed bolters of the Lowndes county delegation. Carson and Maull, two colored members from Lowndes, took breakfast with Spencer early in the morning of the day of Spencer's election, at the Madison House. Barber told them Spencer had made up his mind to give each of them an office. "Spencer was present, and promised each of them a route agency on railroads."

Hinds told Barber that he had "fixed Mancil," a democrat at the Capitol, by increasing the number of trips per week on some postal route that Mancil had as contractor or sub-contractor, thereby increasing his pay from three to six hundred dollars.

Governor Smith heard Hinds say he had "fixed" a democratic Senator, "so that he would not be present to vote on the Miller-Martin contest."

W. V. Turner proves that Hinds had money which he dealt out freely to the colored members of the Court-house body. Men came to him who had no money; he referred them to Hinds, and they came back with ten and twenty dollar bills.

"It was generally understood that Hinds was Spencer's cashier, and any member that needed money could get it from him." "I saw Calvin Goodloe, on one occasion, bring a thousand dollars into the room of Mr. Spencer while I was there, and paid it to Spencer. Mr. Spencer seemed disappointed that it was not two thousand, and stated as much. Spencer said that he had spent two or three thousand dollars already. Goodloe said he would get another thousand for him. This was while the election of Spencer was pending in the Court-house Assembly."

"I inferred, from what was said and from what I knew of the current history of the campaign, that the money was used for securing Spencer's election to the U. S. Senate."

John Cashin says—"On or about the day of Spencer's election, Jones (colored Senator from Lowndes) came to me to get a hundred dollar bill changed. He called me off into a side door at my place of business and pulled out three one hundred dollar bills from his vest pocket. I said to him, 'what is that?' He repied, 'This is Spencer,' at the same time holding the money up in his hand. He told me at the same time not to say anything about the money he had, as he wanted to give Carson $50 and Maull $25. He said he could control their votes at any time."

"It was understood that each one of them was to get one hundred dollars, and he did not want them to know how much he had got."

"I have also spoken several times to Jones about this matter. I subsequently changed each one of the hundred dollar bills."

"It was the common talk and inquiry, 'How much did you get?' This talk was among the members of the Court-house Assembly, and others seeking positions through Spencer. I frequently heard it said, now is your time; if you don't get it before the election, you will not get any thing.' Jones told me he got money from Spencer for himself, Maull and Carson."

Barber says it was understood that Jones was to get $300 for remaining in the Court-house body and supporting Spencer.

James S. Perrin testifies that he saw Gilmore, Senator from Sumter, come out of Hinds' room with $300, which he said was for Senator Black, who threatened to leave his seat in the Court-house body; that Johnson, Walker and Goldsby, members of the House, got money from Hinds; and that Mancil had an interview with Spencer with reference to his leaving the Capitol Assembly to defeat a quorum there.

It was a part of Spencer's plan to defeat a quorum in the House at the capitol on the 3d day of December, 1872, to prevent that body from electing a U. S. Senator. To effect this, bribery and drugging were resorted to. The expenses of Peddy, a member of the House from Lee county, were paid by Charles Pelham, a part of the money having been furnished by Spencer, through Brainard, and he absented himself. Mancil was procured to absent himself by the means already stat d, and Stribling, a democrat from Washington county, was enticed into a gambling saloon and made drunk, and dosed with opium or some other powerful narcotic until his life was nearly destroyed to secure his absence from the House of Representatives at the capitol.

A friend of Spencer had first offered Stribling a large sum to induce him to quit the Capitol Legislature and join the body at the Court-house. This he indignantly refused.

James S. Perrin, informing Hinds of his purpose, got $20 from *him* and lost it at cards with Stribling. This was intended "as a bait," to lure him into deeper play. These facts were stated to Hinds. On the evening of the 2d of December, Lou Meyer, George Ellison, and James S. Perrin went up to the top story of the Madison House, Hinds came up where they were and gave Lou Meyer $100, who gave it to George Ellison, remarking to him, that "if these fellows don't work Stribling nobody can." They then went to the Rialto, a drinking and gambling saloon, and Perrin becoming alarmed withdrew from the party. The others went to play with Stribling. They drugged the liquor with a narcotic, and he was found there next morning alone, in a condition described thus by Dr. Freeman: "I found him with all the symptoms of poisoning with opium, and considered him in a dangerous condition, and treated him accordingly." For two days afterwards Stribling was incapable of either mental or physical exertion, and he had narrowly escaped death.

Another means of influencing members of the legislature

and others to support Spencer for the Senate, was a free drinking saloon kept in one of the rooms comprising his apartments, in the Madison House, and under his immediate control. M. D. Brainard, who claims that he first projected the plan of a separate legislature at the Court-house, presided as tapster at this bar, and dispensed wines, liquors, and cigars, without charge to Spencer's friends. Spencer could not witness such generous liberality without emotion, and prevailed on Brainard to accept from him $100 to help pay expenses. The negroes also drank and smoked there until it was supposed to be better to assign them to a separate place where they could more fully enjoy an exclusive privilege of drinking with their own color. Accordingly Spencer gave to W. V. Turner plenary authority to procure such a place and treat Spencer's colored friends at his expense. John Cashin's saloon was selected. Champagne, liquors, cigars, shrimps and other luncheon was freely distributed so that, in a day before the election the bill run up to $44.85. This was charged to Spencer and the bill sent to him, and he paid it. On the night before the election (while a portion of his people were standing guard over the delegation from Lowndes,) and on the day of the election, the colored free drinkers and free-lunches of the Court-house assembly, ran up another bill against Spencer at Cashin's saloon to the amount of $162.00. After the election Spencer refused to pay this bill, repudiated Turner's authority to contract the debt, and advised Cashin to indict him and put him in the penitentiary for obtaining his goods under false pretences.

He abused Turner for "a damned dead beat," and treated him otherwise with dintinguished contempt. Spencer could scarcely have felt real animosity towards Turner, for he wrote Turner a letter on the 7th of October, 1874, in which he addressed him as "My dear Sir," asked his assistance as a stump speaker in the election of Mr. Doster as circuit judge, and for "our ticket generally," and subscribed himself as "Truly your friend, George E. Spencer."

It is not because Mr. Spencer refused to pay such a bill to such a person, or under such circumstances, that your committee call attention to these facts; but, in their opinion, such a proceeding in a Senatorial election, at least by one then holding the office and power of a Senator is a gross scandal on that high office; and the influence thus obtained over colored men, who have but recently attained to the capacity to represent large constituencies, in the legislature, and are unduly liable to temptation, is dangerous to the great interests of the State, and to public morals.

Hinds and Moulton had a conversation, (probably the same that Governor Smith heard) relative to an agreement between Senator Edwards and Glass to pair off in the Miller-Martin contest, in which Hinds said (speaking of Edwards) "he is fixed, I will answer for that." Moulton states that at the time said convesration occurred it was of vital importance to Spencer that Miller should be seated, "Spencer told me in Washington that it must be done—that his seat depended upon it—that it was of vital importance and was the key to the situation." "He said his friends in the United States Senate regarded it as necessary, (and so advised him,) to seat Miller, and if it was not done it was doubtful whether he could retain his seat." The same view of this matter was taken by other very prominent members of the Spencer party. Hinds was returned to Montgomery and got $1,990 from Mr. Mitchell, of which $1,000 was furnished by Spencer directly, and doubtless the balance indirectly. This was on 17th January, 1873.

The Senate, under the Attorney-General's plan, was democratic by one majority. All the officers elected by the Senate were democrats. To meet this state of case the plan was devised by Hinds, Betts, Pelham, Whiting and others, to get an agreement between Edwards (democrat,) and Glass (republican,) to pair off in the Miller-Martin contest, for ten days, and then to have Glass to break his promise. That he did so in the most shameless manner is beyond question. Glass and Edwards left Montgomery at the same time, from the same depot, but on different roads, for the avowed purpose of going home. Edwards lived 150 miles from Montgomery, in a place difficult of access, and remote from railroads or telegraphs; Glass lived within 40 miles of Montgomery, at Tuskegee, to which place there was a line of railway. Glass, in charge of Betts, went a few miles out of Montgomery, left the train, got into a close carriage, returned to Montgomery, secreted himself in a room in the Madison House, prepared for him by Hinds and Betts, and remained secreted, with a guard over him, until the moment the vote was to be taken in the Senate on the Miller-Martin contest.

While so secreted his presence in Montgomery was not generally known to many of the leading republicans, and the democrats had no suspicion of it. It was a secret in the keeping of Spencer's managers. McKinstry knew it and visited him in his place of seclusion, as Glass testifies. He was the presiding officer of the re-organized Senate, and knew the purpose of Glass' concealment. Glass got his leave of absence on the 28th January for three days, which on the next day was enlarged to ten days, but was not entered on the journals. But on the 30th January, at 12 o'clock, the Senate took up the reports on the Miller-Martin case, and the question was put on the motion to substitute the minority report for the resolutions acccompanying the report of the majority of the committee. At that moment Betts had a close carriage at the door of the Madison House, and upon an agreed signal being given him from the balcony of the capitol, he put Glass in the carriage and took him to the capitol.

Brainard describes Glass' entry to the Senate chamber as follows : He knew that Glass had been secreted in Montgomery for the purpose of breaking his engagement with Edwards. He says—"It had been intimated to me that Mr. Glass *would arrive from Macon* before the vote was taken in the Martin-Miller contest. I also had hints that Mr. Glass was about the capitol keeping out of the way. While the ayes and noes were being called Mr. Glass dropped in with a cotton umbrella under his arm, an old grey shawl over his shoulders, and a lean carpet-bag in his hand. He was dusty, and had the appearance of having just come off a journey. I went to the capitol to enjoy the tableau and was not disappointed." This statement from one of Spencer's "mana-

5

gers," is a fitting introduction to a statement of another part
of the same scene from another.

Robert Barber, the clerk of the House, and one of Spencer's most influential managers, says as follows: After stating
that in a caucus of the managers for Spencer it was decided
upon that Miller was to be seated, upon the consolidation of
the two bodies, in his contest with Martin, he was asked the
question "How was this to be accomplished?"

A. We were to sustain Lieutenant Governor McKinstry in
his rulings, whatever decisions he might make."

"2. State fully how McKinstry's rulings were to be sustained; by what persons, and by what means."

"A. To carry out the plan agreed upon, and to get Mc-
Kinstry to rule so as to seat Miller before an absent Senator
(Edwards) returned, it was thought necessary for McKinstry
to rule so as to cut off debate and secure a final vote. It was
thought, if McKinstry so ruled, that the democratic members
would bolt, or withdraw from the Senate, or have a fight. To
provide for the latter contingency, picked men were procured,
and were by agreement in the Senate Chamber, in the lobby."

2. "Who were these men?"

"A. W. H. Betts, Charles Pelham (then a circuit judge),
Sam. Oliver, M. G. Candee, Milo Barber, J. J. Hinds, and a
rough from Georgia whose name I do not know, and some five
or six others whose names I can not remember; some from
Mobile."

Thus it is proven that McKinstry's rulings, which are de-
nounced by every respectable Republican in the State, were
pre-arranged by a caucus of Spencer's "managers," viz: C.
C. Sheets, Charles Pelham, W. H. Betts, J. J. Hinds, R. P.
Baker, D. C. Whiting, and Robert Barber. They were conceived in the most deliberate fraud, and sustained by a picked
crowd of men provided for the purpose. McKinstry, while
he supposed he was backed by this posse, defied, bullied, and
threatened Senators on the floor, whose appeal to the Senate
he refused to put, and said to the Secretary, when called on
by Senator Parks to put the motion, he dared not put it to
the Senate; and for the purpose of intimidating Senators, he

made a demonstration as if for battle, by emptying the water
from a heavy pitcher, and opening a drawer in his desk, to
intimate that he was prepared with deadly weapons. A wise
forbearance on the part of Senators alone prevented a scene
of violence and bloodshed.

Barber thus further states the plan agreed upon which this
combined demonstration of force and fraud was designed to
consummate: "It was generally understood amongst 'the
managers' that Senator Glass was to pair off with Senator
Edwards in the vote in the Miller-Martin contest. That Glass
was to go over to the depot with Edwards, and return back to
the city seemingly or apparently unknown to Edwards—the
idea being to make outsiders believe that they both left the
same day."

"They did both go to the depot on the same day and at
the same time."

"Glass returned without the knowledge of Edwards, and
was secreted in a room in the Madison House."

"To give Glass an excuse for breaking his pledge with Senator Edwards, I served a subpœna on him which was given
me by Charles Pelham to execute on him as a witness in some
case in which Pelham was an attorney. I went to the Madison House to execute this writ, and found R. P. Baker doorkeeper for Glass. I asked him to execute the subpœna by
handing it to Glass, which he did."

"Glass was kept out of sight until the vote was being taken
in the said Martin-Miller contest. He was informed by signal
from the front of the capitol the very moment his presence
was required. He appeared in the Senate in time, and did
vote for seating Miller. I understood he was to be paid $300
or $500 for breaking faith with Edwards."

It is needless to pursue this matter any further. Barber
and Glass concur in all the material facts touching this dis-
graceful fraud. Glass denies that he received any money.

The value of this denial, on such a subject, as contrasted
with the other evidence by which the fact of bribery is strongly
indicated, will be more apparent when we remember that, at
the close of his deposition, he states that what he said to the

committee, the moment before he was sworn, was all false, and was so stated because he was not under oath.

The Senate arraigned him at the last session for these crimes, and he resigned to escape the investigation.

Recurring to the fact that the two organizations, each claiming to be the General Assembly, existed in Alabama in November and December, 1872, your committee deem it their duty briefly to examine some of the evidence, submitted herewith, which they think bears upon the question of the legality of the two bodies.

Your committee are firmly convinced that the lawfulness of either of the two bodies, claiming to be the legislature of Alabama, must be determined by the solution of the question, which body most nearly conformed to the Constitution and laws of the State, in the credentials of its membership and in its organization; and that, judged by these tests, the Assembly at the Capitol was the lawful Legislature of the State. Governor Parsons, who was the Speaker of the House in the Court-house Assembly, testifies to the opinion that the Assembly at the Capitol *was the regular and lawful General Assembly of Alabama from the time it was organized until Governor Lindsay went out of office.*

This opinion he held at the time the Court-house Assembly elected him Speaker, which was six days before Lindsay's term expired. He was, by common consent, the most important and influential person concerned in the Court-house Assembly.

Without him, that organization could never have been made or sustained. He led the desperate emeute against civil government in Alabama, to gratify a too earnest desire for the domination of the Republican Party.

The Court-house assemblage was organized, not because of any necessity, but for party purposes, and as an experiment, in the hope that Governor Lewis, when he should be inaugurated, would recognize that body as the Legislature of Alabama. Governor Parsons further states his opinion, *that the recognition by Lewis of the Court-house body destroyed the legality of the Legislature at the Capitol, and established the Court-*

*house body as the lawful Legislature;* and this is the legal foundation on which this revolution in the State government was rested.

Your committee do not find it necessary to make any argument to sustain the proposition that the Governor of Alabama can not, at his pleasure, make a Legislature by his recognition of it, or destroy another by withholding such recognition.

The Constitution confines the legislative power to a separate body of magistracy, and makes it, in this respect, entirely independent of the execvtive department.

But such was the opinion of the leaders of the Court-house body, and it prevailed to the overthrow, for a time, of constitutional government in Alabama, and to the disturbance of the peace of the State, to an extent never before experienced by our people.

The leaders of the Court-house body were incited to this movement through partizan zeal, and claimed that it was necessary to enable the Republican party to enjoy the fruits of a victory gained in a popular election.

This was not a justifiable reason or motive for a proceeding so harsh, and so clearly opposed to the laws and Constitution of Alabama. There was a clear and easy way provided by law to settle these questions, and the law should have prevailed.

The law is always entitled to the respect of all the citizens of the State. These laws and this Constitution were in fact enacted by the Republican party; but by whatsoever party they were enacted, obedience to them was due from every citizen, and especially from those who claimed the power to legislate for the people.

No political party can have claims to power, or to the honors and emoluments of office, that are paramount to the duty of obedience to the laws of the land, particularly in the delicate matter of transmitting the powers of the State government lawfully, regularly, and peacefully from the hands of one set of officers to those of another, in conformity to the choice of the people, as expressed in the elections.

From the testimony of Gov. Parsons, it is obvious that the ruling motive in the project to organize a separate Legislature at the Court-house was to secure to the Republican party the organization of the two houses of the General Assembly. Whether or not his fears of losing this advantage were well founded, the evil consequences of a revolution in the State at that time were too serious to be balanced against the mere danger of losing a United States Senator to a political party, or of losing any power or patronage it might otherwise exercise.

It was not a just view of the subject to assume that any body of representatives would defraud their colleagues of the right to seats in the General Assembly, when those rights were legally established.

The apprehensions expressed by Mr. Parsons that a Democratic organization of the General Assembly would result in the adoption of a new constitution, in which the rights of colored people would be abridged or destroyed, have been refuted in the most unquestionable manner. The immense vote for the ratification of the constitution, ordained by a convention of whom nine-tenths were Democrats, includes a large number of Republicans, black and white, and is the best evidence of the justice of the provisions of the instrument, and of the fallacy of Gov. Parson's apprehensions.

There was no necessity for the organization of the body that met at the Court-house in November, 1872. It placed the good and law-abiding people of the State in the power of the worst class. It was the only plan by which George E. Spencer could gain the mastery over the better men of his own party. To this extent it succeeded, and some of the most respected and influential men of the Republican Party in Alabama, have testified in substance that while Spencer was not in fact the choice of his party, his power to defeat its legislative organization, and his known willingness to do so if he could procure an election by the Democratic party, compelled his toleration, and gained for him the support of men, who, under other circumstances, would have spurned his claims to a seat in the Senate.

It was not true that the Democratic party sought an alliance with him, or would for any consideration have elected him to the Senate ; but he contrived to give currency to such an opinion, and thereby forced his party to nominate him for the Senate. The evidence in the case shows, in the opinion of the committee, that the body by which he was elected was not a legislature.

During the election of the members to the legislature he used means to secure to himself their votes, that abused the army, the post-office, and the revenue departments of the Government. He brought the evils of war upon the people ; caused them to fly from their homes, and to abstain from voting.

He prostituted his office to the purposes of bargainings and bribery to secure votes for his re-election. He corrupted United States officials, for whom he had procured federal appointments, and forced his appointees, under threats of removal from office, to pay money, and, some of them, to commit high crimes to obtain money to assist him in his election. He caused men to be appointed to sinecure positions in the custom-house, post-offices, and the offices of collectors of internal revenue, with the intent and understanding that, while in office, they would not be required to render any service to the Government, but would get their pay; and, while so paid, they would employ their time in securing pledges of votes and influence to re-elect him to the Senate.

He paid, and caused to be paid money to members of the Court-house Assembly, to secure their votes for him.

He paid, and caused to be paid, money to members of the Legislature to a defeat a quorum at the capitol, and thereby to prevent the election of a Senator by that body, and his most trusted agent, J. J. Hinds, caused a member of that body to be drugged and almost killed to prevent his attendance at the capitol.

He dealt in the offices of the United States as merchandise to secure money, and to gain votes in his re-election to the Senate. His managers, with his concurrence, caused a State Senator, for a money consideration, to break his pledge of

48

honor with another Senator, having pre-arranged the scheme, and thereby attempted to secure his seat in the Senate of the United States.

Through his said managers he procured the presiding officer of the Senate to connive at this fraud, and to rule, in violation of all parliamentary law and usage, so as to unseat a Senator elected by the people, and to seat in his place a partizan of Spencer, who was not elected by the people, and held no certificate of election.

He caused the lobby of the Senate to be filled with armed retainers to overawe Senators on the floor, and to sustain by force and violence what he had achieved by fraud.

He used his powers and influences, and the money he controlled through his position as a Senator to debauch men in office, and out of office, so that in his conduct he was working evil continually.

Your committee further ask the action of the General Assembly upon this report, and that the Memorial to be addressed to the Senate of the United States shall be based upon that action, and that the Commitee be allowed further time to consider said Memorial in connection with the action of the General Assembly, and to report the same.

W. G. LITTLE, JR., *Chm'n.*
WM. H. PARKS,
*On the part of the Senate.*
THOS. H. PRICE,
LEROY BREWER,
D. E. COON,
*On the part of the House.*

DECATUR, ALA., Sept. 4th, 1872.
*Hon. W. V. Turner, Wetumpka, Ala.:*

MY DEAR SIR—I am just leaving for New York to attend a meeting of the Nat. Ex. Committee. Collector Miller positively told me he would recommend you for an inspectorship in the Custom-house. Why he has not done so is more than I can tell. He worries me nearly to death by making promises he does not [fulfill]. I can't stand it much longer. Enclosed I send you a money order for $30; would send you more if I had it to spare. I have sent your letter to Miller, with one of my own, and have asked the old man what he means by making promises that he does not keep, and if he fails, you shall have something else. I hope you will keep a sharp lookout in Elmore and Autauga.

In great haste, your friend,

GEO. E. SPENCER.

I will be in Montgomery on the 23d and would like to meet you there.

WASHINGTON, September 14, 1872.

MY DEAR SIR: Your confirmation as inspector of customs was forwarded to Collector Miller yesterday, at $4 per diem pay. Go at once to Mobile, be sworn in, and apply for leave of absence until after the election, which Collector Miller will arrange for you. Show him this letter; he will understand it.

In haste, truly yours.

GEO. E. SPENCER.

Hon. W. V. TURNER, Wetumpka, Ala.

DECATUR, ALA., Oct. 19th, 1872.

MY DEAR SIR: I have received all your letters; until after the election, I have no time to answer letters; I have not one day out of twenty, and then have a bushel of letters to write and answer, and can only give attention to the most pressing. When this "cruel war is o'er" I will promptly answer the letter of all my friends. I asked Captain Whiting to send you to Macon and Russell counties, and hope he has done so. Please look out for my interests wherever you go, and believe me to be your friend,

GEO. E. SPENCER.

UNITED STATES SENATE,
December 16th, 1872.

DEAR SIR: Yours of 9th at hand. I have just mailed a letter to Collector Miller, requesting your payment and retention in Custom-house, in positive terms.

I hope there will be no further trouble.

Truly yours,

GEO. E. SPENCER.

HON. WM. V. TURNER, Wetumpka, Ala.

WASHINGTON, D. C., Oct. 7th, 1874.

MY DEAR SIR: I wish you would do me the personal favor to go to Lowndes county, and take the stump for Mr. Doster, and our ticket generally. You can do good service there, and it is very important that Doster should be elected.  Your prompt action in this behalf will be appreciated by.

Truly your friend,<br>GEO. E. SPENCER.

HON. W. V. TURNER, Montgomery, Ala.

[*Private.*]  DECATUR, ALA., Oct. 16th, 1872.

DEAR BARBER: I have just returned home from West Alabama, and find that Whiting has gone to New York, and has left word for me to go to Montgomery; I cannot for two or three days leave here.  I wish you would write me the news what Whiting has gone to New York for?  And the prospects, etc., etc.  Write me a long letter by return mail, and tell me all that has occurred.  Was Stanwood beaten in Lowndes?  I have heard nothing in a week.  Have you heard of any troops having been ordered to the State?  Can't you manage to get White off the Legislative Ticket in Dallas?  Parsons has a deep laid scheme to elect himself, and has gone to New York to try and raise money to be used in the Legislature.  I have news direct from him.  See Beach and Coon and urge them to see that White is taken down.  Be sure and write me everything that is going on.

In haste, sincerely yours,<br>GEO. E. SPENCER.

DECATUR, ALA., Oct. 22d, 1872.

MY DEAR BARBER: I have just returned from Louisville, where I have been to see General Terry about troops for Alabama.  I have had a company of Cavalry sent to Livingston, a detachment to Pickens county; a company of Infantry to Eutaw; a company to Demopolis, and a company to Seals' Station, Russell county; also, a squadron of cavalry to report to Marshal Thomas, at Huntsville.  I wish Randolph, Deputy U. S. Marshal, would use the company at Opelika in making arrests in Tallapoosa, Randolph and Cleburne, as ——— suggests.  I will be in Montgomery Thursday morning to attend the meeting of the State Committee.  I would go sooner, but cannot, as it is important I should stay here to-morrow.

I wish you would go to Talladega and block that game; I must not, however, be known in the matter.  The troops mentioned above will all be in their respective places in two days from now; some have already arrived.

In haste, truly yours,<br>GEO. E. SPENCER.

# MEMORIAL.

*To the Honorable the Senate of the United States:*

The memorial of the General Assembly of the State of Alabama respectfully invites the attention of your honorable body to the condition in which the State of Alabama stands, in its representation upon the floor of the Senate of the United States.

Your memorialists, the General Assembly of Alabama, respectfully represent to your honorable body that George E. Spencer, who now sits as one of the Senators from Alabama for the term beginning on the 4th day of March, 1873, has not been elected either by the concurrent or the joint vote of the Senate and House of Representatives which form the legislature of the State of Alabama, and therefore is not entitled to hold the seat claimed by him.

Your memorialists do not now question the propriety of the decision of the Senate in recognizing the right of Mr. Spencer to take the seat of Senator from Alabama on the 4th day of March, 1873, by virtue of the certificate of his election which he presented under the hand of the Governor and the great seal of the State. That document on its face entitled him to the seat, and authorized him in all respects to exercise the functions of a Senator, until its validity was successfully questioned.

While your memorialists do not question the decision of your honorable body in seating Mr. Spencer, the State has never conceded his election, or his right to represent it in the Senate; and as a sense of duty they owed to the people of the State, at the last General Assembly of Alabama, the session of 1874–5, the Senate and House of Representatives adopted the following resolutions:

"Whereas, in the opinion of the General Assembly of Alabama, Hon. George E. Spencer does not rightfully occupy a seat in the Senate of the United States, as a Senator from Alabama;

"*Be it resolved by the House of Representatives, the Senate concurring*, That a joint committee, to consist of two Senators and three members of the House of Representatives, be appointed to investigate, examine and report to the two houses of the General Assembly the facts relating to his alleged election as Senator, and the means by which such election was procured, and his credentials as a Senator were obtained.

"*Resolved 2.* That said committee, or a majority of them, may sit during the session of the General Assembly, and during the recess, at any place in this State, and shall have authority to send for persons and papers, and to call witnesses before them to be examined on oath, and to employ a clerk to keep the record and proceedings of the committee.

"*Resolved 3.* That said committee report with all convenient speed a memorial to be addressed by the General Assembly to the Senate of the United States touching the claims of George E. Spencer to a seat in that body as a Senator from Alabama, and shall report to the two houses the evidence taken under these resolutions."

In accordance with said resolutions a joint committee was appointed by the Senate and House of Representatives for the purposes expressed therein, and in the recess of the Legislature proceeded to examine witnesses and take their depositions in writing; which, with the report of said committee adopted by the General Assembly of Alabama, is herewith (with this memorial) presented to your honorable body for its information, and as a denial of right, as against the presumptive evidence offered by Mr. Spencer, to the seat occupied by him.

Your memorialists do not ask, that upon any investigation your honorable body may order of the conduct of George E. Spencer, you will confine said examination to the testimony submitted herewith. Notwithstanding Mr Spencer had full opportunity to cross-examine said witnesses, and to introduce any testimony in his favor to explain or rebut their evidence, or to be represented in person, or by counsel, before said investigating committee. Your memorialists do, however, respectfully ask that your honorable body will examine the report and evidence herewith submitted with this memorial. The evidence thus taken establishes a state of facts that makes it necessary that the State of Alabama should vindicate her right to be represented in the Senate of the United States, by a person chosen by a body, and in a manner that is legal, and not by means that defy the laws, and by a body that was revolutionary; and further, the facts established make it necessary that the State should vindicate her honor against the imputation of being represented in the Senate of the United States by a person whose alleged election was procured by corrupt practices, which are scandalous to the dignity of the State.

Upon the facts presented in said report and accompanying evidence, which, in the opinion of the General Assembly, will be strengthened by a further examination of witnesses and documentary evidence.

Your memorialists, the General Assembly of Alabama, submit most respectfully to your honorable body the following propositions, touching the alleged election of George E. Spencer, and his fitness to represent the State of Alabama in the Senate of the United States, and respectfully ask the consideration thereof, viz:

1. The means which he used (while he was a Senator of the United States) in attempting to secure the election of a majority of the Legislature that would support him for re-election to the Senate.

2. That the body by which George E. Spencer claims to have been elected to the Senate of the United States was not in fact or in law the General Assembly of Alabama, at the time of the election of George E. Spencer, and never was. There never was a quorum in the Senate that voted for said Spencer, and the records and journals of the General Assembly show that fact. The body that voted for Spencer was organized as a party necessity, and to elect Spencer.

3. By unlawful and corrupt practices, and by bargains made by Geo. E. Spencer and other persons, with his knowledge and approval, both before and at the time of his alleged election, with members of the body by which he claims to have been

elected, he procured the influence and votes of members of said body for the office of Senator of the United States.

4. That, being a Senator at the time of his alleged re-election to the Senate of the United States, the said George E. Spencer corruptly used the influence, power and patronage of his said office to procure influence, assistance and votes from members of said body, by which he claims to have been re-elected to the Senate of the United States on the 3d day of December, 1872.

5. That by like fraudulent and corrupt practices, and to defeat the election of a Senator by the General Assembly of Alabama at the time appointed by law, the said George E. Spencer, and others by his concurrence or connivance, did prevent the attendance of members of the General Assembly at the Capitol, and did so defeat a quorum of the houses of said body.

6. That afterwards, when a plan had been suggested by the Attorney General of the United States, which was adopted for the re-organization of the General Assembly, the said George E. Spencer and others with his connivance, in order to deprive a Senator of his seat in said body to which he had been lawfully elected by the people, and thereby obtain confirmation of his said election to the United States Senate, fraudulently and corruptly conspired to oust said Senator from his seat, and did prevent him from occupying the same during more than one entire session of the General Assembly of Alabama.

7. That said George E. Spencer, while endeavoring to secure his re-election to the Senate, and in order to get money to accomplish his said purposes, and while he was a Senator of the United States procured persons, who had been appointed to office of trust in the United States Government, to convert the public money in their charge to his use, and to commit peculations for his advantage.

These and other matters which are established by the testimony taken on said investigation, seem to require that the State of Alabama and the Senate of the United States, should take such measures as will secure to the State a person lawfully elected, and a fit representative to the Senate of the United States, and one that is worthy and qualified to occupy a seat in that high tribunal.

Your memorialists respectfully state that Geo. E. Spencer was not legally elected Senator from Alabama, nor was he ever voted for by a body, having a quorum of elected members, or a quorum of certificated members, as the Journals of the General Assembly of Alabama will show.

Your memorialists respectfully pray of your Honorable Body, that you will take the report of the committee accompanying this memorial as a part of the same; that you will examine the evidence attached thereto taken by said committee, and that the right of said Spencer to the seat he now holds, may be inquired into, and his claim thereto be declared invalid, and said seat be declared vacant.

# EVIDENCE

TAKEN BEFORE THE

# JOINT COMMITTEE

OF THE

## GENERAL ASSEMBLY OF ALABAMA,

*Appointed to examine and report to the two Houses of the General Assembly the facts relating to the alleged election of Hon. George E. Spencer, as Senator in the Congress of the United States, the means by which such election was procured and his credentials as a Senator were obtained.*

# EVIDENCE.

March 18, 1875.

The Joint Committee consisting of Messrs. W. G Little, jr.,
and W. H. Parks, of the Senate, and Messrs. Thomas H. Price,
Leroy Brewer and Datus E. Coon, of the House of Representatives of the General Assembly of Alabama, appointed under
the following joint resolution :

WHEREAS, in the opinion of the General Assembly of Alabama, Hon. George E. Spencer does not rightfully occupy a
seat in the Senate of the United States as a Senator from
Alabama :

*Be it Resolved*, By the House of Representatives, the Senate
concurring, That a joint committee to consist of two Senators
and three members of the House of Representatives be appointed to investigate, examine and report to the two Houses
of the General Assembly the facts relating to his alleged
election as Senator, and the means by which such election
was procured and his credentials as a Senator were obtained.

*Resolved*, 2. That said committee, or a majority thereof,
may sit during the session of the General Assembly and during the recess, at any place in this State, and shall have authority to send for persons and papers, and to call witnesses
before them on oath, and to employ a clerk to keep the records and papers of the committee.

*Resolved*, 3. That said committee report with all convenient
speed a memorial to be addressed by the General Assembly
to the Senate of the United States, touching the claims of
George E. Spencer to a seat in that body as a Senator from
Alabama, and shall report to the two Houses the evidence
taken under these resolutions;

Met in the city of Montgomery on the day above named.

On motion of Mr. Brewer, Mr. Little was elected chairman
of the committee, and J. H. Francis was employed as clerk.

The committee then adjourned to meet in Mobile, Ala., on the 28th day of April, 1875.

MOBILE, ALABAMA, }
April 28, 1875. }

The committee met pursuant to adjournment.
Present—Messrs. Brewer and Price.
A quorum not being present, the committee adjourned until 10 a. m. to-morrow.

MOBILE, ALABAMA, }
April 29, 1875. }

The committee met pursuant to adjournment.
Present—Messrs. Little, Parks, Price, Brewer and Coon.
On motion of Mr Parks, it was agreed that Gen. John T. Morgan be admitted to the sessions of the committee as counsel for the State, and that Mr. Spencer be admitted in person or his counsel.
On motion of Mr. Price, it was agreed that the committee sit with open doors, unless otherwise ordered.
Mr. Little, the chairman of the committee, submitted the following copy of a letter which he had written to Mr. Spencer:

APRIL 22, 1875.
*Hon. Geo. E. Spencer, Washington City:*
Dear Sir—The committee appointed under a resolution of the General Assembly of Alabama, to enquire into and investigate how you procured your election as Senator from the State of Alabama to the Congress of the United States, will meet in the city of Mobile on Thursday, April 29, to proceed with said investigation, and this is to notify you. You can be present if you see proper to do so.
W. G. LITTLE, Chairman
of said committee.

On motion of Mr. Brewer, it was agreed that Hon. George E. Spencer be informed by telegraph of the meeting of the committee, and that he could appear in person or by counsel before said committee if he desired to do so.
The chairman, Mr. Little, subsequently announced that he had telegraphed Mr. Spencer, as instructed by the committee, and had received a reply from the telegraph office at Washington informing him that the dispatch of Mr. Little to Mr. Spencer was delivered at 1.15 o'clock, p. m., Nov. 20, to Mr. Spencer.
The committee then proceeded to take the testimony of

### JOHN J. MOULTON,

of the city of Mobile, who being duly sworn, says:

I know George E, Spencer. I was present in the city of Montgomery on the day before the organization of the General Assembly on the 18th of November, 1872, at the court house. I returned to Mobile and went back to Montgomery about the 24th of the same month. I went to Montgomery by appointment with Mr. Spencer, when I first went up; but he was not there when I returned from Mobile to Montgomery. I think I went at the instance of Mr. Spencer. I was not in Montgomery the day of the election of U. S. Senator by the court house assembly. I was there between the time of organization and the election of Spencer, and saw him there at that time. When I went on the last occasion I took a considerable sum of money with me—either a letter of credit or a check for $5,000, or about that amount. The letter of credit was on Josiah Morris & Co.

Questions by General Morgan.

Q. Was there any other time you took money to Montgomery about the time of the election for U. S. Senator?

A. The first time I took a bill of exchange on New York for $5,000, drawn by T. P. Miller & Co. The next time I took money—it was $2,500, or about that amount. The records will show.

Q. At whose instance or request did you take this money?

A. I cannot remember distinctly as to the first money. At the second time at the instance of Spencer. This last money was taken after Spencer's election by the court house assembly and about the time of Attorney General Williams' proposition of compromise was made.

Q. Do you know Jerome J. Hinds?

A. I do. He lives at Decatur, Ala.

Q. What were the relations between he and Spencer?

A. Very intimate.

Q. During the period of which we have been talking, did you pay over any money to Hinds?

A. I did.

Q. Did you take receipts?

A. Yes, for some amounts, but can not say as to all.

Q. Did you pay any money on Hinds' order?

A. I paid only to him.

Q. How much did you pay Hinds?

A. I can not say exactly. I took his receipt for $1,800 at one time. I can not tell all. That was on the occasion of the organization of the legislature at the capitol, after Spencer's election by the court house assembly.

Q. Had you paid Hinds any money before this ?

A. I don't think I had.

Q. Did you owe Hinds any money ?

A. I did not.

Q. For what purpose did you pay him this money ?

A. I paid it over on a dispatch at the request of Spencer.

Q. For what purpose was the money paid ?

A. I must answer from the surroundings.

Q. What was the purport of the dispatch ?

A. It read in substance as follows : "Meet Hinds in Montgomery" on a given day (which I think was Friday); "bring funds." Signed, "Geo. E. Spencer." The dispatch was dated at Washington.

Q. Did you owe Spencer any money ?

A. I did not. After Spencer's election he paid me, on the 4th of December, 1872, $2,200.

Q. What was your understanding of the use that was to be made of the money you paid to Hinds?

A. The short of it was, the fight was to be made over in the Martin-Miller contest in the Senate, and the money was to be used in seating Miller.

Q. What money do you refer to?

A. The $1,800.

Q. About how much more than the $1,800 did you let Hinds have ?

A. After he gave me the receipt, he came to me for other sums. I can't remember the amounts.

Q. How much money did you let Hinds have in all these legislative transactions, or Whiting, or any other person?

A. I can't fix it definitely in my mind. I think it less than $4,000.

Q. What were the relations between Whiting and Spencer ?

A. They were intimate.

Q. What was Whiting engaged in ?

A. He had some sinecure position under the federal government. He drew pay all the time, and was chairman of the Republican State Executive Committee.

Q. Did you see any of this money you paid to Hinds or Whiting paid out to any one ?

A. I saw Hinds pay some out.

Q. To whom, and what amounts?

A. The only sum I saw paid was a hundred dollar bill. Hinds and I were walking up to the capitol. We saw a man approaching, and Hinds said, "there is a man I want to give a hundred dollars. I have paid out all the money you let me have." I took out a hundred dollar bill and gave it to Hinds.

He handed it to the gentleman, who Hinds said was a member of the legislature and a Democrat. I could not tell the man's name. I might do so if I had a list of the members to look over.

Q. Did he tell you to whom he paid the money, or any part of it?

A. He said he wanted a $500 dollar bill to pay Mr. Glass, which I let him have. This was after the reorganization. It may have been just at the time. Both bodies were at the capitol.

Q. Do you know of any other moneys Hinds or Whiting used?

A. I do not. There is a dispute about the money Whiting received. It is alleged he used it for his own purposes.

Q. Was this your own money?

A. Yes, sir, all of it.

Q. Please look over this list of members of the General Assembly, and see if you recognize the name of the person to whom you saw Hinds pay the $100 bill.

A. (After examining list.) I can not recognize the name.

Q. Was the Martin-Miller contest pending when the $500 and the $100 were paid by Hinds?

A. It was.

Q. Were you at that time a man of wealth, Mr. Moulton?

A. I was very much embarrassed.

Q. What was the grounds upon which Spencer made these requests?

A. To help his election as U. S. Senator.

Q. What claim had he upon you upon which he depended to require from you these large sums of money?

A. I was holding office which was under his control. He never attempted to use that directly. It was an important and valuable office. My sons were also holding office.

Q. Without any specific fact being made known by Mr. Spencer, did you not consider that was the ground upon which he made the demand?

A. It was understood the large sums were to be refunded by Spencer.

Q. Did Spencer know your resources for obtaining large sums of money?

A. I do not think he took it into account. When I became largely involved, I notified him I must be protected in my private interests and otherwise. Prior to his election as senator, I told him my financial condition. I told him I must have $10,000 to settle my accounts with the government. He said he would let me have the amount, promised me that I should have it. He has never let me have it, and I paid it out of my private means. He told me to wait until he was elected to the Senate and he would have $10,000 left, he thought, and I should have every dollar of it. I told him I intended to resign as postmaster of Mobile. I said to him, "I can't stand this any longer." He replied, "don't resign. I will stand by you till hell freezes over." Mr. Petherbridge came to me for a settlement of my accounts. I drew on Spencer for $5,000 by telegraph. My draft was not honored, nor has it ever been paid. This was about July 11, 1873.

Q. Did you ever demand other sums of him?

A. I did not. The demand for $5,000 was shortly after his election. I drew by telegraph and he replied, "I am out of money."

Q. Did Mr. Spencer, by telegraph or otherwise, ever intimate the use of post office money for political purposes?

A. He did not.

Q. Did he assure you you would be protected by the postoffice department or through his influence, or any other influence, for the use of post office money for political purposes?

A. No. I had a conversation with him in Montgomery at the time I asked him for the $10,000. I told him I was discouraged. I told him I was going to resign unless that money was paid. He said, don't do it. I replied, I would be compelled to do so. He replied, don't do it. I will stand by you. I can make it all right in Washington.

Q. Did you understand that he meant to indemnify you out of his own resources, or that through his influence he could protect you?

A. I did not believe, from my knowledge, he could pay me out of his resources; but I knew he had had control of about $15,000 of an election fund during the campaign, and from his further statement to me, that he would have $10,000 left.

Q. How long after you separated from him in Montgomery before you drew upon him for $5,000?

A. About two months.

Q. Did you make great sacrifices for the money advanced for him?

A. I did.

Q. Did you pay to any other persons besides Hinds and Whiting any moneys in Montgomery, or turn over any moneys?

A. No sir, I think not.

Q. Did Spencer or his friends say to you at any time before or after his election, that the object of the meeting of the court house assembly was to secure the election of an U. S. Senator?

A. He did not. His friends evidently had that in view.

Q. Who were the active friends outside of the legislature in urging his election?

A. There were a number.

Q. Who were regarded the leaders?

A. Hinds was very prominent. Whiting did what he could. Hinds has always been nearer to Spencer than any other man. It was thought Hinds had always to be pacified to secure Spencer's favor. This has been the case since Spencer's election. They are very intimate and live in the same house.

Q. Were there any other active men for Spencer in the lobby?

A. Governor Smith and all the Federal office holders in the State were doing all they could. I do not think if Spencer's election had been certain that the court house legislature would have been organized.

By Mr. Little—

Q. Do you state that this money was used directly or indirectly to secure the election of Mr. Spencer?

A. That was understood to be the purpose. There is no doubt such was the case.

Questions by Gen. Morgan—

Q. After the election of Spencer and the plan of the organization of the legislature had been proposed by Attorney General Williams, did you receive any telegrams from Spencer?

A. I did. He telegraphed me from Washington to go to Montgomery to meet Hinds and to bring funds. In this dispatch, or in a dispatch or letter received about this time, Spencer stated that the fight had to be made over again.

Q. How much money did you take to Montgomery at the request of Spencer to be handed to Hinds?

A. About $2,500 or $3,000 in a letter of credit on Josiah Morris & Co.

Q. Did you afterwards furnish any money to any one else to be used for the benefit of Spencer.

A. I afterwards received a dispatch, on the 10th or 11th day of January, from Hinds, drawing upon me for $500. I received two or three dispatches from him the same day. He said he must have the money, that it was absolutely necessary. I telegraphed him to call upon Bingham, who had funds in his possession of mine, who would pay him about $250; which he did.

Q. Did Hinds telegraph for these funds on his own account or Spencer's?

A. Unquestionably on Spencer's. I never had a business transaction with Hinds.

Q. After that time did you, in any way, furnish any moneys to Hinds, or any one else, on Spencer's account?

A. I did not.

Q. Were any requests made by Hinds, Whiting, or any one else, for money to be used in these legislative transactions for Spencer's benefit to which you failed to respond?

A. No other.

Q. Was Petherbridge in Mobile at the time Hinds' dispatch was received?

A. He was.

Q. Will you fix some day upon which the conversation occurred between you and Spencer, in which you told him you would resign?

A. I think it was on the first or fourth of December, 1872. I am inclined to think it was two or three days before his election occurred.

Q. Why was it that you demanded $10,000 of Spencer when you had not advanced that amount?

A. I don't think I demanded it. I stated to him I must have that amount. For eighteen months before this drafts had been drawn upon me by different persons for political purposes at Spencer's instance, and in this way I had advanced a large amount of money, in which I was assured I would be protected by Spencer. It was in this way the sum had accumulated that I told Spencer it must be refunded to me. The amount I had thus advanced exceeded $10,000.

Q. Did he ever deny to you his liability to refund this money to you?

A. He did not in any respect.

Q. Were any of these drafts drawn by Whiting or Hinds?

A. They were.

Q. Were they large amounts in the aggregate?

A. They were.

Q. In the latter part of 1872 did you tell Spencer you were broke?

A. I think I told him I was bankrupt.

Q. Did you tell him or give him to understand that the heavy drafts made upon you was the cause of it?

A. Spencer knew it, and always recognized it in his conversations with me.

Q. Was all this prior to the request to furnish money to Hinds at Montgomery?

A. It was.

Q. Have you any recollection of Hinds having told you to whom he paid money, or that he wanted money in connection with Spencer's election?

A. He told me in conversations that various persons wanted money; that this man wants so much (naming the man), and that one wants so much, but I cannot recall the names of the persons mentioned. The question was asked in my presence, whether the senator who paired off with Glass would not return on a particular day, referring to the day upon which the Martin-Miller contest was to be decided. Hinds spoke up and said that he (referring to the Senator) had been "fixed."

Questions by Mr. Parks—

Q. Might not Hinds have referred to the agreement made between this Senator and Glass?

A. He undoubtedly referred to that, but conveyed the idea that there had been some arrangement made between himself (Hinds) and that Senator. When it was suggested that the Democratic senator might return, Hinds spoke up and said, "he is fixed, I will answer for that."

Q. Was that in the conversation in which he said "I want so much for this man and so much for that?"

A. No sir! It was more than a month afterwards.

Question by Mr. Coon—

Q. Did you understand at the time Hinds used the expression "he is fixed," that he meant that money had been used?

A. I did so understand it. It was understood that the disbursement of money was Hinds' business, on account of General Spencer.

Questions by General Morgan—

Q. At the time the last conversation named occurred, was it considered a necessity to the security of Spencer's seat in the senate that the Martin-Miller contest should be settled in favor of Miller.

A. It was considered of vital importance. Spencer told me in Washington that it must be done; that his seat depended upon it; that it was of vital importance, and was the key to the situation.

Q. What did Spencer tell you of a conversation held with his friends in Washington in regard to the contract between Martin and Miller?

A. He said his friends in the United States Senate regarded it as necessary, and so advised him that it was necessary to seat Miller, and if it was not done it was doubtful whether he could retain his seat.

Q. Did Spencer, while you were in Washington, in any of the conversations had with him on this subject, request or require of you to aid him in this matter?

A.   No sir, if you refer to his being seated in the senate. These conversations occurred after I had furnished money as before stated to Hinds.

Q.   You spoke of a dispatch, on yesterday, received from Spencer, in cypher; to what did that dispatch relate?

A.   The dispatch requested me to furnish Hinds with money. It could only be read with a key, which both Spencer and I had.

Q.   Was Spencer in Montgomery during the Miller-Martin in contest.

A.   I don't think he was.

Q.   Who was his chief agent and manager in Montgomery?

A.   J. J. Hinds.

Q.   Do you know of any promises of office made by Spencer or his agents in consideration of supporting him for U..S. Senator?

A.   I do not of my own knowledge.

Q.   Do you know of such as stated by Hinds?

A.   I heard Hinds say if a certain member of the legislature stands firm he shall have a certain federal office, which he afterwards did get.

Q.   Did you hear Hinds say if George Duskin stood up to Spencer in his election for U. S. Senator, he would be appointed to a federal office?

A.   I did hear him say so.   My recollection is that Hinds was commissioned by Spencer, who was on the ground, to go directly to Duskin and make the bargain with him.

Q.   Did he get the office?

A.   He did and now holds it.

Q.   Had not Duskin withdrawn from the court house assembly before this time and started home?

A.   He had.   The pledges made to him were not satisfactory and he demanded a more responsible underwriter; at least so I understood it.   When he received the pledges demanded he returned and took his seat.

Q.   Do you know, as coming from Hinds or Spencer, the promise of federal office to any other members in case they supported Spencer for Senator?

A.   I know of none.

Questions by Mr. Little—

Q.   Did not J. C. Goodloe decline to go into the court house assembly for some time after its organization?

A.   Yes sir.

Q.   Before he went into the court house assembly, did you not hear the subject of his getting a federal office discussed?

A. It was understood that he was to be provided for.

Q. Was he subsequently appointed to a federal office?

A. He was. He received the appointment of collector of the port of Mobile.

Q. Who did you hear discussing this proposition relative to Mr. Goodloe?

A. Hinds and others of Spencer's friends.

Questions by Mr. Coon—

Q. Was it not your understanding that Senator Wilson of Montgomery was originally opposed to Spencer's second election?

A. I understood he was considered doubtful and needed to be looked after.

Q. Was it not your understanding that he was to receive the post office at Montgomery?

A. I did not so understand it at the time but learned it afterwards.

Q. Did Wilson finally obtain the post office at Montgomery and did he vote for Spencer?

A. He obtained the post office. The records will show how he voted.

Q. How much money did you advance in the Spencer-Warner contests?

A. About $2,000, in Spencer's interest, and at the request of H. Ray Myers.

Q. Previous to your appointment as post master of Mobile, how much money had you advanced in Spencer's interest?

A. Upwards of $2,000.

Questions by Gen. Morgan.—

Q. Did you at any time borrow any money from Gen. Spencer?

A. I did not.

Q. Did you borrow $2,250 from him the day after his election as U. S. Senator in Montgomery?

A. He gave me that amount. I did not borrow it.

Q. Why did he give it to you?

A. It was to refund moneys I had advanced for him in large sums as heretofore stated.

Q. In the cypher telegram spoken of in your evidence heretofore, did he demand of you that you should take money to Montgomery to pay the $2,250?

A. He did not. He said to come and bring funds.

Q. Has Spencer ever demanded of you since that time that you should refund to him the $2,250 or any part of it?

A. No, sir, he has never done so.

Q. Did you have a key to the cypher dispatch sent by Spencer?

A. I did.

Q. Did you have a key when the dispatch was received?

A. I did not and went over to Mayer's house and we read it together, he having a key. I told him this meant business; there was more work.

Q. Did that dispatch tell you to meet Spencer or Hinds?

A. Hinds. Mayer saw the dispatch and knew its contents.

Questions by Mr. Coon—

Q. Did you ever return any of the $2,250 voluntarily?

A. I have never paid one dime of the money.

Question by Mr. Price—

Q. Was Mayer present when Spencer handed you a package containing $2,250 in Montgomery, or did he participate in that transaction by way of carrying messages or otherwise between yourself and Spencer about the matter?

A. Mr. Spencer never handed me a package containing $2,250 at Montgomery or at any other time or place. Spencer did hand me a bank check for $2,250 drawn to his order and by him endorsed, and when he handed it to me it was in a room when no one was present. I never mentioned the matter to Mayer until a long time afterwards. This is the only check or money I ever received from Spencer.

JOHN. J. MOULTON.

#### W. H. LEWIS

Being sworn, says:

I was clerk in the post office in Mobile when Mr. J. J. Moulton was post master. Mr. Moulton obtained the place for me. I do not know Mr. Spencer. At one time I was in the money order department, and was afterwards made assistant post master. Mr. Moulton kept his bank account with T. P. Miller a short time before he went out of office. Remittances to the money order office were deposited either at the Custom house, at the First National Bank or at Miller's. Mr. Moulton drew drafts against the money so deposited.

Q. What property did Mr. Moulton have at that time?

A. But little other than his salary as postmaster.

Q. When he went out of office were his accounts behind?

A. They were, and my mother (Mrs. Moulton) had to raise the money out of her private means to settle them. This was about the middle of February, 1873.

Q. Do you know of any demands made upon Mr. Moulton

by any party at Montgomery to aid in the election of Mr. Spencer?

A. I do not.

W. H. LEWIS.

JAMES GILLETTE

Being sworn, says:

I was United States Commissioner for the Southern District of Alabama in 1872.

Questions by Gen. Morgan—

Q. Did you issue a warrant for the arrest of three persons from Marengo county, claiming to be representatives to the general assembly, just before the time for its annual session in the year 1872?

A. I did, and for two or three others not members.

Q. Where were you when the warrant was issued.

A. The warrant was issued at Montgomery on the affidavit of B. R. Thomas, who claimed to be a member from Marengo county. It was prepared by Alexander White and U. S. District Attorney Minnis.

Q. Where was the warrant returnable?

A. I desire to say that as supervisor of elections I considered my jurisdiction extended over the State. I was appointed by the United States Circuit Court, Chief Supervisor of Elections in the State. In the matter of the investigation of election troubles I considered my jurisdiction extended over the State. I do not know where the warrant was returnable. The records will show. The parties came before me in Mobile and waived examination.

Q. Was Gen. Spencer in Montgomery when the warrant was issued?

A. He was there when I left. I do not know whether he was there when the warrant was issued.

Q. Did you not go to Montgomery to commence that prosecution?

A. An affidavit was first made before me at Mobile, prepared by W. W. D. Turner. I sent the warrants to the marshal. I thought, upon further consideration, that the warrants ought to be recalled because the evidence was insufficient. I wrote to withdraw the warrants and went to Montgomery to see that they were withdrawn. When I arrived there, Mr. Thomas appeared before me, and made affidavit of the facts on his own knowledge, and issued new warrants. The parties were arrested, and were brought before me in this city. After waiving an examination, I bound them over to appear at the next term of the U. S. District Court. I turned the papers in the case over to the district attorney, and this is the last I ever heard of the case. The parties were brought to Mobile, during or about the time of the first assembling of the legislature in 1872.

Q. Were you in Montgomery when they were in Selma?

A. I do not know.

Q. You do not know the round they took?

A. I do not, except from rumor.

Q. Did you not know the purpose of the issue of the warrant was to prevent the participation of the Marengo members in the organization of the House of Representatives of the General Assembly.

A. I did not know any such thing. My knowledge of the case was purely official.

Q. What other officer in the southern district of Alabama had the right at that time to take bail?

A. I think there were two commissioners in the neighborhood of Demopolis, Mr. Wayne and Mr. Meredith, of Sumter, were commissioners.

Q. Who made the affidavit upon which the first warrant was issued?

A. A colored man. He was clear at first, but I talked with him afterwards and was not satisfied, and had some misgivings as to his statements. I had never seen him before.

Q. Did you know B. R. Thomas?

A. I did not know him before I met him in Montgomery.

Q. Do you know whether he is any more honest than the negro?

A. He made a more intelligent affidavit.

Q. Did you say the affidavit was prepared when you arrived in Montgomery?

A. Mr. White and Mr. Minnis were preparing it, or brought Mr. Thomas before me shortly after my arrival.

Q. Did you get back from Montgomery on the Monday or Tuesday of the week of the assembling of the court house assembly.

A. I do not remember.

Q. When in Montgomery, did you issue any other warrants?

A. I do not remember.

Q. Did you not issue warrants for the Barbour members?

A. I do not think I did. I am pretty certain I did not; but the records will show. I wish to state in reference to the warrant issued for the Marengo members and the board of supervisors for that county, I had in my office as chief supervisor, certain reports and tally lists made by the U. S. supervisor at Demopolis of the vote cast in the city of Demopolis, and the report that a large number of votes, some seven or eight hundred, contained in one box. had been thrown out by the county board of supervisors. This report made it my duty to investigate the whole matter, even if no subsequent affidavits had been made.

Q. Were these reports official?

A. They were, and were made by sworn officers.

Q. Do you know who were the supervisors?

A. I do not. Two were democrats and two were republicans. I do not remember who signed the report of the frauds. The box I speak of was thrown out by the county board of supervisors. The federal supervisors charged that the votes had been improperly thrown out.

Q. In issuing this warrant upon the negro's affidavit, did these reports influence your action?

A. Only as to there being probable cause.

Q. Why, then, did you think it necessary to recall the warrant?

A. It was a matter of grave importance. I could have investigated the alleged frauds in my capacity of chief supervisor without arresting any one. The colored man was not an aggrieved party, as Mr. Thomas subsequently claimed to have been. At any rate, I withdrew my first warrants upon a deliberate opinion that public interest would not suffer thereby, and only issued fresh warrants when compelled to do so by clear and undoubted testimony.

Q. Did you think the white man who was interested in the case was more to be trusted than the colored man who had no interest, and was supported by the supervisors' report?

A. I thought Mr. Thomas, who claimed to be the rightfully elected member, and seemed to have full knowledge of all the facts of the alleged fraud by which he was deprived of his certificate, was the most interested party. The question of respectability or color had nothing to do with the matter. It was purely a matter of evidence.

JAMES GILETTE.

PHILIP JOSEPH

Being sworn, says:

I was in Montgomery in November, 1872, at the time of the organization of the court house assembly. I had a conversation with Gen. Spencer before or shortly after its organ-

2

ization. It was before his election. The conversation was regarding party affairs. His candidacy for the U. S. senate was mentioned. There were no other candidates for the place at that time. There had been considerable opposition to him.

Questions by Gen. Morgan—

Q. Do you know of him or his friends having used any money to secure his election?

A. From my own knowledge I do not.

Q. From what source did you learn that money had been used?

A. From persons belonging to the court house organization. I would prefer not to give their names. I mean members of the court house assembly.

Q. Was the information you received from a member of the court house assembly?

A. He was not a member.

Q. Do you know of money having been paid to any one to secure his support of Spencer?

A. Not of my own knowledge.

Q. What was the object of the court house movement?

A. 1st. To give to the republicans control of the State; and 2d. To elect Spencer.

Q. Were you in the caucus at the U. S. court room on the day of the organization of the court house body, or in any caucus of the general assembly?

A. I was in several caucuses, but do not know of any special thing that was done.

Q. Who were the most active men outside of the members, in supporting Spencer for senator?

A. I noticed Mr. Brainard. J. J. Hinds seemed to take great interest, as did also Whiting.

Q. Were you advocating or opposing him at that time?

A. I can't say I ever advocated his election.

Q. Did you oppose him up to his election?

A. I ceased opposition when I found those who might have defeated him had given their adhesion to him.

Q. Did you then become his advocate?

A. I did not.

Q. How did those who had been opposing him come to quiet their opposition?

A. I heard rumors, but had no personal knowledge.

Q. Were they prevailing at the time?

A. I heard them. My understanding was some promises of federal patronage had been made. It was generally understood that Spencer controlled all the federal patronage

·· except local post offices, and these also if he took interest in them. This idea prevailed among some of the members of the general assembly.

Q. Did you hear any member of the court house assembly say that office had been promised him if he would vote for Spencer?

A. I heard members say offices had been promised, but did not hear them say offices had been promised them.

Q. Please give the names of the members you heard say this.

A. I prefer not to do so.

Qestions by Mr. Price—

Q. Was the impression made on your mind by any expression of any member of the court house assembly that Spencer used money or official patronage to secure his election?

A. A member stated to me that federal patronage had been promised, but I know of no money having been used.

PHILIP JOSEPH.

HARRY C. THROWER

Being sworn, says:

I know Geo. E. Spencer when I see him. I have no personal acquaintance with him. I was in Mobile at the time the court house assembly was in session at Montgomery.

Questions by Gen. Morgan—

Q. Do you know any persons who were members of that Legislature who afterwards received appointments to Federal office?

A. I do.

Q. If you have heard such persons say that they received Federal offices in consideration of supporting Spencer for U. S. Senator, state who the persons were and the conversations had with them on the subject.

A. I had no conversations with persons who were members of the Legislature, but had conversations with other persons who were up there at Montgomery supporting Spencer.

Q. Who were they?

A. George E. Yarrington and John G. Osborne.

Q. What offices did they receive?

A. One is detective for the U. S. Revenue Department, the other is a gauger in the same department.

Q. What did they tell you that occurred between them, and Spencer, or in regard to the means by which they had secured their appointments?

A. They said they had obtained their appointments by having used influences upon members in securing Spencer's election.

Q. What means did they say they used?

A. By getting men who had not made up their minds which Legislature to go into to join the body that elected Spencer.

Q. Did they say what influences they used, whether persuasive or some other means?

A. They stated that Spencer authorized them to promise Federal office to doubting members, if they would join the court house legislature. These members did not get the promised offices and they were making merry over the fact.

Q. Do you remember the names of any of the members who had been induced by promises of federal office to join the court house legislature?

A. I remember J. C. Goodloe. It was stated that Spencer could not have been elected unless Goodloe went over to the court house assembly and supported him. He was a long time making up his mind which legislature he would join. He was finally induced to go to the court house legislature, as was stated to me, by promises of being made collector of the port of Mobile, which office he now holds.

Q. Do you know of any other persons who were at Montgomery using their influence to secure Spencer's election who have since received federal appointments.

A. I do. Lou H. Mayer, Frank Y. Anderson and H. Ray Myers.

Q. Where do these parties reside?

A. H. Ray Myers resides in Canada, the other two in Mobile.

Q. At the time of Spencer's election by the court house assembly, what position, if any, did you hold?

A. I was inspector of customs at Mobile.

Q. Were you well acquainted with persons holding federal office in the custom and internal revenue department in this city at that time?

A. I was.

Q. State whether any tax or contribution was made upon such federal officeholders while Spencer's election was pending?

A. A demand was made on every federal officeholder in the building for money for Spencer, with the understanding that if they did not pay they would be turned out of office.

Q. What was the purpose of the contribution?

A.  It was stated General Spencer had sent here for money and must have it.

Q.  Why was the levy made on federal officeholders?

A.  It was understood that these offices were under Spencer's control and the officers could be removed at his pleasure.

Q.  What was Spencer's necessity for money at that time?

A.  It was understood he needed the money to carry the legislature to elect him.

Q.  How much did you pay, and how much was assessed to you?

A.  I did not pay—they just took it.  There were two or three assessments.  Forty dollars at one time, twenty at another, and I think fifteen at another.  I signed vouchers for the full amount of my monthly pay, ranging from $120 to $124. At the time I was assessed $40, I received $80 on the voucher for $120; at the time I was assessed $20, I received on the voucher for $124, $104; at the time I was assessed $15, I received on the voucher for $120, $105.  At the same time I signed the vouchers, I gave orders on the collector, authorizing said amounts to be deducted from my salary.  All of the federal officers did the same; they were assessed in the same proportion and for the same purposes.  We all received a letter from the deputy collector, D. C. Rugg, stating that if we did not feel disposed to pay these assessments that our resignations would be accepted, as there were others who would pay liberally for the positions.  I intended to save the letter, but lost it.

Q.  When did you receive this letter?

A.  I think it was just after the general election in 1872.

Q.  Do you know of any officers in the custom house or revenue department who drew pay, but performed no service?.

A.  I know that there were several whose names were on the pay roll of the inspectors who drew pay and performed no duty.  I made out the rolls nearly every morning.  I think J. W. Dereen was one, J. K. Greene another.  Greene left here about two months before the election and never returned. The other names I cannot now remember.

Q.  Were these men afterwards elected to the Legislature?

A.  I know J. K. Green was a member of the Legislature from Hale county at the time and was afterwards re-elected. I think Dereen was a Senator at the time and was also re-elected.

Q.  Were Green and Dereen members of the court house assembly?

A.  I think they were.

Q.  Do you know of any person now holding a position in the custom house, drawing pay, who performs no duty.

A.  Yes.  D. C. Whiting holds the position of appraiser of merchandise at the port of Mobile and is very seldom here. He is absent now and has been absent most of the time for six months.  He is incapacitated from holding any office, having lost his mind.  A man by the name of Townsley is performing his duties for $30 per month, for which Whiting receives over $200 per month.  Mr. Frank Y. Anderson holds the position of special U. S. Treasury agent by special appointment of Spencer.  He receives about $125 per month. There is no duty connected with the office.  He was appointed an inspector of customs and ordered by collector Goodloe to report to the chief inspector for duty, which he refused to do.  Goodloe then told him he had no further use for him and refused to allow his name entered on the roll of inspectors.  Anderson afterwards wrote to General Spencer asking a different appointment and obtained the office of assistant treasury agent.

HENRY C. THROWER.

MOBILE, ALABAMA,  
May 1, 1875.

The committee met pursuant to adjournment.
Present—Messrs. Little, Parks, Price, Brewer and Coon.

HON. J. P. SOUTHWORTH,

being sworn, deposes and says :

I belong to the Republican party.  Was first appointed district attorney of the United States, in May, 1864, for the southern district of Alabama ; was subsequently appointed for the northern and middle districts, and held that position for a year.  My term expired in May, 1873, and George M. Dustin succeeded me.  I came to reside in Alabama in February, 1869.  While in this office I took an active part in general politics, and to a considerable extent in other States. I thought the organization of the assembly known as the court house legislature, at Montgomery, in November, 1872, was unlawful, unconstitutional and revolutionary in the extreme, and I still think so.  I was not in Montgomery while that body was in session.  There were influential and prominent republicans in Alabama who regarded that organization as I did.  Judging the tree by its fruit, I am satisfied that the re-election of Mr. Spencer to the United States Senate was the chief purpose in view in that organization.

By General Morgan—

Q. State whether that opinion prevailed at the time amongst the Republican party in Alabama?

A. I am satisfied it did. When I say the Republican party I mean the intelligent members of that party. I know J. J. Moulton, the ex-postmaster at Mobile; I was district attorney, and it became my duty to investigate alleged defalcations of said Moulton, who was then postmaster of Mobile. The first intimation I had on the subject came from Mr. Petherbridge, an agent of the postoffice department. Moulton was found to be in arrears to the Government of the United States in the sum of about $23,000. The loss was made good by the personal friends of Mr. Moulton in Mobile, after which he was indicted and prosecuted for the embezzlement in the circuit court of the United States at Mobile, at which time. and on that account, the hostility of Mr. Spencer became more marked towards me. He had never liked me because I was the friend of General Warner; I had an interview with Mr. Moulton and Petherbridge together; Moulton's defalcation related chiefly to the money order fund, which he had mainly deposited to his personal credit in the banking-house of T. P. Miller & Co., in Mobile, and had drawn out of the bank on his personal checks. In the interview with the agent of the Government, I saw a telegram from Geo. E. Spencer to Moulton, which read, in substance, "come to Montgomery, (on some day named, I think it was Friday), meet Hinds and bring funds." The dispatch I saw may have been a copy. This was in January or February, or March, 1873; the date of the dispatch I cannot state, I think it was during the time of the session of the court house legislature; I have no doubt that was the date. After I had learned these facts from Petherbridge, and had been informed by him that Moulton had said, in a defiant way, that the money had been used for Spencer's electioneering purposes, and that Spencer would stand by him to the bitter end, and on the morning of Moulton's arrest, when he was brought to my office by the marshal, Moulton expressed a wish to go to the city building and see his brother, who was then the mayor of Mobile; I told him to go with the marshal; he expressed a dislike to be on the streets with the marshal and asked me to take him there; I consented and went with him. Judge Moulton came from the bench where he was presiding in the mayor's court; we went to his private room and sent for him, and he came immediately. As the judge came in the room John Moulton said to him "Judge, they have arrested me after all." The judge replied, "Just as I expected, when you were flourishing you were led and controlled by that damned Spencer and those other damned scoundrels of his, but when you get into trouble, as you have in this matter in using the funds to build up Mr. Spencer, you come to me; I can't help you, I shall not try; let the men who got you into this trouble get you out, I shan't try it. I said to John Moulton I thought a motion to adjourn would be in order, and we returned to my office. During the day C. F. Moulton came to my office and went on John Moulton's bond for his appearance to answer this offense.

I made no effort to conceal Mr. Spencer's connection with this matter, but was free to express my view of it, and afterwards told it to the attorney general. The case went on, and, after a continuance, which was ordered at one term by the attorney general, was, at a subsequent term, tried before Judge Woods and a jury. The jury did not agree on a verdict and the case was subsequently *nolle prossed*, after I went out of office. The case was *nolle prossed* by the order of the attorney general on the recommendation of Mr. Hays, General Spencer, and perhaps others. In giving the language of other persons, above, I was following my recollection of the substance of what was said, and am satisfied I have stated them pretty accurately. When I went to the city building, on the day mentioned, I was strongly convinced that the money that Moulton was short in his accounts had been used, in part, for the personal electioneering purposes of Spencer, to procure his re-election to the senate. When I heard the conversation between the brothers, (the Moultons) I had no doubt of it, and did not hesitate, on proper occasions, so to express my conviction. One of these proper occasions was a subsequent interview with the attorney general, in which I said to him, in substance, that it would be even-handed justice to punish Spencer instead of Moulton. Spencer was active in requesting my removal as district attorney.

Q. Who had the chief or virtual control of Federal patronage in Alabama at the time of these transactions?

A. Geo. E. Spencer.

Q. Was his sway, in this regard, materially divided or shared in by any other person as it related to the custom-house and post-office at Mobile?

A. It was not. He was considered amongst Republicans in Alabama as the chief dispenser of public Federal patronage, and it was known that he favored those only who contributed to his personal preferment or adhered to his personal fortunes. After his election to the United States Senate by the court house assembly, it was a known fact that those who obtained Federal appointment or employment in Alabama, were those who had assisted in his election, and in some instances those who had voted for him or afterwards sustained his course in the combined or fusion legislature. To instance, Wilson was made postmaster at Montgomery; Cochran, postmaster at Selma; Goodloe, collector of the port of Mobile; the brother of Miller (senator of Butler and Conecuh, who had the contest with Martin) a Scotchman, fresh from Scotland, and then not naturalized, and quite an inexperienced youth, not much over twenty-one years of age, was made deputy collector of the port of Mobile; Chisholm, who was a conscript member of the senate of the court house body, but never took his seat in the fusion legislature, was given a place in the custom house; General Dustan was appointed chief special treasury agent at Mobile, and still holds the office; Geo. M. Duskin was appointed district attorney for the southern district of Alabama; Hon. Nick McAfee was appointed to succeed Judge Minnis as district attorney for the middle and northern districts of Alabama; P. G. Clarke was made postoffice agent in Alabama, and now holds the office. Others of the body, I am well assured, were promised good places by Spencer and his supporters, and have failed to get them. Before this legislature met there was a strong body of Republicans who agreed to oppose Spencer's re-election to the senate of the United States; of this number were Messrs. Alexander White, and Lewis E. Parsons, and they were strongly pledged to use all proper means to defeat him. Mr. Parsons has had a Federal appointment, but was not confirmed by the Senate; Mr. Pennington was a member of that body, and was soon afterwards made governor of Dakota, which office he now holds. These instances, and a general and free discussion of this subject amongst Republicans, satisfied my mind that most of the members of the court house body had some promise of office, place or preferment from Spencer, and that he has rewarded all of them as far as possible. There has been much grumbling amongst the disappointed.

JOHN P. SOUTHWORTH.

HON. ALEXANDER M'KINSTRY

Being sworn, says:
I was lieut. governor of the State of Alabama in November, 1872; I took the oath of office between the 23rd and 26th of that month; I was notified of my election to that office by a

committee of the capitol legislature; I remember Mr. Manning of the House and Mr. Martin of the Senate as being members of that committee; my election was ascertained by the capital legislature; the vote by which I was elected was not counted by the court house legislature; my commission as lieutenant governor was signed by Gov. Lewis; the certificate of the secretary of state is the commission; Mr. E. H. Moren was lieutenant governor of the senate up to my installation into office; after my installation I took my seat in the court house legislature, after I had been notified by Gov. Lewis that he recognized that body as the legislature; I found J. L. Pennington presiding in that body; I had not been there until I went to preside; I did not agree that I would go there as soon as I was installed into office; Geo. E. Spencer was in Montgomery when I took my seat—my impression is he was; he was a candidate before the court house body for United States Senator; I do not think any one else was spoken of as a candidate; Geo. M. Duskin was a member of the senate of the court house body. After the plan of the attorney general was submitted, both bodies—the capitol and court house—kept organized, Duskin was weak and had to be persuaded along. The first I knew of his weakness was on the bill relating to taxation; I mean by weakness, he manifested a disposition not to attend; he did not come, and had to be sent for.

Q. Do you know of any argument or persuasion that was used with him to induce him to attend?

A. I told him I thought he ought to stand up.

Q. Do you know of his having left the city at any time and starting home?

A. I know I did not see him in his place, and he was absent.

Q. Do you know of any assurance he had from Spencer, or any of his friends, that he would be appointed United States district attorney if he stood firm?

A. I do not know.

Q. Did Spencer or Whiting ever give you information that Duskin would be appointed district attorney?

A. I think not. I have no recollection of anything of the sort.

Q. Do you know of Spencer having promised office to any person?

A. I do not.

Q. Do you know of Spencer or Hinds, or Whiting, during the legislature of 1872-3, having promised the position of collector of the port of Mobile to any one?

A. Not of my own knowledge; I was opposed to Spencer's election, and had but little to do with him; the respectable portion of the Republican party of the entire State were opposed to the election of Spencer, so far as I know, but we were compelled to let matters take their course in order to keep the court house body together; there were some men who would not have him, and we were forced into electing him; it was considered a party necessity.

Q. Was there any understanding among the leading members of the court house body that certain offices had been promised certain officers by Gen. Spencer?

A. There was a current rumor, which I credited, that his influence would be used for the purposes indicated.

Q. State, as far as you are able, to whom these offices were to be secured?

A. I do not know that I can fix any one in my mind.

Q. Was it understood that Mr. Goodloe was to get the office of collector of the port of Mobile?

A. That was a rumor.

Q. Was this rumor credited among the members of the court house legislature?

A. It was among some.

Q. Did not Mr. Goodloe stand out for some time, declining to take a seat in the court house or capitol legislature?

A. I do not know; he did not come to the court house assembly for some time.

Q. Did any person, within your knowledge, information or belief, use any argument to induce him to go into the court house assembly?

A. I have no recollection about it. I did not know Goodloe before.

Q. How many persons who were members of the court house assembly have since received federal appointments or places of preferment, and what are their names?

A. Pennington has been appointed governor of Dakota; Duskin district attorney U. S., southern district of Alabama; Wilson post master at Montgomery Goodloe collector of the port of Mobile; P. G. Clarke special agent P. O. D.; Cochran post master at Selma; Gen. Dustan treasury agent; senator Baker U. S. marshal, northern district of Alabama; Chisholm, a senator, U. S. inspector customs; Dereen post master at Demopolis; McAfee U. S. district attorney. I can remember no others.

Q. Did Spencer or his immediate friends regard you with sufficient confidence to let you into their secrets.

A. I think not. What I gathered in regard to the places he promised persons was in current report.

Q. Have persons, who were active in supporting Spencer, since received federal appointments?

A. I think they have. Hinds and Whiting were active, and have received appointments.

Q. Do you believe Spencer was the choice of the republican party of the State for U. S. senator?

A. I do not.

Q. Do you believe the court house organization could have been maintained until your inaugural, and that of Gov. Lewis, without the assistance of Spencer in that body?

A. I do not.

Q. Do you not know that Spencer's friends insisted on his election as a *sine qua non* to their remaining in that body?

A. I do not know.

Q. Do you believe it?

A. I do.

Q. Upon what is your belief founded?

A. From my position in the whole matter and the surroundings.

ALEX. McKINSTRY.

JAMES R. EAGIN

Being sworn, says:

I am assistant postmaster and cashier of the post office in this city. I held the position from 1865 to 1869. I was then out of office during Bromberg's administration, but have been in office since that time. I was a clerk during the administration of Moulton, and kept the cash accounts of the post office proper, but not of the money order department.

Q. Do you know of any money that was furnished out of the post office funds while you were with Moulton, to Hinds, or Whiting, or Spencer, or to any other person for Spencer?

A. I do not know that it went to Spencer's use.

Q. Do you know of any money furnished from the post office for political purposes?

A. I know money was furnished by the post office employees and deducted from their wages.

Q. Do you know of any persons whose names were on the post office rolls who performed no service?

A. Spencer Terrill did no service that I know of. John Truyear, both colored men, and a white man, whose name I can not remember.

Q. Do you know of any draft drawn by Spencer upon Moulton?

A. I do not.

Q. Do you know of any draft drawn by Spencer in favor of Moulton?

A. I know of a draft drawn in favor of Spencer, and by him endorsed to Moulton. The draft amounted to about $2,000 or $2,200. The draft was used to replace money that had been taken out of the drawer to be used for political purposes, as I understood, the draft remaining as so much cash or government funds, which had been taken out and the draft deposited in its stead.

Q. What political purposes was the money used for?

A. All the information I have on the subject was derived from Moulton.

Q. Where did Moulton keep his accounts?

A. His money order accounts were kept with Miller & Co., and the post office deposits were made in the U. S. depository in the custom house. The draft I have spoken of was cashed out of the post office money proper.

Q. Do you remember any other draft cashed by Mr. Moulton out of government funds?

A. I know of only one more, which was drawn by Lou. H. Mayer for $25, which I think was signed by him, as chairman of, I understood it, of a political organization.

Q. During the administration of Moulton who did you understand had control of or the dispensing of federal offices?

A. Spencer, as I understood.

JAS. R. EAGIN.

### LOU. H. MAYER

Being sworn, says:

I hold the position of collector of internal revenue, and have held it since May, 1873. I was promoted from the office of assessor to that of collector by the commissioner of internal revenue. I do not think Mr. Spencer had anything to do with my promotion. I learned he was not in Washington when the appointment was made.

By Gen. Morgan—

Q. In 1872, who was the most influential republican in Alabama in reference to the dispensing of federal patronage?

A. I know what is expected for me to say. But I do not know.

Q. Who was the most influential in 1873?

A. I think Mr. Hays, as he had Reynolds appointed contrary to Spencer's wishes. After that time, Spencer was most influential in relation to dispensing patronage of all the congressional delegation.

Q. Through whose influence did Mr. Goodloe get his appointment?

A. Through Mr. Spencer's, though Sheets and White assisted.

Q. Through whom did Wickersham obtain his appointment?

A. I don't think he had any friends but Turner. He was opposed by the whole delegation.

Q. Were you in Montgomery at the time the election for U. S. senator was pending in the court house assembly?

A. I was there on Monday, Tuesday and Wednesday. Spencer was elected on Tuesday.

Q. Did you see Spencer, Hinds and Whiting there?

A. I did.

Q. Had you received a request to go to Montgomery?

A. No, sir. I will take that back. I may have been requested by my friends here to go there.

Q. What was your object in going to Montgomery?

A. To assist in Spencer's election.

Q. Did you carry any money with you?

A. Just enough to pay my expenses. I borrowed to get back, or I think so.

Q. Do you know of any money having been used in securing Spencer's election?

A. I do not. It was rumored that Warner or Wickersham was about to buy up some of our members. I went to Spencer and told him of it. He said he could not help it, and to be careful not to make any promises.

Q. Was General Spencer before that a friend of yours?

A. I have always regarded him as one of the best friends in the world. I would do as much for him as any man in the world.

Q. After Spencer's election, did you return to Montgomery in the interest of Spencer?

A. I returned in my own interest to secure the office of revenue collector.

Q. Did you meet J. J. Moulton in Montgomery?

A. I did. I met him on the street leading to the capitol. He asked me where Spencer was. I told him he was in a saloon or restaurant. He asked me to go to him and tell him to send him what he promised. I went to Spencer and told him what Moulton said. He replied that he would see Moulton afterwards. Moulton came in and I saw Spencer hand him a package of money. Some time later, when we returned to Mobile, Moulton brought me a telegram, written in cypher, from General Spencer, dated at Washington, requesting

Moulton to return the money he had loaned him; that he would be in Montgomery shortly, on Friday, or some day soon after, and to bring or send the money he had loaned him, that he would need it. Moulton then informed me that it would be very hard for him to raise that amount of money at this time; that he expected to have a longer time.

Q. About what time was Moulton arrested for defrauding the post office department?

A. It was on the following Monday after Petherbridge's arrival.

Q. You say Moulton brought the telegram to you?

A. He brought it to me to read. It was to the effect that he was to bring or send the money to Montgomery.

Q. Did Moulton ever bring any other dispatch for you to read?

A. I do not know.

Q. When did you inform Moulton you had a key to Spencer's dispatches?

A. I did not inform him, that I recollect. I think he was present when we bought the three dictionaries that were keys.

R. Do you know any reasons why a demand of a debt due from Moulton to Spencer should be sent in cypher?

A. Yes, because General Spencer would hesitate to make a public demand upon his personal friend (as Moulton then was) for money loaned him purely out of friendship, and I know that General Spencer agrees with me in not believing that our telegrams are kept as confidential in the telegraph office.

Q. To whom were the three dictionaries given?

A. One to Spencer, one to Whiting, and I retained the other. H. Ray Myers may have had one. I do not know who had them, so many of us understood it. I have not my copy now. I do not remember having given Moulton one. He knew the cypher as well as I did, and might have bought a dictionary. He might now have my copy.

Q. If Moulton knew the cypher why did he come to you to read the dispatch?

A. I had the book.

Q. You have stated that you know this money had been loaned by Spencer to Moulton, and that it has not been repaid, except $1,500. How do you know this?

A. Moulton and Spencer have both told me so. I have no other knowledge of the matter. Moulton told me in a buggy riding about the time of his troubles that he had paid Spencer only $1,500 of the loan.

Q. Did you aid Moulton in getting out of his troubles?

A. I aided him all I could. I endorsed for him to the extent of $1,000 and afterwards paid the amount.

Q. When did Spencer tell you Moulton had repaid the loan?

A. He told me in March of this year.

Q. Had he ever told you so before?

A. Just on the eve of the last State election, in October, 1874, he asked me as he had done before what were the chances of getting the $750 out of Moulton. He had written to me before this about it. I am not positive.

Q. Did Moulton go to Montgomery to pay the money as requested by Spencer?

A. He went to Montgomery, but don't know whether he paid it or not.

Q. If Moulton told you he had paid the money to whom did he say he paid it?

A. I don't remember in whose hands Moulton told me he paid it or when.

Q. Before this had you ever received any money from Moulton?

A. I frequently borrowed $50 or other small amounts from him and returned the same. I do not remember that I received any larger amounts from him.

Q. Did you ever collect a draft or drafts drawn on Moulton?

A. I may have collected a draft for $50, while we were running the *Herald*. I am positive for no larger amount. I never saw any draft drawn by Spencer, Hinds or Whiting, on Moulton.

Q. At the time Moulton asked you to ask Spencer to send him what he promised, did you know what Moulton meant?

A. I did not. Moulton told me afterwards that it was $2,250 that Spencer loaned him.

Q. Did you know Mr. Widmer?

A. I did.

Q. Do you know Mr. Fritz?

A. I do.

Q. Do you know whether Mr. Spencer got any money from Mr. Fritz?

A. I know he did not.

Q. How do you know it?

A. Because Spencer wrote me he had not got any from him, and Mr. Brasher, the Revenue Agent, informed me he had investigated the case and that he found no evidence that Spencer ever got any money from him.

Q. Do you know what was Mr. Widmer's reputation as an officer?

A. He was, in my opinion, one of the best officers in the country, and a correct man. I arrived at this opinion simply from the examination Mr. Widmer permitted me to make of his books and from the clear and comprehensive instructions he gave me verbally as to my duties as collector to which office I daily expected to be appointed.

Q. If Widmer were to tell you on his dying bed that he had loaned Spencer $5,000 and Spencer were to tell you that he had not, which one of them would you believe?

A. I would believe Mr. Spencer.

Q. What men here (in Mobile) are in federal positions who were members of the court house assembly and voted for Spencer?

A. J. O. Goodloe, Collector of Customs, Geo. M. Duskin, United States District Attorney, C. W. Dustan, Special Treasury Agent; Mr. Chisholm, Inspector of Customs. Goodloe was appointed through Spencer's, and White's and Sheets' influence; Gen. Duskin and Dustan through Mr. White's and Mr. Hays'. I think Mr. Chisholm was retained in his place because he was a good officer and needed no influence to retain his place.

Q. Was Mr. Chisholm in office prior to the election of Spencer?

A. I think he was.

Q. Had he ever been suspended?

A. I do not know.

Q. Do you know whether he had a position in the custom house when he was in the court house assembly?

A. I do not.

By Mr. Price—

Q. How long have you known Gen. Spencer intimately?

A. Probably since 1870.

Q. What is the ground of your intimacy?

A. Congeniality of sentiment and feeling.

Q. When and how did you discover that congeniality of sentiment and feeling?

A. In 1870–71, and from personal association afterwards.

Q. Where was that personal association?

A. In Washington.

Q. For how long?

A. For three months. We have associated since.

Q. Was the attachment mutual?

A. I think it was.

3

Q. How do you know it was mutual?

A. I think I have his confidence as much as any man in Alabama.

Q. How has he shown it?

A. By entrusting me with his confidence.

Q. Have you any reason to feel under obligations to Spencer, except from your social relations with him?

A. Oh, yes! He got me the appointment of assessor of revenue in the year 1871.

Lou. H. Mayer.

### GEO. L. PUTNAM

Being sworn, says:

I was post master in Mobile and went out of office when Moulton went in. I was removed upon the recommendation of Spencer and Turner, without there being any defalcation on my part. I received a complimentary letter from the Department as to my conduct of the office. There were no charges against me or complaints from the Department, or any other source.

Q. Who was the person who was in Mobile manipulating the matter of your removal?

A. H. Ray Meyers was the principal man, and represented himself as the agent or spokesman of Senator Spencer. Lou. Mayer also participated, but not so actively.

Q. What demands did Mayer make of you with the understanding that if you did not pay you would be removed.

A. He demanded considerable sums of money from me. He obtained pretty much all I had. In one item I paid $10 per week to support a paper run in the interest of Spencer as against Warner.

Q. Did Meyer make any complaint of your politics.

A. I became aware of the fact that Meyer represented to others and to Spencer that I was not loyal to Spencer's interest, and could not be trusted to carry out his policy. In a conversation had with Spencer about a year ago, he informed me that Meyer had deceived him in this matter.

Q. State as fully as you are prepared to do, any demands that were made by Meyer upon Moulton, as a consideration of his being appointed your successor as postmaster of Mobile, and what amounts of money were, or were promised to be paid by Moulton?

A. John J. Moulton at that time was money order clerk in the post office under me. Meyer lodged and roomed at his house. Moulton's account at one time was short about $1,600.

This was discovered by Mr. Eagan when I was in Washington. Moulton borrowed the money and made up the deficit. I was aware that he was an applicant for the office of post master of Mobile. I notified the Department that I had removed Moulton for this and other causes. I also notified Spencer and the President in person of these facts before Moulton was appointed. I knew that Meyer was drawing on Moulton heavily for money, representing to him all the time that he would get the office. It was understood here amongst the Republicans that Spencer could only be controled through Meyers. Whatever Meyers promised, it was understood that Spencer would carry out.

Q. Do you remember any instance when Moulton paid Meyers any money?

A. A dispatch was sent by H. Ray Meyers to Moulton, which was seen by Mr. M. C. Osborne, requiring Moulton to send him $500; that that would fix Turner all right, referring to Moulton's appointment as postmaster and my removal. I remember that one of Spencer's complaints to me, when I was in Washington, was that Meyers represented to him that I was too stingy to contribute what I should; that I did not do my share in that line; that I had refused to make assessments on my clerks, which were demanded, or complained that I had not done by Meyers. I told my clerks that they could pay of their own accord if they desired to do so; that I would not require it of them.

GEORGE L. PUTNAM.


JAMES S. PERRIN

Being sworn, says:
I reside in Monroe county; I am a Republican and have never voted any other ticket.

By Mr. Little—

Q. Have you ever held any office under the federal government?

A. I have held two; special assistant assessor of revenue for the first Alabama district, and deputy United States marshal for the Southern District of Alabama. I was appointed assistant assessor of revenue in July, 1872, and continued in office until January 1st, 1873. I was appointed marshal in October, 1874.

Q. Through whose influence were you appointed to office?

A. Through George E. Spencer, at that time United States Senator.

Q. Why were you appointed?

A. To assist in organizing the Republican party, and in Spencer's re-election to the United States Senate, by assisting in securing the election of members to the legislature favorable to him.

Q. Were you at Montgomery in 1872, during the time the court house assembly was in session, before and during the time the election of Spencer was pending?

A. I was.

Q. What was the object and purpose of the court house assembly?

A. It was to place the legislature in the hands of the Republican party and elect Spencer.

Q. Why was it necessary to organize at the court house for those purposes?

A. We knew the Senate was Democratic, and unless Miller and Chisholm were seated, who we knew were defeated, we would not have a quorum of Republican Senators.

Q. Was it conceded that Miller and Chisholm were not elected?

A. It was so conceded by the leading Republicans who were familiar with the facts. It was considered a party necessity that Miller and Chisholm be seated.

Q. Was there anything done by Gen. Spencer and his friends previous to the general election, by which to secure a majority of Republican members in the general assembly?

A. There was, by his friends.

Q. What was done?

A. I wrote to Gen. Spencer in Lou Mayer's presence, that under the Enforcement Act we could get affidavits and have Democratic members arrested and detained until the legislature was organized by the Republicans, and his election as Senator secured. Lou Mayer was present when I wrote the letter. I read it to him and he approved its contents, and wrote a letter to Spencer himself, stating to me that it was in furtherance of the plan I proposed.

Q. Afterwards was this plan acted on, and if so, when and where, and what was done?

A. The missing members were arrested while on their way to Montgomery, at Selma, and were carried via Meridian to Mobile where they waived an examination, gave bond and were released. No indictment was ever found against them, and there was no further prosecution. I do not think it was ever intended that they should be indicted or prosecuted.

Q. Was there any understanding between you and Spencer by which you were to be appointed United States Commissioner, for the purpose of issuing warrants to make arrests in the furtherance of Spencer's election?

A. There was an understanding. I think I have letters to that effect from Spencer, which I will furnish the committee if I can find them. These letters were received after my first letter to Spencer suggesting the plan of arresting parties under the Enforcement Act mentioned heretofore in my testimony.

Q. Were you ever appointed United States Commissioner?

A. I was not. Judge Busteed alleged that it could only be done in term time, and the appointment could not be made in time to carry out the plan.

Q. Was J. J. Hinds in Montgomery during the session of the court house assembly, and pending the election of Spencer?

A. He was.

Q. What was the relation between him and Spencer during the pendency of his election, and what post did he take in securing his election?

A. He was very intimate with Spencer and occupied the same rooms at the hotel. They occupied three rooms, one for private interviews, another for cigars and whisky to which a man attended, and the other I suppose was their bed room. These are all the rooms I saw them in. Hinds was considered as Spencer's private cashier.

Q. By whom was he so considered?

A. By the leading members of the Republican party inside and outside of the legislature.

Q. What were your relations to Hinds and Spencer at that time?

A. Very intimate; but Spencer committed himself more confidentially to Hinds that any other person.

Q. Were your surroundings and position of a character that admitted of your knowing the means by which Spencer's election was secured?

A. They were.

Q. Will you state as near as you can recollect whether any of the Republican members hesitated to go into the court house assembly, or threatened to leave, and if any, what inducements were offered them to take seats therein or remain?

A. Thomas D. McCaskie hesitated to go into that body because he stated it to be illegal on account of the want of a quorum in the Senate, and that he believed the capitol the legal place of assembling. Meyers and I induced him to go there because we stated it would be the salvation of the Republican party, and we also promised to secure him, through

Spencer, the office of Weigher and Guager of Customs of the port of Mobile. We were authorized to make the promise by Hinds for Spencer. McCaskie did afterwards take his seat in the court house assembly and there remained. Jacob Black, of Barbour, threatened to leave and go to the capitol. I saw Gilmore, of Sumter, come out of Hinds' room with $300 in his hand. He stated to me this was the amount. I asked him what he was going to do with it. He said it was for Black. I remarked that that disease was becoming infectious and must be stopped.

Q. What did you mean by "disease?"

A. Whenever a member of the court house assembly became dissatisfied he was called a sick or diseased member. The medicine given was *greenbacks.*

Q. Did Black remain?

A. Black recovered. He remained with the court house assembly, and I know nothing of his disaffection.

Q. Proceed with the other names?

A. Johnson and Walker, or Goldsby, all of Dallas, met me on the street in front of the Madison House. They asked me to loan them money, stating they wanted to go to Selma. I told them I had none with me then. One of them said he was sick of the way white Republicans were treating colored Republicans, especially of the way Turner had been defeated for Congress. They stated that on this account that they were in favor of electing Turner to the United States Senate, and if they would go to the capitol the Democrats would vote for Turner before they would for Spencer. I told them if they were sick Hinds had some medicine that would cure them, and to go up and see him at the Madison House. They went.

Q. Did you see them afterwards?

A. In about an hour afterwards I met them on the steps of the hotel with money in their hands. I asked them if they got any. Walker or Goldsby said he had got enough to take him to Selma. Johnson added, "and to come back again, winking," giving me to understand he had gotten a good deal more. I heard no more complaint from them, and they were afterwards warm supporters of Spencer.

Q. Did J. C. Goodloe take his seat in the conrt house assembly at its organization?

A. He did not.

Q. What part did he take in the organization of the legislature or election of Spencer?

A. He was regarded by the leading republicans as a secret agent of Spencer to ascertain and report the proceedings of the capitol legislature, which he did.

Q. Was it understood that he would take his seat in the court house assembly when Spencer's election came up?

A. It was understood that he would come down and record his vote for Spencer when needed.

Q. Was any promises made in consideration of his services for Spencer and his vote for him?

A. It was understood that Spencer would use or had used his influence in receiving the payment of certain large war-claims Goodloe had before the court of claims in Washington. There was also promised the collectorship of the port of Mobile.

Q. Do you know of any moneys being used or promises being made to members of the General Assembly directly or indirectly to induce them to support Spencer for United States senator?

A. I met E. J. Mancil on the street, near the Madison House in Montgomery, and told him that he might take a little snuff and sneeze as well as other people. He replied that he made nothing out of the Stanton legislature, but signified his willingness to go; at the same time telling me that if I ever divulged upon him he would kill me. I told him that he would then be guilty of two felonies, "murder" and "bribery," and he would be sure to go to the penitentiary. I then took him up and introduced him to Hinds and Spencer, telling Hinds in an under tone that he was a fit subject, I left the room after we had all taken drinks and cigars, leaving him with Spencer and Hinds. Mancil left the city and remained absent until after Spencer's election and the legislative troubles were settled.

Q. Was Mancill a democrat or republican?

A. He was a democrat and a member of the capitol legislature.

Q. What was the object in having him leave the city?

A. To destroy the quorum of the capitol legislature, in order to make it appear that the court house legislature had the strongest claims to legality.

Q. Were means used to get other democratic members from the capitol legislature for the purpose first stated? If so, what were the means and who were the members?

A. Yes, William Stribbling of Washington county. I went to Hinds and got twenty dollars from him, telling him I wanted to inveigle Stribbling. another member of the capitol legislature, into a game of poker and let him win; it was to keep him away from the capitol. It was the purpose to let this be but a bait so that we could get him there again, and at the proper time get up a game and get him drunk and keep him away from the legislature.

Q. State whether you carried out this purpose.

A. I went to the Exchange and lost the money in playing poker with Stribbling and McHugh, in Stribbling's room; I prolonged the game for some time in order to ascertain if they had a taste for card playing; I lost more than the twenty dollars, giving my due bill for the balance; I found that Stribbling liked the game and could be manipulated in this manner, but McHugh took no further stock.

Q. How did you further carry out your plan?

A. Lou Mayer, George Ellison and I, after I communicated this to Hinds, went up into the top story of the Madison House; Hinds came up where we were and gave Lou Mayer $100, who gave it to George Ellison, remarking to Hinds that if these fellows don't work Stribbling nobody can; this was the evening before Spencer's election.

Q. How did you use this money?

A. We went to the Rialto, a gambling saloon, and George Ellison brought Stribbling into the bar, where we took a drink; I called for beer and they called for a different drink; I saw the clerk handling two or three different bottles, and I feared something was wrong and left him with Ellison; from the manipulation of the bottles by the clerk in mixing Stribbling's drink, I preferred to go no further in the matter; Ellison took Stribbling off, telling me he would fix him; I saw nothing of Stribbling for several days, but the next morning Ellison told me that Stribbling was all right, and that we need not give ourselves any further trouble about him; we succeeded in keeping Stribbling away from the capitol legislature as long as it was desired by the friends of Spencer.

Q. After the plan of the attorney-general was submitted for the fusion of the two legislatures, was there any plan agreed on among leading republicans in the consolidated legislature in order to make it appear that the court house assembly was a legal organization?

A. Yes, by the seating of Miller in the Senate, at all hazards, in the place of Martin.

Q. Was that plan carried out?

A. It was.

Q. If you know how it was carried out, state how.

A. Only from hearsay, I had left the city.

Q. What became of Chisholm on the consolidation of the two Legislatures?

A. He left the Senate and resumed his duties in the custom house.

Q. Did he offer any contest for his seat?

A. He did not; it was admitted by Chisholm and all oth-ers that he had no right to the seat; he took his seat in the court house legislature to make a quorum and to elect Spen-cer.

Q. Was it understood by the republicans that there was no quorum in the senate of the court house legislature, and that Chisholm and Miller were seated to make a quorum?

A. It was.

Q. State, if you know, any persons who were promised positions or were given money for their support and influence in Spencer's election?

A. Lou H. Mayer, myself, M. G. Candee, George Ellison, Goodloe, McCaskie, Wilson, P. G. Clarke, Duskin, McAfee, Cochran, McKinstry, John Lamb, Whiting and Foster were promised offices, and others whose names I can not recall. Those who were given money I have already spoken of, so far as I remember.

Q. In the order in which you have named them, give the offices promised.

A. Lou H. Mayer was appointed internal revenue collector. I wrote to Spencer at the request of Mayer, asking for his appointment. Spencer wrote to Mayer and told him to be quiet, his appointment would be made. He showed me the letter; and to show me that Spencer was true to his promise he was assured that his name had been printed on the letter heads for this district by the department at Washington. This was shortly after Spencer's election. Mayer told me himself Spencer promised him the office. I was assured by Lou Mayer on behalf of Spencer that I would get the deputy collectorship. Candee came to me and asked me if I would withdraw my claims for the deputy collectorship in his favor, and Mayer would accept, he (Candee) would influence Rey-nolds to appoint me to a good position in the custom house with like salary, which was agreed upon. Candee subse-quently informed me that Reynolds would appoint me to the position of inspector of customs, and I refused to accept the position.

George Ellison was to be appointed deputy collector of customs in Rugg's place, for services rendered in assisting in procuring Spencer's election. He worked with the weak-kneed democrats. The office was abolished or consolidated; and Ellison was tendered an inspectorship and commissioner, but resigned at my suggestion. I know Ellison was recog-nized by Spencer as one of his friends at Montgomery pend-ing his election.

Goodloe and McCaskie I have heretofore named.

Wilson, Clarke, Duskin, McAfee, Cochran and Whiting were all provided for as promised.

McKinstry, Lamb and Foster were not provided for as promised.

Q. Who was regarded as the dispenser of federal patronage pending Spencer's election as senator.

A. Senator Spencer.

Q. What contributions were levied, if any, for political purposes upon federal office holders?

A. From five to ten per cent. were levied on the monthly salaries of federal officers. These funds were supposed to go into the hands of the treasurer of the State executive committee; but I never saw any of it and do not know what became of it.

Q. Do you know where the money come from that was expended at Montgomery to assist in Spencer's election, or any portion of it?

A. I heard a considerable portion of it came from J. J. Moulton to J. J. Hinds. I received my information from the friends and supporters of Spencer.

Q. Was Spencer the choice of the republican party for senator?

A. His support came from the office holding element, or those expecting office.

Q. Why was it the office holders submitted to contributions?

A. Because their tenure of office depended on Spencer's will.

Q. Why was it the office holders supported Spencer so unanimously?

A. Because the devotion to Spencer's interest, who controlled the patronage of the State, was the surest way to retain their places.

Q. Do you know of troops having been brought into the State just before the general election in 1872, for the purpose of influencing voters?

A. I do.

Q. State freely and particularly about it.

A. Troops were brought here at that time for the alleged purpose of protecting the federal revenue officers in the performance of their duties. This was the ostensible object, but the real object was to parade the troops through the country with United States Marshals having pretended warrants and exhibiting them for the purpose of intimidating the people and driving persons from the country. These warrants were taken by the marshals into neighborhoods and exhibited to persons who would inform the parties that the marshal was after them. They would then leave the country or get out of the way. The "warrants" were simply papers folded with no writing on the inside, but names were on the outside on the folds. Spencer wrote to Mayer that he had procured troops to be under the control of the revenue officers, and Mayer so informed me. Acting on this information I made a requisition for troops, and proceeded with them and the marshal, who had the pretended warrants and exhibited them as I have indicated.

Q. Was there any outrage upon which this requisition was based, or was there any necessity for the protection of officers?

A. There was no real necessity for the troops.

Q. Was there any pretended or alleged necessity? If so, state what it was.

A. There was. I shot a hole through my own hat with my own pistol and wrote to Lou H. Mayer that I had been set upon by men in ambush and K. K. K., which he perfectly understood was not the case by a previous understanding. I had the troops with me at that time; I was in advance and out of their sight when I shot the hole in my hat. I ran back and deployed them as skirmishers and we advanced upon the supposed K. K. K's with an intrepidity that reflected credit upon the troops, who knew no better than that there was a real foe before them.

Q. Why did you do this?

A. It was to satisfy the department at Washington that the presence of troops was necessary, and to prevent their recall.

Q. Was this reported to the department at Washington as a real outrage?

A. It was. I saw it mentioned in several Northern papers.

Q. Were the troops retained?

A. They were kept by me as long as they could be made use of as a political machine.

Q. Who reported this pretended outrage to Washington?

A. I made a report to Mayer and he reported to Washington.

Q. In whose interest were you and Mayer acting?

A. In George E. Spencer's; to secure at all hazards a. legislature that would elect him to the U. S. Senate.

Q. What connection did Spencer have with the execution of this plan of operations?

A. He was acquainted with our plan of operations and was instrumental in having troops placed at our disposal to carry out the same.

Q. In your efforts to reduce the capitol legislature below a quorum, what other acts were done?

A. None that were carried into effect; it was understood that if it became necessary, that I should go to Evergreen and send a telegram to Mr. Barnett, of Monroe county, that his wife was in a dying condition, and to come home immediately; the dispatch was to be signed "Nick Stallworth," to make it more plausible.

Q. Do you know any active part taken by Lou Mayer to promote Spencer's election other than you have stated?

A. None; only that he stated to me that Black had tendered his resignation as revenue officer, in blank; it was understood the resignation was not to go into effect unless the right of Black to his seat in the Senate was contested on account of holding federal office, when it was to date the day before his election as senator in 1872; this took place in Montgomery, pending Spencer's election.

Q. What called you to Montgomery during the organization of the court house assembly in 1872?

A. I was there, as were all the federal office holders, in the interest of Spencer; we wanted to keep our places, and we knew the best way to do so was to work for Spencer, and if he did not reward us he would go back upon his promises, which he did in some cases.

Q. Did Hinds or Spencer write you to come to Montgomery?

A. Hinds wrote me to come or be there; I have not the letter with me; I may have it at home; Lou Mayer told me Spencer said he expected us all to come up.

Q. Did you meet J. J. Moulton at Montgomery?

A. I did.

Q. Did you see him using money, or hear him say anything about using it in the interest of Spencer?

A. I did; he owed me some money and I asked him for it; he said he would have to use all he had or could get in the Spencer election.

Q. Do you know any thing concerning the proposed letting a contract for carrying the mails on the Alabama river?

A. It was understood between Hinds and myself that Spencer's influence was pledged to secure me a contract for carrying the mail on the Alabama river, between Montgomery and Mobile, in the year 1873.

Q. Why was this contract tendered you?

A. In part as a consideration of my support of Spencer for the United States senate.

Q. Did any thing pass between you and Hinds in reference to carrying the mail on this route?

A. The understanding was that I was to have the contract and I made an arrangement with the Mobile Trade Company for carrying the mail, by which I would have left a profit of several thousand dollars ; I informed Hinds of this fact, and wrote him urging the establishment of the route and my appointment according to the understanding; Hinds answered me, telling me that I would have to divide ; I wrote I would not divide.

Q. What did you mean by "divide?"

A. That he would take the greater part of the profits.

Q. Did you get the contract?

A. I did not ; the mail is being carried over that route at this time.

Q. Did you ever receive any instructions as to troops under your control, and if so, what were they?

A. I received instructions from Lou Mayer, the collector of revenue under whom I was acting, not to use the troops for political purposes; which meant, by a previous understanding with Mayer, that I should use them for political purposes, as there was no necessity for them.

Q. Why was that dispatch sent you?

A. It was to make the dispatch a matter of record to satisfy the department, and which he afterwards told me he made known to the department. The reason why the telegram was first sent was on account of a difficulty I had with a newspaper man at Evergreen, who was publishing a newspaper at that place, and who had written an article charging that the troops were being used for political purposes.

Q. In your testimony on yesterday, you spoke of the people being intimidated by the presence of federal troops and the warrants displayed by the marshals, what do you mean by "intimidation?"

A. They were more afraid of arrest by troops and trial by federal judges, than the negroes are of the supposed kuklux. I arrive at this conclusion from handling troops in the country.

JAMES S. PERRIN.

WM. R. CHISHOLM

Being sworn, says :
I reside in Florence, Ala., when at home. I am inspector

of customs at this port. I have held that position since August, 1872.

Q. Did you hold any position in the State government at any time in the year 1872?

A. I was a candidate for the senate in that year, in the counties of Limestone and Lauderdale. I received information that justified me in going to Montgomery, and after arriving there, further investigation was made by a committee appointed by the court house senate. They made a favorable report, and I was seated in the court house senate.

Q. Who was your opponent in the canvass?

A. Daniel Coleman.

Q Were you elected or defeated in that election?

A. My impression is that I was legally elected. I arrived at this conclusion after arriving at Montgomery, and frauds were made known to me.

Q. You did not think, before you went to Montgomery, you were elected?

A. I did not know definitely. I thought so from rumor.

Q. How many votes did you receive?

A. I do not remember.

Q. How many did Coleman receive?

A. I do not know.

Q. What information did you receive that took you to Montgomery?

A. I can not say definitely from whom I received letters.

Q. Do you remember the nature of the information?

A. It was of a general character.

Q. Did any one advise you that it was necessary, as a party necessity, that you come?

A. I did not receive such advice.

Q. What was the nature of the information that caused you to go to Montgomery?

A. I can't tell definitely the nature of the information.

Q. Was it suggested that you could get a seat if you came?

A. I had good cause to go there and inaugurate the investigation. I did not seat myself.

Q. What was the nature of the information that carried you to Montgomery?

A. I received a communication that I might be seated on a thorough investigation. The investigation was inaugurated and I was seated.

Q. Were you seated in the court house assembly?

A. I was.

Q. How long were you in Montgomery before you took your seat in the court house assembly?

A. I was seated in the early days of the assembly.

Q. Were you seated the second day?

A. I can not say. I do not think it the first or second day. An investigation was had.

Q. What kind of an investigation?

A. A committee was appointed that investigated the matter.

Q. What did you lay before the committee?

A. I had not a great deal to do with it. I had witnesses examined. Mr. J. H. Price was one, and Mr. M. Goldsmith was another.

Q. Did you produce these witnesses before the committee?

A. I did.

Q. What did you propose to prove by them?

A. To give statements in regard to the election. It was stated a great many votes were thrown out, and it was said the same cause existed for throwing out votes for Coleman as for myself. These witnesses had stated this to me.

Q. Who was on this committee?

A. I only remember Mr. Doster.

Q. What was the report?

A. It was favorable.

Q. Is it in the journals of the court house senate?

A. I do not know.

Q. Was a journal kept by that body?

A. There was.

Q. In the investigation, were the ballots before the committee?

A. I think not.

Q. What was the nature of the testimony?

A. A great many votes were thrown out that should not have been. I don't know how long the committee was investigating.

Q. Did you ever give any notice of contest?

A. I did not.

Q. Did you ever hold any certificate of election?

A. I did not.

Q. Did Mr. Coleman hold a certificate?

A. I think he did.

Q. How long did you retain your seat in the court house assembly?

A. Until the compromise of Attorney General Williams was agreed upon.

Q. Did you apply for your seat in the consolidated legislature?

A. I did not.

Q. Did you not fail to claim your seat because you knew you were not elected ?

A. I did not. I thought I was elected, but I knew there was no use to contest in a democratic senate.

Q. You say the senate was democratic ?

A. My impression is that by the time I could get up a contest the senate would be democratic.

Q. Do you not know the senate was republican at that time ?

A. Mr. Gilmore died and left a democratic majority. I believe on the first reorganization the senate was republican.

Q. Was it not a conceded fact by the republicans that you could not successfully contest the seat of senator Coleman ?

A. I did not feel justified, from my impressions, in making the contest.

Q. Why did you not feel justified in making the contest if you believed you were elected ?

A. I knew there was a good deal of expense connected with the contest, and I felt satisfied I would not be seated.

Q. Was it not because you felt your opponent had a better claim to the seat ?

A. It was because of the expense, delay, and other causes.

Q. Did your opponent, Daniel Coleman, have a certificate of election before and after the fusion of the two bodies ?

A. He did.

Q. Is he still senator ?

A. He is.

Q. Has any one ever contested his seat ?

A. I think not.

Q. If you had not taken your seat in the court house legislature, would there have been a quorum in that body ?

A. I think there would have been a quorum without me.

Q. Was Baker a member of the court house assembly from the 3d district, and if so, did he contest his seat in the fusion legislature ?

A. He was, but did not contest his seat.

Q. What was the object of the meeting of the court house assembly ?

A. To counteract the movement of the democrats in seating members not entitled to seats.

Q. Were there not members of the court house assembly who were not elected, or who failed to contest for seats in the fusion legislature ?

A. There were members in the court house assembly who did not contest for seats in that body, and who did not apply for seats.

Q. If you and Mr. Baker and Mr. Miller had not taken your seats in the court house assembly, would there have been a quorum in that body?

A. There would not.

Q. Was not the ultimate purpose of the court]house[leg-islature the election of Spencer?

A. I can't say it was, particularly. It was thought[dem-ocrats had obtained seats who were not entitled to them, and it was to counteract this movement and to secure the seats of members who had been excluded from the capitol legislature.

Q. Was it considered a party necessity?

A. It was so considered in order to give these members their seats.

Q. Was Mr. Spencer the choice of the republican party for the office of U. S. senator?

A. He was.

Q. Were there any promises of money made to members for their support of Spencer?

A. Not to my certain knowledge. I was not promised any.

Q. Do you know of any money being used by Spencer or his friends to secure his election?

A. I know of none.

Q. Who was the most ardent supporter, or who occupied the most confidential relations with Spencer?

A. I think Gov. Smith was intimate and a warm supporter.

Q. What were the relations between J. J. Hinds and Spencer?

A. They were good friends.

Q. Did they occupy the same rooms at the hotel?

A. They stayed at the same hotel.

Q. Do you know of Hinds having used any money in Spencer's election?

A. I do not.

Q. How many of Spencer's friends in that election, inside and outside of the legislature, now hold federal office?

A. I do not know how many. There are several who sup-ported him now holding federal office. General Dustan is one, Duskin another, McAfee another, Goodloe, myself, Cochran. Wilson was appointed but has since been removed. Clarke another.

Q. Did you call on General Spencer during the session of the court house legislature?

A. I have been in his room and met him frequently. He and I are friendly.

4

Q. Did Gen. Spencer write or telegraph you to come to Montgomery?

A. He did not.

Q. Did Hinds?

A. I do not think he did.

Q. Who did?

A. John Price of Florence consulted with me first on the subject; we knew a United States Senator was to be elected, and we went to Montgomery together.

Q. Did you or not know your presence was necessary in Montgomery to make a quorum in the court house assembly?

A. I did not consider that question.

Q. Did you not discuss that question when you arrived at Montgomery?

A. I do not remember that it was discussed.

Q. How did you make your claim in the court house assembly for a seat?

A. I made no formal or written application.

Q. Did the idea originate with you to make the claim?

A. I had received statements that justified me in the opinion.

Q. Did you make any claim before the committee was appointed?

A. I made no formal or written claim.

Q. Do you know how the committee came to be appointed?

A. I do not know at whose instance the committee was appointed.

Q. What was the first notice you got of the appointment of such committee?

A. I got notice shortly after the committee was appointed.

Q. Were you not present when the arrangement was made?

A. I was not.

Q. How long after you got to Montgomery before you received notice of the appointment of the committee?

A. It was in the early days of the session; I won't say it was the first or second day.

Q. You have stated that you never made any formal or written claim to a seat before the committee was appointed; now state whether you made any demand of any sort, or claim, before the committee was appointed?

A. No, I did not; it was my intention to have the matter investigated.

Q. Did your action in going to Montgomery and taking a

seat in the court house assembly have any reference to the election of Spencer?

A. It did not, because I was not satisfied as to who would be the candidate.

Q. Would you have gone to Montgomery had it not been for the pending senatorial election?

A. Yes sir.

Q. Were you in Montgomery while the Martin-Miller contest was pending?

A. I was.

Q. Was it the understanding that Miller was to be seated?

A. I do not know.

Q. Don't you know that Senator Glass was secreted to be brought in to vote in the Martin-Miller contest?

A. Not of my own knowledge; I know he was paired off with Senator Edwards.

Q. You seem to be so defective in memory, have you a good or bad memory?

A. I think I have a tolerable good memory, but cannot remember events in every particular that transpired two or three years ago.

Q. Who is considered to control the federal patronage in this State to a greater extent than any other man?

A. General Spencer.

Q. Is it not by that means he secures the influence of office holders?

A. I can't speak for others.

Q. Through whose influence were you appointed?

A. I would not say it was altogether through Mr. Spencer's; I had many friends in the Republican party.

Q. What Republicans were excluded from the capital legislature who applied for admission as members of that body?

A. I think that Mr. Black was excluded, and the Barbour delegation were not permitted to take their seats; also, General Dustan.

Q. Do you know whether Mr. Black applied for a seat in the capital legislature?

A. I think he did.

Q. Was he refused admission?

A. I don't know.

Q. Don't you know Mr. Black took his seat in the court house legislature on its organization?

A. He did; I, also, know he was afterwards seated in the capitol legislature on a contest.

Q. Why was Mr. Black seated on a contest in the capitol legislature?

A. Because it was established, beyond a doubt, he was elected.

Q. Why were you not seated on a consolidation of the two legislatures ?

A. I made no effort to be seated.

Q. Don't you know Mr. Black was seated under the compromise of Attorney General Williams, and there was no contest ?

A. I think that was the case.

Q. Don't you know on the consolidation of the two legislatures the Senate was Republican ?

A. I think it was.

Q. If the Senate was Republican why did you not contest for your seat ?

A. I had sufficient reasons for not making it.

Q. Did you believe you could succeed ?

A. I did not.

Q. You have stated you held your appointment to a Federal office before Spencer's election ; did you hold such office during the session of the court house assembly ?

A. No sir, I was removed from the position dating from the day of the general election by Mr. William Miller, Collector of Customs.

Q. When were you reappointed ?

A. I was reappointed, perhaps it was in February ; it was after I had left Montgomery and gone home.

Q. Did you have a new commission issued to you ?

A. I did for the same place I held before.

Q. Why were you removed ?

A. I don't know the exact cause unless it was he had received information that I had been elected to the Senate.

Q. Was not that removal at the time understood to be for the purpose of qualifying you for holding your seat in the senate ?

A. I had no understanding on the matter ; I knew nothing of it until I received notice in Montgomery.

Q. Was this done before you took your seat?

A. I received the information while I was in my seat in Montgomery ; the removal dated and took effect from the day of the election.

Q. Did your pay stop on the day of the election ?

A. It did, and I received no pay up to the time of my appointment.

Q. Did Mr. Miller have any right to stop your pay dating back of the notice of removal ?

A. I do not know what Mr. Miller's powers were.

Q. It is unusual thus to discharge an officer ; why was it done in your case ?

A. I can't say why Mr. Miller did it.

Q. Did you understand it, or did you enquire into it?

A. I did not understand it, I enquired into it however.

Q. Did you perform any duty from the date of your discharge up to the time you received notice of it ?

A. I did not ; I was off on leave.

Q. Had your leave expired ?

A. It had not.

Q. If you were holding office to-day and were discharged, your discharge to take effect back of the date of your appointment, would you question the power of removal ?

A. I would question the right to stop my pay dating back. That would be a different case.

Q. You say you enquired into the cause of your removal, what explanation did you get ?

A. All that Mr. Miller said was, the understanding was I was elected and he would remove me.

Q. How do you think Mr. Miller found out you were elected before you did ?

A. I do not know from what source he derived his information.

Q. You say you were reappointed some time in February, was this after Spencer's election and the consolidation of the two legislatures ?

A. It was.

Q. How can you say then, in answer to the question as to who procured your appointment, that you held your appointment before ?

A. It did not occur to my mind at that time that I had been removed for a few weeks.

Q. You now say you did receive a federal appointment after Spencer's election.

A. I was reappointed.

Q. Through whese influence ?

A. I can't say it was altogether through Spencer's influence. He was friendly to me. A good many republicans recommended me.

Q. Do you know whether he exerted his influence to have you appointed ?

A. I think he did.

Q. You say you had performed no duty since the day of the election up to the time you received notice of your removal, why were you reappointed to an office to which no duties were attached ?

A. At the time I was away from here on a leave of absence. The office has duties attached to it.

Q. Did you ever draw pay for a time when no services
were rendered?

A. No sir, except when absent on leave.

Q. How long were you absent on the leave you have mentioned?

A. I was absent a month or more.

Q. Are you sure you never signed a pay roll or receipt
embracing the time between the day of the election and the
time of the meeting of the court house assembly?

A. I am not sure I did not.

Q. Are you sure you did not receive the money for that
time?

A. I am sure.

Q. If you signed such a pay roll and received no money,
what was done with the pay roll or money?

A. I don't suppose any money was issued upon such a
pay roll.

Q. If any was issued who got it?

A. I don't know. I got none.

Q. Did you draw your per diem during the time you were
in the court house assembly?

A. I did.

WM. R. CHISHOLM.

### JOHN W. MILLER

being sworn, says: I reside in the city of Mobile and am
engaged in the banking business, and am a member of the
firm of T. P. Miiler & Co. I know J. J. Moulton, former
postmaster of this city.

Q. Have you any information as to where Mr. Moulton
kept his bank account, during the time he was postmaster and
shortly before his removal?

A. He did business with us dating about a year before
his removal up to that time.

Q. Do you remember the date of his removal?

A. I think it was January, 1873.

Q. Do you know any thing of the nature of the fund deposited with you?

A. It was my information they were public funds, from the
fact that a great many small drafts from postmasters were
deposited from different sections of the country. I understood them to be public funds; though his account on our
books was in the name of John J. Moulton.

Q. Do you remember his depositing a draft at any time for the sum of $2,250?

A. Our general ledger shows that there was a deposit made on the 7th day of December, 1872, of $2,250. On referring to the deposit ticket on which the character of the deposit is described, I find that the deposit consisted of a draft drawn by the First National Bank of Montgomery on the Commercial Bank of Mobile.

Q. How can we ascertain to whom the draft is made payable?

A. By referring to the National Commercial Bank of Mobile or the First National Bank of Montgomery.

Q. Did Moulton at any time in the Fall of 1872, or early part of 1873, draw any money through your bank, for use in Montgomery?

A. I don't remember the exact time, but think it was the latter part of 1872, he called at our bank and obtained a letter of credit for $2,500, addressed to Farley, Smith & Co., of Montgomery. It was all used. (The examination of Mr. Miller was suspended until he could examine his books and papers, when it was resumed.)

Q. You mentioned in your evidence on yesterday, a draft for $2,250, which you were requested to produce, have you been able to find it?

A. I have. (The witness here presented the draft, as the one spoken of before by him, marked Exhibit "A," as follows:

$2,250.     THE FIRST NATIONAL BANK OF MONTGOMERY, }
                MONTGOMERY, ALA., Dec. 4, 1872.  }

"Pay to the order of Geo. E. Spencer twenty-two hundred and fifty dollars in currency.

To National Commercial Bank, Mobile, Ala.

E. R. MITCHELL, Cashier.

Endorsed by Geo. E. Spencer and John J. Moulton.

Q. Will you deliver the original, of which the above is a copy, to the committee?

A. I will deliver it to the committee, subject to the order of "National Commercial Bank" of Mobile. It is a voucher to them for the amount. The draft is marked Exhibit "A."

Q. You also testified yesterday about a letter of credit for $2,500 to J. J. Moulton, have you refreshed your memory on that subject?

A. I have found the original copy in our letter-book, and herewith furnish a copy, which is hereunto annexed and is marked Exhibit "B," which original is dated Dec. 19, 1872.

Q. Can you now state correctly how many drafts were drawn against this letter, or what amounts or what dates, and when drawn?

A. There were two drafts drawn, one for $1,500, another for $1,000, both dated at Montgomery, Dec. 21st, 1872, drawn on us by John J. Moulton, in favor of Farley, Smith & Co.

Q. Have you the original drafts, and will you deliver them to the committee.

A. I will do so with a receipt for the same, subject to our order.

The drafts are hereto annexed, and are marked Exhibits "C." and "D."

JOHN W. MILLER.

## EXHIBIT "B."

OFFICE OF THOS. P. MILLER & Co., Bankers, <br> 28 St. Francis St., Mobile, Ala., Dec. 19, 1872.

*Messrs. Farley, Smith & Co., Montgomery:*

DEAR SIRS—Mr. John J. Moulton's draft on us for twenty-five hundred dollars will be honored by us if drawn through your house on us during the next ten days. Let this letter accompany the draft.

Yours truly,<br>THOS. P. MILLER & Co.

## EXHIBIT "C."

$1,500.                    MONTGOMERY, ALA., Dec. 21, 1872.

Pay to the order of Farley, Smith & Co. fifteen hundred dollars, value received, and charge the same to account of

JNO. J. MOULTON.

To Messrs. T. P. MILLER & Co., Mobile, Ala.

## EXHIBIT "D."

$1,000.                    MONTGOMERY, ALA., Dec. 21, 1872.

Pay to the order of Farley, Smith & Co., one thousand dollars, value received, and charge the same to the account of

JNO. J. MOULTON.

To THOS. P. MILLER & Co., Mobile, Ala.

WM. MILLER

Being sworn, says:
I reside in Mobile. Was collector of the port of Mobile from February, 1872, to May, 1873.
By Mr. Little—

Q. Did W. R. Chisholm hold any office in the custom house during your term of office?

A. He was appointed inspector in the early part of the year 1872. I think I am certain he was acting during the summer of that year.

Q. How long did he hold that position?

A. My impression is that soon after the general election in November, 1872, I got the information or impression from him that he had a seat in the legislature, and he did not propose to draw any pay during the time he was in the legislature.

Q. Did you remove him from the position?

A. I did not. I regarded it as a withdrawal for the time being. There was no formal removal or resignation.

Q. About the commencement of the legislature did you notify him that he was removed?

A. I did not. I notified them all—all who were elected to the legislature—that I would not pay them for the time they were in the legislature, or held any other office.

Q. Did Chisholm render any service while he was in office?

A. From five to ten days would cover the entire service rendered by him.

Q. Did he draw pay for all the time of his appointment?

A. He did.

Q. When was Chisholm removed, or when did he go out of office?

A. About the 5th of November, 1872.

Q. Were more persons appointed to office in the custom house in 1872 than were needed?

A. I think there were.

Q. For what purposes were these supernumeraries appointed?

A. For the political influence of the appointees.

Q. Were you suspended at any time from your position as collector?

A. I was.

Q. Was there any communication between you and Spencer as to your reappointment?

A. I received a telegram from Spencer informing me that Warner's name would be withdrawn, and to meet Hinds in Montgomery. I met Hinds in Montgomery. I think Spencer wrote me a letter, sending it by Hinds. At any rate, I got a letter from Spencer at about that time, in which I was informed that I could confer with Hinds and H. Ray Myers, and that they would name the men from whom to select employees in the custom house. After conferring with Myers personally, and with Hinds by letter, I went on and made re-- movals and changes, and wherever I thought it at all consistent with my duty, put in the men they named. Among these appointees were Chisholm and Dereen. Hinds insisted that Chisholm should be made chief inspector. I appointed him an inspector, but not chief inspector. H. Ray Myers told me soon after I got the telegram named from Spencer, that he had had a meeting with the negroes and had determined upon a list of names to be appointed.

Q. Who was the chief dispenser of federal patronage in Alabama?

A. I think Spencer was.

Q. What was the relation between Spencer, Hinds and H. Ray Myers in political affairs?

A. I regarded them as fast friends, each one endeavoring to seek the promotion of interest of the others, both political and otherwise.

Q. What was the understanding at the time these supernumerary appointments you have spoken of were made, as to how long their term of office should last?

A. The supernumeraries were appointed to continue in office until after the election in November, 1872. The others until there was cause for removal.

Q. What was the power of the collector of the ports, in appointing and removing inspectors?

A. He had the right, under the regulations, to remove inspectors and to appoint temporary inspectors whenever he deemed it necessary.

Q. What is the customary method of discharging inspectors?

A. To give them notice in writing, or verbally, that their services are not wanted. .

Q. Was Chisholm ever discharged in this way?

A. He was not. He was informed some time early in November to make out his voucher for the number of days he considered himself in office for that month.

WM. MILLER.

MOSES S. FOOTE

Being sworn, said:

Q. Where did you reside in the year 1872, and what was your business?

A. I resided in Mobile, and was engaged in the banking business.

Q. Did you have any business transactions in your bank, in the Fall of 1872 with Lou H. Mayer or John J. Moulton?

A. I did, with both of them.

Q. What was the nature of the business?

A. Taking money on deposit and discounting paper.

Q. Who personally made the deposit?

A. John J. Moulton, who was then post master of Mobile.

Q. In whose name was the account entered?

A. In the name of W. H. Lewis, agent. He was engaged in the post office department at the time.

Q. Do you know what funds were so deposited?

A. I do not know, unless it was post office money?

Q. What reasons have you for thinking it was post office money?

A. I ascertained the fact from Moulton himself at the time.

Q. What was the amount of this deposit?

A. Twelve hundred and forty dollars, Oct. 31, 1872.

Q. Why was the deposit made?

A. As a collateral for a discount.

Q. What was the amount of the paper, discount and time?

A. Two thousand dollars and, I think sixty days.

Q. Who obtained the discount?

A. L. H. Mayer, assessor of internal revenue, at the time, and John J. Moulton, post master.

Q. The deposit being less than the accommodation, what other security did you have, if any.

A. The endorsement of Hon. C. F. Moulton and Caleb Price, Esq.

Q. Was the paper met at maturity?

A. No, it was extended.

Q. Do you know the necessity for extension; if so, state it?

A. I was informed by both, Mr. L. H. Mayer and Mr. Moulton, that Spencer had gone back on them, he having told them that $25,000 was set apart for political purposes to carry the State, by the Republican National Executive Committee, and that they had been authorized in anticipation of this amount to make the loan or any money arrangements necessary, and that Spencer had not provided the means promised, and they therefore asked for further time. Mayer stated, at the same time complaining of Spencer, that he (Spencer) knew that Moulton had used post office money, and that he (Mayer) had pledged his wife's jewels and all the money he could get, as well as revenue money, to pay these accommodations. These matters were stated as a basis for further extension.

Q. Was there any other money transactions with you about that time by these parties, or either of them ; if so, what were they ?

A. Yes. I accommodated Mr. Mayer, upon his application by cashing the pay rolls of his assessments, the money not having arrived from Washington in time, the pay rolls having been properly endorsed and certified by the assessor and collector.

Q. Was there any further transactions with Mr. Mayer of this nature ?

A. There was. He applied to me to cash the pay rolls of three assistant assessors at the same time. The application was made on the first of the month for pay during that month, which I declined to do, unless properly sworn to before the assessor, L. H. Mayer, and certified as correct by John J. Foster, as collector of internal revenue, all of which was done, and therefore the accommodotion was granted. A similar request was made the following month upon the same character of paper, but was declined.

Q. What were your reasons for declining the second request ?

A. Two reasons. 1st. He said it was to be used in sending men into the country for political purposes; that they intended to carry the State for Grant and Spencer. 2nd. I was satisfied that the pay rolls certified and sworn to thirty days before they were due was unlawful. I called Mayer's attention to that fact, and asked him what he meant by such conduct. He replied ; "I know what I am doing, and have the approval of the department and will be sustained."

Q. Have you any information tending to show that George E. Spencer was connected with any of these transactions ?

A. Only the fact that on one occasion Moulton drew from his pocket a letter in the presence of Mayer, I think, and stated that it was a letter from Spencer, authorizing them to make money transactions and pledging to them the $25,000. This statement was made pending the negotiation for the loan of the $2,000.

Q. Did you call on the collector for an explanation of why he certified to these pay rolls in advance? If so, what did he say?

A. I did, and asked him why he certified to these accounts so far in advance of their being due, and what would he do in case any of these parties should die in the meantime. He replied, he and Mayer would have to pay them between them ; that they were riding him to death in this Spencer matter, and that he was tired of it and did not intend to repeat it.

Q. During these transactions did you learn any fact tending to show that Mayer was to receive any reward for his services from Spencer?

A. Yes. Mr. Mayer informed me that if Grant carried the State, Spencer would be elected to the United States Senate, and he would then, through Spencer, be appointed collector of internal revenue at Mobile over Dr. Foster, when the offices of collector and assessor were consolidated. Moulton also told me that Mayer would get the appointmont.

Q. Did Mr. Mayer ever ask any other accommodation from you?

A. He did. He came to me and wanted one or more thousand dollars. He wanted to deposit as collateral U. S. postage stamps. I declined to make the loan.

MOSES S. FOOTE.

The committee then adjourned to meet in Montgomery tomorrow at 11 a. m.

MONTGOMERY, ALA., May 6, 1875.

The committee met pursuant to adjournment at the capitol. Present: Messrs. Little, Parks, Price and Brewer.

W. H. HUNTER

Being sworn, says:

I reside in the city of Montgomery. I resided in Lowndes county in 1872. I am a Republican in politics. I was a member of the lower house of the general assembly of this State in 1872 from Lowndes county.

Q. At the organization of the general assembly, were you a member of the court house or capitol legislature?

A. I was a member of the court house legislature, so called.

Q. Was it considered by the leading Republicans of the general assembly that there was a quorum in the Senate of the court house assembly?

A. Not without the seating of certain members that had no certificates. Among the number were Chisholm, Baker and Miller.

Q. What was the object and purpose of the organization of the court house body?

A. The intention and object as stated to us in caucus and secret sessions was to effect a permanent organization of the two bodies of the general assembly of Alabama with Republican majorities in both branches, the principal object being to secure the election of a United States Senator, for which office Spencer was a prominent candidate, but against whom there was considerable opposition. This opposition gave way when the agreement gained credence that if Spencer was not elected no one would be.

Q. Do you know of any other means used to overcome this opposition?

A. The argument was used by the party leaders that it was a party necessity to keep the majority in the court house body and to elect Spencer.

Q. Was J. J. Hinds in Montgomery pending the election for United States Senator by the court house assembly?

A. He was.

Q. What were the relations between he and Spencer?

A. They appeared to be very intimate and confidential. Hinds was constantly among the members urging them to vote for Spencer, and to maintain the court house organization. He was with Spencer constantly; they come to Montgomery together, and Spencer occupied a suit of rooms in the Madison House, and I suppose Hinds occupied the same rooms. If any one had to be looked after, or was regarded as a little weak on the Spencer election, it seemed to be Hinds' special business to look after him; he was regarded as Spencer's cashier and agent; I was informed by colored members that the night before Spencer's election an oyster supper was given the colored members of the court house assembly by Hinds in Spencer's interest.

Q. Do you know whether any members of the court house assembly were disaffected towards that organization when it first assembled, and at first declined to take seats?

A. It was understood there were several disaffected members to that movement; of which number was Senator Goodloe, who, although present, did not join or participate with them until just previous to the election of United States Senator.

Q. Was there any reason given why Goodloe finally took his seat in that body?

A. None, except it was understood that his receiving the collectorship of the port of Mobile was to be his compensation.

Q. If after Spencer's election you had any conversation with Goodloe with reference to his appointment to the collectorship of the port ot Mobile, state what it was.

A. I had a conversation with Mr. Goodloe, in which I expressed surprise at the appointment of Reynolds to the collectorship of the port of Mobile instead of him (Goodloe); I said to him, "I thought it was the understanding you was to get that office;" his reply was: "It will all come out right yet!"

Q. Was he subsequently appointed to this office?

A. He was.

Q. Do you know from your own knowledge, or from a general understanding with the leading Republicans that other members were to receive Federal appointments?

A. The Federal patronage of Alabama was to be divided among the members of the assembly who supported Spencer; I remember the name of Geo. M. Duskin, who was to be appointed United States District Attorney; this was the general understanding. A short time after the election of Spencer, and about the time of the reorganization under the terms of the attorney general, I proposed to run as a candidate for speaker of the house of representatives; Senator Spencer said to me that he could procure for me the appointment of consul to Alexandria, Egypt. After the reorganization, and a day or two before the day upon which I attempted to bring on an election for United States Senator in the consolidated or reorganized legislature, D. C. Whiting showed me a telegram from Spencer, who was then in Washington, in these words: "Shall I have Hunter appointed now, or wait until the legislature adjourns; I think the latter plan preferable." (Signed) "Geo. E. Spencer." The appointment referred to was the consulate to Alexandria, which had been filled by a Utica, New York, man, two weeks previous to the date of the dispatch, and the fact published in the Associated press dispatches, of which Spencer was fully aware.

Q. Can you give any explanation of this conduct of Spencer?

A. I am satisfied he was aware of the fact that I intended to make an effort to elect a United States Senator by the consolidated legislatures, and that this was an effort to forestall my action.

Q. Do you know of any money having been used to secure the vote of any member of the general assembly for Spencer?

A. I know that January Maull received $25; he stated to me that Carsons received $75, and Jones $400, which was stated to be a fund for reimbursing for money expended in the campaign. I, although a member of the Lowndes delegation and a supporter of Spencer, received nothing, nor was I tendered any money, although I had expended ten times the amount of the others.

Q. Did Hinds use any money in securing Spencer's election?

A. He seemed to have plenty of money and had a way of making it known; I saw him with it frequently; he seemed to be liberal with it, and left the impression upon me that he was there ready and prepared for any emergency in Spencer's interest.

Q. What seemed to be Hinds' special business there at the time?

A. He seemed to be there specially in the interest of Spencer, who was a candidate for United States Senator, in electioneering for him among the members and upon the streets.

Q. Was J. J. Moulton there at the time?

A. I remember his being there the evening of the temporary organization under the plan of the attorney general.

Q. Among the candidates before the court house assembly for United States Senator, who was your choice?

A. General Spencer.

W. H. HUNTER.

ROBERT BARBER

Being sworn says:

I reside near the city of Montgomery; in 1872 I was clerk of the lower house of the court house assembly, and, also, of the consolidated legislature.

By Mr. Little—

Q. What was the object of the court house assembly?

A. To get a Republican organization; we did not think we could get it at the capitol, but the main object was to secure the election of Spencer.

Q. Was the object, during the campaign, previous to the general election, directed to the election of members of the legislature, with the view of electing a United States Senator; if so, who, and what steps were taken?

A. Yes, Geo. E. Spencer. Gen. Spencer said he had reliable information that Parsons would be a candidate against him for the place, and must be defeated.

Q. How did he propose to accomplish this?

A. He sent me to Talladega county for the purpose of getting out an independent candidate.

Q. Who was to be the independent candidate, and what inducements were to be offered him?

A. A man named Wood, who resided near Syllacauga, and was a Republican of considerable influence; I was instructed by Gen. Spencer to inform Mr. Wood that he would see that all the expenses of the canvass would be met. When

I reached the place, I found Parsons would not be a candidate, and did not execute the plan.

Q. Was there any other plan for securing Spencer's election or defeating other parties?

A. Peter G. Clarke and H. Ray Mayer were sent to Dallas by Spencer to defeat Alexander White, who was supposed to be in Parsons' interest.

Q. What plan was adopted for defeating White?

A. They were to arrange with Beach for him to be a secret candidate against White, whose name was to be left off the tickets which were to be printed at Washington; the tickets were printed with about one-half with White's name upon them and the other half left blank. When the tickets arrived White discovered the omission and had his name printed in the blank.

Q. If arrangements were made for any other county state what they were and the county?

A. A crowd of us went over to Lowndes to beat Stanwood and a colored man, known opponents of Spencer, and put in Hunter and two colored men favorable to Spencer, in which plan we succeeded.

Q. In carrying out these plans was any money used?

A. In the Lowndes county trip Spencer gave Whiting $300 to defray expenses.

Q. Have you any written communication relating to the plans you have mentioned touching the use of troops in Alabama?

A. I have some letters which I do not care to produce, as they are of a private character.

Q. Do you say you have them in your possession?

A. I do; but wishing to violate nothing like confidence, will not produce them unless required to do so by the committee.

(The witness was permitted to consult with his attorney.)

Q. As it is improper to ask of the contents of the letters when you have them in your possession, we are put to the necessity of requiring you to produce them; will you do so?

A. I produce the letters, here they are (handing them to the chairman); I ask that the committee have copies made, and allow me to retain the originals.

(A copy of these letters is hereto appended, marked exhibits E. and F., and are a part of this testimony).

Q. Do you know these letters to be genuine?

A. I know Spencer's handwriting; they were written and signed by him, and bear the impress of his seal or motto used by him.

5

Q. I notice in the letter of October 22, 1872, the expression, "I wish Randolph, Deputy United States Marshal, would use the company at Opelika in making arrests in Tallapoosa, Randolph and Cleburne, as —— suggests;" please explain the meaning of this expression?

A. I received a letter from Randolph county before the date of these letters, suggesting that if troops be sent into the counties named that enough voters would be run out of them, through fear of arrest, to secure the election of Republican representatives from those counties, and the letter of October 22 was in reply to a letter written to Spencer, conveying to him this information.

Q. Was your connection with the Republican party and Spencer of a character to enable you to understand their and his plans?

A. I was familiar with their and his plans all the way through; I was assistant secretary of the Republican State Executive Committee.

Q. What were the relations between Hinds and Spencer?

A. Hinds was the confidential man and represented Spencer fully in every particular. He had the control of every movement made.

Q. Do you know of any money being used by Hinds or Spencer or by any one for Spencer to secure his election; if so state it and who were the special friends of Spencer working in his interest pending the election before the legislature, and what was done?

A. The special friends of Spencer were C. C. Sheets, member of Congress; Col. W. H. Betts, D. C. Whiting, J. J. Hinds, already mentioned, Hon. Charles Pelham, A. R. Baker, present U. S. Marshal for Northern District of Alabama, and myself. These are the men who had the special management of Spencer's election. I was informed in our conferences that all the money necessary to secure Spencer's election was provided and in the hands of Hinds.

Q. Were any means used upon the Lowndes county delegation of the court house assembly to induce them to remain in said assembly and to support Spencer; if so, state fully about it.

A. It was generally understood by the managers of Spencer's election, the night before his election, that the Lowndes county delegation, except Hunter, were disaffected and would not be present to vote for Spencer, and would thereby defeat his election, there not being a sufficient number left on joint ballot to elect a senator. We were informed that $2,000 had been raised to disaffect these members, and that the money was subject to the order of Senator Jones, which was afterwards ascertained not to be the case, but not knowing better at the time, I was instructed to inform Senator Jones that we had $2,500 subject to his order, conditioned upon his holding the Lowndes county delegation in the court house assembly. We ascertained Jones was attending a colored ball and sent J. N. Beach, a government detective, to interview Jones and report. Sandy Bynum, John C. Hendrix and myself were selected to watch the Lowndes county delegation in the lower house of the assembly, except Hunter, all night, and not lose sight of them. Betts was to take special charge of Senator Jones, and was instructed, if necessary, to offer him the $2,500. I was to watch the representatives all night, which I did. Just before day Daniel Norwood, assistant sergeant-at-arms, came out of the house where they were staying and I gave him five dollars to go in and wake up Carson and Maull and tell them I wanted to see them. They came out and I invited them to the Madison House, where breakfast had been ordered by Senator Spencer for their especial benefit. I then went to Senator Spencer's room and informed him that I had them. He told me to bring them up to his room, which I did. I told Carson and Maull, two of the representatives from Lowndes, that Spencer had made up his mind to give each of them an appointment. Spencer was present and promised each of them a route agency, one on the Western Railroad. I have forgotten the other. The promise was made in my presence. During the night, while on watch, I left Bynum on watch and went to Spencer's room and suggested to him to send to Lowndes for Bryant, who came the next morning, and I understood received $300 from Hinds. This seemed to fix the Lowndes county delegation all right. The legislature convened that morning; the Lowndes members were present and voted for Spencer.

Q. Were there any promises made or inducements offered to other members of the court house assembly?

A. Many of the members were promised offices. I was authorized by Spencer to promise as many offices to members as I thought necessary to secure their support.

Q. Was J. C. Goodloe promised any position?

A. Not in my presence; but it was understood that he was to receive a federal appointment, and that, at the proper time, he would join the court house assembly; but that he was to remain in such a position as to have access to and the confidence of the capitol assembly until his vote was needed at the court house to elect Spencer. He attended the caucusses of the capitol assembly and ascertained all he could of its movements by going to the rooms of members and con- versations, reporting all that he learned and heard to Spen- cer.

Q. Were any influences used upon members of the capitol legislature in furtherance of the plan to secure Spencer's election?

A. Yes. We were trying to defeat a quorum of the capi- tol legislature constantly. I was given to understand we had succeeded in defeating a quorum by the disaffection of a man named Mancill, whom Hinds had informed me he had "fixed," to use his own expression, by increasing the number of trips per week on some postal route that Mancill had as contractor or sub-contractor, thereby increasing the pay to $600. I think the contract was for $300 and he increased it to $600. I was given to understand by the managers, (I mean by "managers," the persons heretofore spoken of as having charge of Spencer's election,) that we had nothing to fear from representative Kelly.

Q. What about Stribbling?

A. Stribbling was turned over to those who played cards. I was given to understand that he was to be drugged, and afterwards learned he was lying somewhere insensible. This was the night before the day fixed by law for the election of U. S. Senator, when the capitol assembly was to proceed with such election. I learned that on that day he was still lying insensible.

Q. Were there any members of the court house assembly seated in that body for the purposes stated who were not elected? If so, who were they?

A. It was the general impression that neither Baker or Chisholm were entitled to seats.

Q. At the time of the fusion of the two legislatures under the attorney general's plan, did either Baker or Chisholm apply for a seat in the consolidated body?

A. No sir, neither of them. They were excluded by the terms of the compromise.

Q. State whether any compensation, or promise thereof, was made to Baker or Chisholm to induce him to enter and remain in the court house assembly as a representative or senator from a certain county?

A. At the time Baker took his seat in the court house assembly, he was a commissioner to take testimony in claims against the United States, and complained that he would lose money by taking his seat, as it was known he was not elected and could not get his pay. I promised him a clerkship, be- ing at the time myself clerk of the house.

Q.  Did he afterwards take any position in the consolidated legislature?

A.  He did.  He was appointed clerk of the committee on internal improvements by Gen. Dustan, the chairman.

Q.  Was there any promise made to him of any federal office?

A.  He told me he had been promised a federal appoint-ment.  I think it was special agent of the postoffice department.

Q.  Did he afterwards receive a federal appointment?

A.  He was afterwards appointed U. S. Marshal for the northern district of Alabama.

Q.  What office was Chisholm to get?

A.  I made the same promise to Chisholm as I did to Baker in regard to a clerkship.  After the consolidation of the two bodies he was appointed to a position in the custom house at Mobile.

Q.  Do you know whether Baker or Chisholm were sent for or came of their own accord to the meeting of the legislature?

A.  I think they were sent for.

Q.  Was it decided upon by the friends of Spencer that Miller was to be seated upon the consolidation of the two bodies, in his contest with Martin?

A.  It was.

Q.  When, where and by whom was this arrangement made?

A.  When—during the pendency of the Martin-Miller contest.  Where and when—in a caucus of the managers heretofore mentioned.

Q.  How was this accomplished?

A.  We were to sustain Lt. Gov. McKinstry in his rulings, whatever decisions he might make.

Q.  State fully how McKinstry's rulings were to be sustained, by what persons and by what means.

A.  To carry out the plan agreed upon and to get McKinstry to rule so as to seat Miller before an absent senator returned, it was necessary, we thought, for McKinstry to rule so as to cut off debate and secure a final vote.  It was thought if McKinstry so ruled, that the democratic members would bolt or withdraw from the Senate, or have a fight.  To previde for the latter contingency, picked men were procured and were by agreement in the Senate chamber in the lobby.

Q.  Who were these men?

A.  W. H. Betts, Charles Pelham, Sam Oliver, M. G. Candee, Milo Barber, J. J. Hinds, a "rough" from Georgia whose name I did not know, and some five or six others whose names I cannot remember, some from Mobile.

Q. Was McKinstry apprised of this plan, and did he co-operate?

A. I don't know that McKinstry was apprised of the plan of their being brought there ; but he knew the men, and we believed he would rule so as to seat Miller at all hazards and would be strengthened by their presence, the object of the plan being to show him he had friends who would back him.

Q. Why was it believed McKinstry would so rule?

A. We thought some dilatory action might be taken by democratic members which would prevent final action in the matter until the return of the democratic senator, Edwards, and it was necessary to have final action on that day and seat Miller, as we feared Edwards might return before the matter was settled.

Q. State what was done to procure Senator Glass to remain in Montgomery in the absence of Senator Edwards and vote on the question of seating Miller over Martin. Give a full statement of all that transpired up to the time Glass took his seat and voted.

A. It was generally understood among the managers that Senator Glass was to pair off with Senator Edwards in the Miller-Martin contest ; that Glass was to go over to the depot with Edwards and return back to the city seemingly or apparently unknown to Edwards, the idea being to make outsiders believe they both left on the same day. They did both go to the depot on the same day at the same time. Glass returned without the knowledge of Edwards and was secreted in a room at the Madison House. To give Glass an excuse for violating his pledge with Senator Edwards, I served a subpœna on him, which was given me by Charles Pelham to execute on him as a witness in some case in which Pelham was an attorney. I went to the Madison House to execute this writ and found A. R. Baker doorkeeper for Glass. I asked him to execute the subpœna by handing it to Glass, which he did. Glass was kept out of sight until the vote was being taken in said Miller-Martin contest. He was informed by signal from the front of the capitol the very moment his presence was required. He appeared in the Senate in time, and did vote for seating Miller. I understood he was to be paid $300 or $500 for breaking faith with Edwards.

Q. Who is A. R. Baker?

A. He was the Senator from Morgan county in the court,

house legislature, and is now United States marshal for the Northern District of Alabama.

Q. In what manner was the signal given to Glass to appear in the Senate and from what place?

A. From the second story portico of the capitol, either by the waving of a coat or handkerchief.

Q. What were the next steps taken?

A. Upon a vote being taken, McKinstry ruled that Miller was seated. Before the result was announced Senator Cobb changed his vote from the negative to the affirmative for the purpose of moving for a reconsideration, which motion he made. President McKinstry ruled the motion was out of order and declined to put it to the Senate. The Senate adjourned with the understanding that Senator Cobb should have the floor next morning.

Q. What was done next morning?

A. The motion to reconsider was renewed by Mr. Cobb. McKinstry adhered to his former decision. Thereupon Mr. Cobb said he would not resort to violence.

Q. What was then done?

A. Senator Parks renewed the motion to reconsider, which McKinstry ruled out of order. Senator Parks appealed from his decision and asked McKinstry to put the appeal to the Senate, which he refused to do.

Q. What was then done?

A. Senator Parks undertook to put the vote himself, and called on the secretary to call the roll. McKinstry said to the secretary, "You dare not do it, sir," at the same time emptying the water out of his pitcher. He then laid his cane on the stand and then opened his drawer. Senator Parks then put the question, but no vote was taken. Senators Hamilton and Cooper crossed over to Senator Parks and urged him to desist. Senator Parks finally desisted and Miller came forward and was sworn in.

Q. Are these the rulings to which you referred in which McKinstry was to be sustained?

A. They are.

Q. Was there any preconcerted plan agreed upon by which the Democratic members from Marengo county were to be arrested immediately after their election or before the assembling of the legislature?

A. The understanding was that they were to be arrested while *en route* to Montgomery and carried to Mobile by way of Meridian or a round about way. They were not to be brought through Montgomery.

Q. By whom was this understood?

A. By the managers?

Q. Do you know whether Gillette was written to, or telegraphed to come up?

A. My recollection is that he was either written to or telegraphed?

Q. Did he come?

A. My recollection is that he did.

Q. What was the purpose of these arrests?

A. To prevent a quorum of Democratic members in the capitol legislature.

Q. Was John J. Moulton in Montgomery pending Spencer's election?

A. I think he was here part of the time.

Q. Do you know of any members having obtained money from Hinds, while they belonged to the court house assembly?

A. Yes. Most of the colored members would get loans from Hinds. I have seen them frequently borrowing money from him.

Q. Did he take any note from them, or was there any promise of repayment on the part of the borrowers?

A. Not that I know of. The money was obtained under the guise of a loan.

Q State whether this money was paid out of the fund provided by Spencer, or out of Hinds' private funds?

A. It was my inference, from all the facts within my knowledge that the money thus furnished came out of the fund that had been provided as I heretofore stated.

Q. Do you know any facts tending to explain the use of troops in the district of which Lou H. Mayer was at the time revenue assessor?

A. Yes. I read a communication from Mayer, setting forth a plan he had submitted to Spencer for the use of troops in that district. The ostensible object was the use of the troops to protect revenue officers in the performance of their duties in the collection of the United States revenue, and the suppression of illicit distilleries; but the real object was to organize the party into organizations called National Guards. I afterwards received a letter from Squires, who was connected with Perrin, reporting progress and stating how many organizations he had perfected. He was complaining that the commanding officer of the troops had got tired of that kind of service, and did not co-operate with him.

Q. Was Hinds a skillful manager of such matters as came before the managers mentioned by you?

A.   Yes, sir.   I considered him one of the shrewdest politicians I had seen—untiring, energetic and unscrupulous.

Q.   What are your feelings toward Mr. Spencer?

A.   I have no personal ill feeling against General Spencer,
but think his course in politics has been the death blow to
the republican party in Alabama.   His test of a man's allegiance to the republican party was allegiance to himself.

ROBERT BARBER.

## EXHIBIT " E."

[Private.]                    (Coat of Arms.)

DECATUR, ALA., Oct. 16, 1872.

DEAR BARBER:

I have just returned home from West Alabama, and find
that Whiting has gone to New York and has left word for me
to go to Montgomery.   I can not for two or three days leave
here.   I wish you would write me the news; what Whiting
has gone to New York for, and the prospect, &c., &c.

Write me a long letter by return mail, and tell me all that
has occurred.   Was Stanwood beaten in Lowndes?

I have heard nothing in a week.

Have you heard of any troops having been ordered to the
State?   Can't you manage to get White off the legislative
track in Dallas?   Parsons has a deep laid scheme to elect
himself, and has now gone to New York to try and raise
money to be used in the legislature.   I have news direct from
him.   See Beach and Coon, and urge them to see that White
is taken down.   Be sure and write me everything that is going on.            In haste,

Sincerely yours,

(Signed)                                GEO. E. SPENCER.

## EXHIBIT " F."

(Coat of Arms.)

DECATUR, ALA., Oct. 22, 1872.

MY DEAR BARBER:

I have just returned from Louisville, where I have been to
see Gen. Terry about troops for Alabama.

I have had a company of cavalry sent to Livingston, a detachment to Pickens county, a company of infantry to Eutaw,
and a company to Demopolis, and a company to Seal's Station, Russell county.   Also, a squadron of cavalry to report
to Marshal Thomas, at Huntsville.

I wish Randolph, deputy U. S. marshal, would use the company at Opelika in making arrests in Tallapoosa, Randolph and Cleburne, as ——————— suggests. I will be in Montgomery Thursday morning, to attend the meeting of the State committee. I would go sooner but can not, as it is important I should stay here to-morrow. I wish you would go to Talladega and block that game. I must not, however, be known in the matter.

The troops mentioned above will all be in their respective places in two days from now—some have already arrived.

In haste, truly yours,

(Signed)                                          GEO. E. SPENCER.

HENRY COCHRAN

Being sworn, deposes and says :

I was a member of the legislature of 1872 from Dallas county. Messrs. Alexander White, Thomas Walker, Joseph H. Goldsby and Ransom L. Johnson were my colleagues representing that county.

By General Morgan—

Q. What federal offices have any of these persons held to which they were appointed since they were elected members of that legislature?

A. I was myself appointed postmaster of the city of Selma. I think Goldsby was appointed after the expiration of his term of office in the legislature.

Q. What is your office worth per annum ?

A. About $2,500 per annum.

Q. When did you receive your appointment to that office]?

A. I think I received my appointment as postmaster some time in February or March, but did not take charge of the office for some two months afterwards. I was confirmed at a regular term of the senate.

Q. Did you visit Washington city about the time of your appointment?

A. I did not.

Q. Were you in the legislature at the time of your appointment ?

A. I was.

Q. How long did you continue to hold your seat before you wrote a paper to the governor of Alabama in reference to your resignation?

A. I can't recollect how long.

Q. Did you write the paper before June, 1873 ?

A. I did.

Q. Did you write any paper?

A. I did, but can't remember its contents.

Q. Can you remember the substance or purport of the contents of that paper?

A. It had reference to a resignation, but I can not remember its purport now.

Q. Was it a resignation?

A. It had conditions in it. I can't say whether it was or not.

Q. What were the conditions?

A. I can't remember.

Q. Was it intended to be a resignation?

A. Not by me, it was not.

Q. Did you send it to the office of the governor of the State?

A. I left it with the private secretary of the governor.

Q. If it was not a resignation, why did you leave it with the governor's secretary?

A. I understood I could not be a member of the legislature and atso postmaster. I afterwards found out it did not apply to me, as I was elected after I was appointed, and I withdrew the paper.

Q. What was the necessity of withdrawing the paper if it was not intended as a resignation?

A. Now I can't give any explanation, for I don't remember.

Q. What did the conditions in the paper refer to?

A. I can't remember.

Q. How long after the paper was left in the office of the governor before you recalled it?

A. I don't give any definite time. It might have been three months or it might have been six months.

Q. Do you think most likely, three or six months?

A. I can't say. I don't remember.

Q. Did you obtain the paper from the governor or from his private secretary?

A. I can't remember.

Q. Had the legislature of 1872–3 adjourned before you filed that paper?

A. I think it was four or five days before the adjournment of that body. It may have been longer.

Q. Did you then abandon your seat and go home?

A. No, I did not.

Q. What did you do?

A. I went down and took charge of my office and went back again.

Q. Did you retain your seat until the adjournment of the legislature of 1872–3?

A. I did. I remember now that I filed the paper heretofore named on or about the last day of the session of 1872–3, as near as I can remember.

Q. After your return from the legislature to Dallas county, did you not tell various people you had resigned?

A. Yes, I believe I did.

Q. Did you not tell me so?

A. I don't think I did.

Q. Did you not tell Gen. Coon so?

A. I think I did. I think I showed him a copy of the paper I filed.

Q. How long was it after your return from the legislature before you told any one you had withdrawn your resignation?

A. I don't recollect.

Q. About how long?

A. I can't give any definite time. I know I withdrew it some time before I told any one of it, notwithstanding I was bothered considerably about it by General Coon, who wanted to be elected in my place.

Q. How long had you withdrawn it before you told Gen. Coon of it?

A. I don't remember.

Q. In the interval between the time you filed your resignation and the time you withdrew it, did you see General Spencer?

A. I don't recollect.

Q. Did you have any correspondence during the time mentioned with him?

A. I think I did. I know I did.

Q. How many letters do you say you wrote him within the time named?

A. I don't know.

Q. Did you write him more than once during that time?

A. I can't say. I never wrote much. The only thing I remember of now is a dispatch enquiring if Coon was beaten in Dallas county.

Q. When was it received?

A. The evening after the election occurred.

Q. When was the election?

A. I do not know.

Q. Was it not in November, on the day fixed by law, on Tuesday after the first Monday in November?

A. I do not remember.

Q. Had you not been in correspondence with Spencer concerning General Coon's election?

A. I can't remember of any correspondence with him on the subject.

Q. Who did you write to in Washington on the subject of Coon's election?

A. I can't remember any one. I might have written.

Q. If you did not write to General Spencer, how came him to telegraph you asking if Coon was elected?

A. I suppose he wanted to know, I can't tell.

Q. At the time you recalled your resignation, did you not come to Montgomery and see Governor Lewis?

A. I did not.

Q. Did you write to him?

A. I expect I wrote to him withdrawing my resignation.

Q. Who asked you to withdraw your resignation.

A. There were several. I think Col. White was the first one.

Q. Who were the others?

A. Several. I cannot remember.

Q. When did White ask you to withdraw it?

A. I can't say.

Q. How long after it was first filed?

A. It might have been three or six months.

Q. What reason had. Mr. White for your withdrawing your resignation?

A. He said there was no necessity for it; that I could hold the office. The colored and white people preferred me to Coon and I preferred to stay there myself.

Q. Was Coon obliged to be elected to fill your vacancy?

A. I don't know. I was in favor of keeping him out if I could.

Q. Did you not know that Gen. Coon from the beginning was opposed to the court house assembly?

A. I did not.

Q. When did you first know it?

A. I never knew it.

Q. Did he not tell you so?

A. He did not. He always led me to believe he was in favor of it; that I swear to positively.

Q. Have you ever heard before this time that Gen. Coon was opposed to the courthouse legislature?

A. I can't say I ever heard he was opposed to it.

Q. Did you not know before your resignation was recalled that Gen. Coon was opposed to the court house legislature?

A. I did not.

Q. Did you not know before that time General Coon was opposed to Spencer holding a seat in the U. S. Senate?

A. He was opposed to Spencer, but I don't know that he was opposed to his holding a seat in the U. S. Senate.

Q. Was he violently opposed to Spencer?

A. I can't say. He is not a violent man.

Q. Was he not decidedly opposed to him?

A. I think he was as decidedly opposed to him as he would be to any body.

Q. Why was he decidedly opposed to him?

A. My opinion is, because he did not appoint him to an office. I heard him say Spencer had gone back on him. I don't think he was opposed to him from any good motive.

Q. What office had Gen. Spencer promised Gen. Coon?

A. I don't know what office.

Q. How did you know Gen. Coon was opposed to him because he did not appoint him to office?

A. From expressions from Gen. Coon.

Q. What were they?

A. One of them was he promised to appoint him collector of the port of Mobile. He did appoint him to an office, or had him appointed.

Q. What was it?

A. Consul to Rio Janeiro.

Q. At what time did Spencer have Gen. Coon appointed?

A. It was a year or more before his (Spencer's) second election.

Q. Were Coon and Spencer then friends?

A. I thought so.

Q. Have you been at any time opposed to Gen. Spencer?

A. I think I was opposed to him when Warner was elected.

Q. Were you then a member of the legislature?

A. I was.

Q. Who did you vote for in that election?

A. For Warner.

Q. As against whom?

A. Goldthwaite and some republican.

Q. Was there a violent controversy between Spencer and Warner?

A. I can't say. I was not into it.

Q. Was Spencer actively engaged in trying to beat Warner?

A. I can't say whether he was or not.

Q. Were not Warner's friends indignant at Spencer for having defeated him?

A.   I think they were.

Q.   Were you not one of the indignant friends?

A.   I took no part except to vote for Warner.

Q.   When did you cease to be a Warner man and become a Spencer man?

A.   I am friendly to both of them now.

Q.   At the time the court house assembly was organized did you desire Spencer elected to the U. S. Senate?

A.   I desired it.

Q.   Were either Mr. White or Mr. Parsons a candidate for the same office?

A.   I don't believe they were.   I never heard of it.

Q.   Did you at that time prefer Spencer over White or Parsons?

A.   I could not prefer either of them to him, as I had no chance, as neither of them was spoken of to me as candidates or in my presence.

Q.   Did you have a personal preference for Spencer over any other person for U. S. Senator?

A.   I had no chance to prefer any one else, no one else was mentioned.

Q.   Aside from all mention of names, did you prefer him over White and Parsons?

A.   I did.

Q.   Had you had any interview or correspondence with Spencer, between the time you voted for Warner and the time you went into the court house assembly?

A.   I had both interviews and correspondence with him.

Q.   How many interviews?

A.   Probably a half dozen.

Q.   Did you have much correspondence?

A.   Not much.

Q.   Were they before your election to the legislature in 1872?

A.   Both before and after.

Q.   In any of those interviews, or in any of that correspondence, did you solicit him to have you appointed postmaster at Selma?

A.   Yes, sir.

Q.   Was it after or before your election that you made the request?

A.   Both before and after.

Q.   Why did you make it after your election?

A.   Because two or three other parties were trying to get it.

Q. Had he refused before the election to get you the appointment?

A. He never refused. He always told me he wanted to get me the appointment.

Q. Were you not a member of the legislature at each time you made the request?

A. I was.

Q. Were you not a member for two successive sessions?

A. I was.

Q. Why did you solicit him after your election in 1872 for the appointment of postmaster, if before that time, while a member of the previous legislature he had promised it to you?

A. Because other men were trying to get it.

Q. Did you expect him to go back upon you because other men were seeking the office?

A. I did not. I did not know what influences politicians would bring to bear on him.

Q. At what time and place did you make the last request?

A. My recollection is, that after his election, he came to me and asked me if Col. White had any objection to my appointment? I told him I did not think he had, and went to see White, who said he had no objection to the appointment. Spencer said it was White's appointment, as it was in his town.

Q. How long after Spencer's election was it that this conversation occurred?

A. It was the day after.

Q. Are you distinct in your recollection of the event just named?

A. I am.

Q. How long was it before his election you had a conversation with Spencer concerning the appointment?

A. It was three months, in the summer. It might have been three months or it might have been three days, to the best of my recollection.

Q. Which was it to the best of your recollection, three days or three months?

A. Three months. I had no conversation with him during the time of the sitting of the court house assembly before his election.

Q. Was it modest deference to the General that prevented your mentioning the subject to him at that time?

A. I felt myself above it, or approaching him about it.

Q. When did you first know he would be a candidate for re-election?

A. I reckon it was a year or two before.

Q. When did you first feel yourself above asking him for the postoffice?

A. When I came here to the legislature the last time.

Q. Have you not already stated that you wrote to him asking for the appointment after you were elected in November 1872?

A. I have.

Q. Did you talk with any one here about getting you the postoffice while you were in the court house assembly?

A. Yes; I spoke to Col. White and nearly all the members, and asked them to sign a petition; I talked to all my friends; I talked to Judge Smith.

Q. Who else?

A. Gen. Morgan talked to me and tried to influence me to go to the capitol legislature, and leave the court house legislature; this was after the election of Senator; he said Spencer would not keep any of his promises, and there was no reliance to be placed in him; that a negro would get the postoffice at Selma, and I would never get it; that a negro had gone to Dawson to make his bond for the office; (I don't know what negro it was) that if I went to the capitol the white folks would think more of me; I stated I did not care who got the postoffice, but I could not desert the court house legislature.

Q. Did any of the persons you have named speak to you about the postoffice before the election of Spencer?

A. I think they did; I was told there would be no doubt about my appointment to the office by my friends.

Q. In the conversation had with Gen. Morgan did he tell you how he knew Spencer had made promises to you?

A. I don't think he did.

Q. Don't you know how he came to know promises came to be made?

A. I do not.

Q. Were you surprised to know he knew it?

A. I thought he was just joking me.

Q. Among the persons who talked with you before Spencer's election you have omitted to mention the names of all; who were they?

A. Maj. Clark was one.

Q. Was J. J. Moulton another?

A. I don't think he was.

Q. Was D. C. Whiting another?

A. No, sir.

Q. Lewis E. Parsons?

6

A.   No, sir; I had a conversation with him afterwards.

Q.   J. J. Hinds?

A.   He was, both before and afterwards.

Q.   When did you have a conversation with him before the election of Spencer and during the session of the legislature at the court house?

A.   I don't remember having any *with him*; he might have had *with me*.

Q.   What was the conversation about?

A.   I don't remember what it was; he might have said I would get the postoffice.

Q.   Where did this conversation occur?

A.   I don't know whether it occurred on the street or at the court house.

Q.   How many conversations did you have with Hinds?

A.   I do not know how many I had with him, or rather he had with me.

Q.   What was said, as well as you can remember, about your getting the postoffice?

A.   He said I might get the postoffice, just as you or any one might say it.

Q.   Was not Hinds at that time an active supporter of Spencer for the Senate?

A.   He was.

Q.   Was he not the most active supporter of Spencer?

A.   He was one of the most active.

Q.   Do you know of any money Hinds spent in the matter of the election of Spencer?

A.   I do not; I never saw a dollar spent in the election.

Q.   Before Spencer's election were you known as one of Spencer's supporters?

A.   I don't know; I think I was, I know myself I was.

Q.   Were you at that time taken into the councils of the leaders of the court house assembly?

A.   I was in the caucus that nominated Spencer.

Q.   Were you in the other caucuses?

A.   I don't think I was; I was in some of them.

Q.   Had you conferences with the leaders of the court house assembly as to their policy?

A.   I don't know that they had any private conferences except to bring about a reconciliation toward the end.

Q.   Did you go to the capitol on the day fixed by law for the assembling of the legislature?

A.   No, sir, I did not.

Q.   Why did you not go there?

A. I was told the Republicans were to meet in caucus at the court house.

Q. When you went to the court house did you intend to establish the court house assembly?

A. I intended to do as the others did.

Q. Did you know that it was intended to establish the court house assembly before you went there?

A. No, sir.

Q. Did you express any opinion in caucus as to whether the court house assembly should be established?

A. I did not.

Q. Did you have any opinion on the subject?

A. I don't remember; I abided by what was done.

Q. Did you believe one of the purposes of that organization was to elect a United States Senator?

A. No, sir.

Q. Did you know an election was to take place for United States Senator?

A. Yes, sir, during the session.

Q. Was the question discussed whether they could elect a United States Senator if they went to the capitol?

A. It was the night before the election, but it was not on the day of the organization of the court house assembly.

Q. Between the time of the organization and the time of election by that body of Spencer, did you know or hear of any arrangement by which any members of that body or other persons assisting in carrying out its policy, were to receive Federal office or appointment?

A. I knew nothing of it.

Q. Did you believe Gen. Dustan was to receive a Federal appointment?

A. I knew nothing of it.

Q. Did you believe he was to receive a Federal appointment?

A. I believed nothing of it, for I knew nothing about it.

Q. Did you believe Calvin Goodloe was to get a Federal appointment?

A. I did not believe anything about it for I did not know him then.

Q. Did you believe Baker or Chisholm were to receive Federal appointments?

A. I knew nothing of it.

Q. Did you not hear the name of some member of the assembly as being likely to get a Federal office?

A. I did not.

Q. Do you recollect calling upon Gen. Spencer at any

time and taking some witnesses with reference to the post-office?

A. I never took any witnesses, or went with any, concerning the postoffice to Spencer.

Q. After the attorney general recommended the fusion of the two legislatures, did you have any conversation with Hinds with reference to the postoffice?

A. I don't think I did.

Q. Did you promise any one that you would adhere to the action of the court house assembly after the fusion?

A. No, sir; I opposed the bond bill; I was not required to do it.

Q. Were you not considered a doubtful Republican then?

A. I was not.

Q. When you went into the court house organization did Hinds or Spencer know you would support Spencer for the Senate?

A. I do not know whether they did or not.

Q. Can you recollect that after the fusion of the two bodies, that Mr. McAfee of Talladega county, on the second Tuesday of the reorganization of the two bodies, immediately after the reading of the journal of the previous day's proceedings, moved to adjourn the house?

A. I do not remember it; I think I was outside and came in as Hunter was being brought to the bar of the house.

Q. Did you not know it was agreed in caucus the night before that the house should adjourn as soon as the journal was read?

A. I did not.

Q. Do you not know the object of the motion was to prevent the election of United States Senator on that day?

A. I do not.

Q. Do you know any understanding existing among the leaders of the Republican party that Miller was to be seated in the Senate?

A. I knew nothing of it until it was brought up in the Senate.

Q. Have you ever told any person you were promised the office of postmaster of Selma before the election?

A. I might have done it.

Q. Would you have voted for Spencer if he had not made you the promise?

A. I would; the postoffice would not have been in the way.

Q. Would you have gone to the court house and remained

there if you had known Spencer would defeat you for the office?

A. I would, as I was elected as a Republican; I would not take into consideration what he had done for me.

Q. If you had no opinion whether the court house body, or the body at the capitol, was the true legislature, and had no desire to elect Spencer, what inducement operated upon you to keep you in the court house assembly?

A. Because I was a Republican, and thought I belonged there.

Q. Did you have any purpose to accomplish or plan to carry out at the time you recalled your resignation from the Governor?

A. No, sir, I had none.

Q. Would you have recalled your resignation if any other person than Gen. Coon had been nominated?

A. I rather think I would.

Q. Were you not in the convention that nominated Gen. Coon as your successor in the office you had resigned, and did you not take part in the proceedings?

A. Yes, I was in the convention and took part in the proceedings; Anderson Smith and Datus E. Coon received a majority of the votes for the nomination.

Q. Whose position was Smith nominated for?

A. I don't know whether it was for the position White resigned or for the place I resigned; the chairman announced there was no vacancy for my place.

Q. Were ballots cast for two vacancies?

A. They were. My memory being refreshed, the ballots first cast were for the seat made vacant by the resignation of Mr. White; afterwards ballots were cast to nominate some one for my place.

Q. Did you inform the convention that you had withdrawn your resignation?

A. I stated I had not resigned and was going to serve.

Q. Had you withdrawn your resignation from the Governor at that time?

A. I think I had.

Q. How long before?

A. I think I had it in my pocket and was going to show it, but was requested not to do so.

Q. Was not the reason of your withholding a public statement that you had recalled your resignation, because you saw that Gen. Coon would receive a majority of votes to fill the vacancy?

A. No. I wanted to serve in the legislature myself my time out.

Q. You were so anxious to serve in the legislature yourself, why did you resign at all?

A. I did it because I thought it would interfere with my other office.

Q. Did you tell Gen. Coon you recalled your resignation to prevent his election?

A. I showed him a copy of my resignation. There were two papers left with the governor's secretary. One was an unconditional resignation, and the other was no resignation at all. It was a copy of a paper prepared for Wilson. I notified the governor at the time how I wished the papers considered. He said if that was the case to leave them with his private secretary; that if I wanted him to use them to let him know or notify the secretary.

Q. Is there any statement you desire to make in explanation of your testimony, or in addition thereto?

A. In alluding to the resignations in my testimony, I desire to say I did not regard them as resignations. There was no bargain and sale as to my office with Senator Spencer or any one else.

H. COCHRAN.

### J. R. HORNER

Being sworn, says:

I reside at Tuscaloosa. I resided there in 1872. I am acquainted with George E. Spencer; have known him since 1865.

By Gen. Morgan—

Q. Were you in Montgomery pending the election of Spencer for the U. S. senate in 1872?

A. I was not.

Q. Do you know of any influences brought to bear in the election of Spencer?

A. I do not.

Q. If you had any knowledge of, or was connected with the management of his election, state it?

A. I had no connection with or knowledge of it?

Q. What are the relations between Spencer and Hinds?

A. I think they are friendly.

Q. Why do you think they are friendly?

A. He stayed at Hinds' house in Decatur.

Q. How do you know he stayed there?

A. I have seen him there, and he stated to me he made that his home when in Decatur.

Q. Did not common rumor in and about the neighborhood of Tuscaloosa, more than two years ago, connect Spencer and Hinds in the post office or mail service?

A. I have heard people give that as their opinion.

Q. Were you ever offered any federal office by Spencer; if so, what or when; or his influence to procure you an office?

A. He offered me his influence.

Q. In connection with what office?

A. That of consul. But this was not connected with or dependent upon any election.

Q. Was this offer voluntary on his part?

A. The promise of influence was.

Q. Was this before the election in 1872?

A. It was before the canvass commenced in that year.

Q. Was Spencer under any obligations to you?

A. No, sir, nor I to him.

Q. Did Spencer advise with you in reference to sending troops to Tuscaloosa?

A. He asked me if troops were necessary to secure a fair election.

J. R. HORNER.

### JOHN CASHIN

Being sworn, says:

I have lived in Montgomery since July, 1868; I have never held any public office; I have a brother a member of the legislature; I have been an active member of the republican party; I have done what was in my power to secure its success; I am a retail liquor dealer; I had a saloon here in 1872 on Perry street; Mr. Spencer owes me a bill in connection with my business; I kept a lunch in connection with my bar; the afternoon of the day before the day of the election for United States Senator by the court house body, W. V. Turner, with several members of the legislature, came to me and stated that Mr. Spencer had told them to get what they wanted on his account; I let them have wine, brandy, whisky and cigars; they run the bill up to $44.85 that night; the persons in company with Turner were colored members of the legislature attached to the court house body; I remember Green, Speed and Mathews; other members of the legislature were going backwards and forwards; I made no charge to these persons, but sent the bill over to Mr. Spencer the morning of the day before his election, and he paid it; it was made out:

"George E. Spencer,

To John Cashin,                      Dr.

For refreshments furnished....................$44.85."

I sent it to Spencer by my bar keeper and he paid him $45 ; during the day and night before his election I continued to furnish the same parties with refreshments on the same account ; a bill was made amounting to $162 ; the morning after Spencer's election he went away ; I presented the bill to Mr. Hinds to whom I had been referred by the parties who had been furnished with refreshments, they stating that he was attending to Spencer's business ; Hinds said he did not know anything about it ; that Spencer gave him no instructions about it ; that he was going to Washington and would see him about it ; the bill has never been paid ; I afterwards demanded pay of Spencer in person ; I took the bill to him and presented it to him while he was in a room of the Exchange Hotel on the first floor ; Mr. Whiting and he were in the room together ; he took the bill and looked at it and said, "I will not pay it ; I have been paying bills enough of that kind ;" I told him I worked for my money and that was all the way I had of getting it ; that he got the benefit of it and had paid the first bill made on the same account ; he replied, "Go and sue Bill Turner for it ;" I replied to him, "You know I can get no money out of Bill Turner ;" he said he would not pay it, and for me to have Turner arrested for obtaining goods under false pretenses ; that he was a dead beat and a fraud ; this was all that was said by him at the time ; Whiting said he supposed Spencer had given Turner no authority to make the bill ; I told Whiting to keep his mouth out of it, as he knew nothing of it ; this was the end of that interview ; last summer I met Spencer again, on Sunday evening after the convention, in front of my saloon.

I asked him to see Turner, who was in the city, and to have a settlement of that bill. He told me he did not want me to bother him any more about it, and if I wanted any money out of him to sue him ; that that was the only way I could get it. I told him he knew damned well I could get no money out of him or Turner either unless they chose to pay it. I remember another interview before this, at the capitol. Spencer was in the lobby. I went in the hall of the house and called Turner out and told him Spencer was there, and I wanted an understanding about that bill.

He went to Spencer with me, and I said to Spencer, "Here is Turner. I want that matter about that bill settled." He drove Turner away by saying, " Go away, I am not going to pay it. I don't want to be troubled with you."

The persons who got these refreshments were supporters of Spencer in the court house assembly. My house was a constant resort for the two days before the election of Spencer for the colored members of the court house assembly. Whenever they ordered it charged to Spencer it was so charged, and only when it was so ordered was a charge made to Spencer.

I knew Carson, Jones and Maull, representatives in the court house assembly from Lowndes county.

By Mr. Little—

Q. Do you know whether Jones is addicted to playing cards, and if he lost any money at any time?

A. (The witness earnestly requested to be excused from answering the question, but being pressed by the committee to answer, said:) "He is addicted to playing cards, and I have known him to lose considerable sums, amounting in all to probably four hundred dollars."

Q. Were you at that time acquainted with many of the colored and white members of the court house assembly?

A. I was.

Q. Did you have conversations with them on the subject of the policy of the court house assembly?

A. I did.

Q. Did you hear of any offices being promised members by Spencer or his friends?

A. I heard members and others say Spencer had made promises of office he had not complied with. Recently, I heard Hunter say he had been promised a place and did not get it.

Q. For what purpose were these refreshments being used as you understood it?

A. For the benefit of Mr. Spencer.

Q. Was there any other house open for Spencer's benefit?

A. Spencer's room was used at the Madison House for white members. Bottles and a jug of whisky were in the room and glasses were sitting out.

By Mr. Price—

Q. You say you know Carson, Jones and Maull, members of the court house assembly from Lowndes county. State any circumstance you know that tends to show they, or either of them, received any money from Spencer on or about the day of his election by the court house assembly, and how much?

A. On or about the day of Spencer's election, Jones came to me to get a one hundred dollar bill changed. He called me off into a side door at my place of business and pulled out three one hundred dollar bills, out of his vest pocket. I said to him, "What is that?" He replied, "This is Spencer," at the same time holding the money up in his hand.

He told me at the same time not to say anything about the money he had, as he wanted to give Carsons fifty ($50) dollars, and Maull twenty-five ($25) dollars. He said he could control their votes at any time. It was understood that each one of them was to get one hundred dollars, and he did not want them to know how much he had got. I have also spoken to Jones several times about this matter. I subsequently changed each one of the hundred dollar bills.

Q. Do you know of any other circumstance tending to show that Spencer used money to secure his election?

A. It was the common talk and inquiry, "How much did *you* get?" "How much did you get?" This talk was among members of the court house assembly, and others seeking positions through Spencer. I frequently heard it said, "Now is your time, if you don't get it before the election, you will not get any thing."

Q. Do you know anything further on this subject?

A. I do, but prefer not to disclose confidence that has been reposed in me.

Q. During the time this talk you heard about, what members received, what sort of intercourse was there between your house and Spencer's room?

A. There was a continual going to and from between my house, Spencer's room and the court house. These were the three prominent centres.

Q. Did you ever hear Jones say he got any money from Spencer in connection with his election?

A. Jones told me he got money from Spencer for himself, Maull and Carson.          JOHN CASHIN.

### EUGETE BEEBE

Being sworn, says:

I was living in Montgomery in 1872-3. I knew Geo. E. Spencer, J. J. Hinds, D. C. Whiting, W. H. Betts and Charles Pelham.

By Gen. Morgan—

Q. Were you at any time in the councils of the court house assembly, or the leaders of the party?

A. I was not.

Q. Who were understood to be Spencer's most influential and active friends in his election before the court house body?

A. The persons you have named, I think, were. I know positively only of Betts.

Q. Please state all that Betts did?

A. I know that I procured a pedestrian to walk down into

Lowndes county for him one night, the roads being impassable at the time. Betts told me he paid the pedestrian $50.

Q. What night was it?

A. Shortly before Spencer's election.

Q. What did he send for to Lowndes?

A. To get Bryant to come up.

Q. What did he want with Bryant?

A. It was stated that Buckley had bought off the Lowndes county delegation, and Bryant was sent for to counteract Buckley's movement.

Q. Did Bryant come?

A. I presume he did.

Q. Did Betts say to you how the influence was to be exerted?

A. He did not.

Q. What time was it that the messenger started?

A. It was late at night. It was thought very necessary to get Bryant here.

Q. Was there any opposition to Spencer in the court house assembly?

A. I know of no organized opposition to him. If there had been I would have known it.

Q. Do you know of any game of cards being played the night before the day an election was to take place at the capitol by the capitol legislature, in which game a democratic member of that body was engaged with D. C. Whiting and other persons? If so, name all the parties engaged in the game.

A. There were D. C. Whiting, Charles Whitney, Geo. Ellison and Stribling, a democratic member from the capitol legislature.

Mr. Stribling asked me on the night mentioned, about 8 P. M., if I could not furnish him a private room to play poker in; that he wanted to take a game with the parties just named, and for me to keep the parties there until he could go and get his cards. He went to the Exchange and got his cards and gave them to a negro boy who waited on the room, and told him when they called for cards to bring those cards in. They then went up into the room and went to playing poker.

Q. Was liquor furnished the party from your bar that night?

A. It was not. They sent out and got their liquor in bottles.

Q. Did you see the party any more that night?

A. I did not. I saw Stribling next morning about 9 or

10 o'clock. He was lying on the lounge, in the room where they had been playing cards, asleep. The dishes were sitting in the room where they had eaten breakfast. The sergeant-at-arms that morning came down after him and took him out the back way and put him in a carriage.

Q. Did you know that evening the other parties were there for a game?

A. They mentioned nothing to me on the subject.

Q. Had you any idea from his conduct that Stribling had been drugged?

A. I had not, and when I heard he had been drugged I laughed at the idea. I think when I know a man's habits, I would know whether he was under the influence of a narcotic or intoxicated from whisky. He was not in a stupid condition when he spoke to me. I simply regarded that he was drunk and down.

Q. You state you heard he had been drugged; was such a report in circulation?

A. It was that day. The report was that he had been drugged at my house.

Q. Do you know which of the parties sent out for liquor that night?

A. I do not.

Q. Did any of the parties apply to you or your bar for liquors that night, after they went up stairs?

A. The did not. They might have taken a drink before going up.

Eugene Beebe.

### JUDGE JOHN BRUCE

Being subpœned and sworn, says:

I am Judge of the United States District Court at this time. I was appointed as successor to Richard Busteed, resigned. I reside in Wilcox county. I am acquainted with James S. Perrin.

By Gen. Morgan—

Q. Do you know anything of the requisition for troops in Wilcox and Monroe counties in 1872?

A. I do not. I may have heard reports in regard to it. I may have seen something in the papers in regard to it?

Q. Did you at any time solicit the use of troops in that vicinity?

A. I have no recollection of doing anything of the kind, and think I did not.

Q. Do you know anything of the use made of troops by

Perrin or Squires in Wilcox and Monroe counties in the year 1872, about the time of the general election?

A. I do not. I have no recollection of ever having seen the troops in Wilcox about the time of that election. I think I did hear something about the operations of Perrin and Squires in Monroe county, but I know nothing of it except by report, never having enjoyed the confidence of those gentlemen, and knowing nothing personally of their plans or operations.

Q. Do you believe you know the reputation of Mr. Perrin among the people by whom he is known for truth and veracity; if so, what is that reputation?

A. I think I may say I do know something of his reputation for truth and veracity by the people who know him in Wilcox county, though I have never had any intimate acquaintance with him, and do not know his real character as well as I do his reputation. It is not very good.

Q. Is his reputation such as would make him a credible witness in your estimation?

A. I should not regard his testimony as entitled to as much confidence as many others.

Q. Have you been an active republican since your residence in the State?

A. I have been a republican and have taken an interest in political affairs. Some may think I have been active.

Q. For what purpose was it your understanding troops were brought into Monroe county in 1872?

A. I know of no troops having been brought there of my own knowledge.

Q. Do you think from your knowledge of Perrin's character, he would be a proper person to put in charge of troops for organizing a political party?

A. I do not think Mr. Perrin a proper man to have the control of troops for any purpose. It is possible, however, Mr. Perrin may be a better man than I think he is.

JOHN BRUCE.

EX-GOV. LEWIS E. PARSONS

Being sworn, says:

I was a member of the legislature of 1872–73. I did what I could as a member of the republican party at the court house organization.

By Gen. Morgan—

Q. Will you state what was the object of the organization at the court house?

A.   I don't recollect that I consulted with any one as to any particular object.   My own object was to prevent the seating of some members from Barbour and Marengo counties who had fraudulent certificates, from information I had before me, and thereby to secure a fair organization of the general assembly.

Q.   Was this the only object of the court house organization.

A.   It was the only object I had.   If others had any other object it was not made known to me.

Q.   If there had been any other object would you have been apt to have known it?

A.   I can't say; I can only state what I know.

Q.   Do you know of any organization of men in the interest of the election of Senator Spencer at any time during the sittings of the court house assembly, or after the fusion of the court house and capitol bodies?

A.   If there was any such combination or organization I know nothing of it.   It is very possible there was.

Q.   Were you an active participant in the election of 1872.

A.   I did what I could to aid in the election of 1872.   I was an elector for the State at large on the republican ticket, and a candidate in Talladega, the county of my residence, for the legislature.

Q.   Have you any knowledge of the objects of the stationing of troops in Alabama during that election?

A.   As far as I know the object was to secure to every legal voter the right to go to the polls and vote once and return to his home without molestation.   If any other use was to be made of troops it was not known to me and would not have received my sanction or support.

Q.   Did you canvass in any other than Talladega county?

A.   I spoke at Florence, Tuscumbia, McNutt's Mills in Franklin county, Huntsville, Wetumpka, Rockford, Lafayette, Dadeville, Opelika and Montgomery.   I may have spoken at other places I cannot now recall.

Q.   From your information and knowledge gained in that canvass, did you believe the stationing of troops in certain localities necessary to secure a fair election?

A.   I then thought it was necessary; I thought it was necessary to have them in the county in which I live, to preserve the peace and to prevent any conflict on the day of the election, which if it took place would result in bloodshed.

Q.   Do you think they were necessary in any other county?

A.   I was not sufficiently informed to have a decided opinion.

Q. Do you know of any troops being used for any other purpose than simply to preserve the peace?

A. I do not.

Q. Were you elected to the legislature from Talladega county in 1872?

A. I was.

Q. Did any friend or emissary of Gen. Spencer visit you for the purpose of getting you to withdraw or have you taken down as a candidate?

A. I had no personal knowledge of such visit, and only knew from being informed of it sometime afterward that such visit was made.

Q. Who was the person you understood was sent?

A. I prefer not to give the name. (Being informed that Barber had testified to the fact.) Robert Barber was the person. It was a long time after the election before he informed me.

Q. Were you at any time at or before your election to the legislature in 1872, a candidate for the U. S. Senate?

A. I was not a candidate, but several friends had suggested to me I might stand a chance to be elected. I had not decided to be a candidate and was not.

Q. Do you know the handwriting of George E. Spencer?

A. I have seen letters purporting to be from him; I would not have known the letters were from him had I not seen his name signed to them.

(The witness was handed the letters of Gen. Spencer, marked Exhibits E. and F., to "My Dear Barber," and requested to read them. After he had done so the examination was renewed.)

Q. In the letter shown you dated Oct. 16, 1872, and addressed by George E. Spencer to "Dear Barber," is the following language: "Parsons has a deep laid scheme to elect himself, and has now gone to New York to try and raise money to be used in the legislature." Is there any foundation in fact for that assertion?

A. Not a particle.

Q. Were you in New York in October, 1872?

A. I was.

Q. In a letter, dated Oct. 22, 1872, addressed by Geo. E. Spencer to "My dear Barber," he uses the following language: "I wish Randolph, deputy U. S. Marshal, would use the company at Opelika in making arrests in Tallapoosa, Randolph and Cleburne, as —— suggests." Did you know of, participate in, or counsel that any such use be made of troops in this State?

A.  I did not.

Q.  Was there, within your knowledge, any understanding or agreement among the leading republicans in this State, in that canvass, that U. S troops should be used for making arrests in Tallapoosa, Randolph or Cleburne, or any other counties, or that they should be put under command of deputy U. S. marshals for any such purpose?

A.  I know nothing of any such understanding or agreement.

Q.  Was not Geo. E. Spencer a prominent member of the party in that canvass?

A.  He was the republican U. S. senator, and was considered the leader of the party in the State.

Q.  Was he not active in the canvass?

A.  I should suppose he was, but I did not see him but once during the canvass, that I recollect.

Q.  At the time of the organization of the court house assembly, did you know Spencer would be a candidate for re-election?

A.  I did not know it, but I had no doubt of it.

Q.  Did you, at the time of the organization, believe that he would be elected?

A.  I did not think about the matter at the time.  The effect it might have upon him or his re-election was not in my mind at that time.

Q.  Was he then in Montgomery?

A.  He was not, as I remember.

Q.  On his arrival in Montgomery, did he announce himself as a candidate?

A.  I suppose he did.  I don't recollect he ever said a word to me on the subject, *pro* or *con.*

Q.  When he announced himself, was he the choice of a majority of the members of the court house assembly?

A.  It is my opinion he was not the first choice of a number of the members.

Q.  Why was he unanimously nominated in caucus, and unanimously elected?

A.  Because it was rumored he would be elected by the capitol legislature if we did not elect him; that he would take enough members from the court house legislature to the capitol legislature to break us up.

Q.  Do you know any fact personally that justified you in believing this rumor?

A.  I do not.  I heard he was invited to meet democratic members at the Exchange Hotel; that he attended, and that the subject of the senatorship was spoken of; and I also heard that within a day or two after, that his attention was called to this meeting, and he said he would stand by the republican party, and sink or swim with it. This was before his election.

Q. Was he nominated because of your faith in his last promise so made, or because the party entertained a real fear that he would abandon the court house assembly and carry off with him enough members to destroy its quorum?

A. I have already stated that we feared if we did not nominate him the capitol legislature would, but it is proper to add that a majority of republican members thought it was due to him to elect him any how, and he would have received the nomination by a majority over any one else in a party caucus, and we did nominate him in caucus unanimously.

Q. Did you believe, if nominated by the capitol legislature, he would accept the nomination?

A. I don't know what others thought, but I thought myself if we refused to nominate him, and the democrats did nominate him, he would accept the nomination.

Q. Did you not believe he had a following in the court house legislature he could take off with him to the capitol?

A. I feared it.

Q. Can you name any of the persons who were his most active friends and supporters for U. S. senator in the court house assembly?

A. A majority of the members in the house were his supporters. Among the more influential were P. G. Clarke, Gen. Dustan and Hunter.

Q. Do you know of any active part taken in Spencer's election by J. J. Hinds, D. C. Whiting and H. Ray Meyer?

A. Meyer was understood to be his friend. The other two gentlemen were here and took an active part in electioneering for Spencer, as I understood.

Q. At the time of the organization, was it not thought Chisholm and Baker were not elected?

A. On the contrary, it was understood that they were fairly elected, and it only needed an investigation to satisfy any fair-minded man of the fact.

Q. Was any report ever made to the effect that they were elected?

A. I don't recollect.

Q. Did either of them claim a seat in the consolidated legislature?

A. I do not think they did.

Q. When in a former answer you have given in this ex-

7

amination, you say your own object in the organization was to prevent the seating of some members from Marengo and Barbour who had fraudulent certificates, from information before you, and thereby to secure a fair organization of the general assembly, in what respect do you mean to assert the certificates they held were fraudulent?

A. I understood the Republican candidates in Barbour and Marengo, for the senate and house, had been elected by decided majorities, and that they had been deprived of their certificates, in what way I did not know; I knew those counties were largely Republican, or had every reason to believe they were.

By Mr. Price—

Q. Had you any knowledge of the returns in the office of the secretary of state?

A. I had no personal knowledge and had not examined the returns.

Q. What other information had you as to the returns made?

A. I had nothing more than reports, I did not see the official returns.

Q. Did your knowledge of the political complexion of those counties enter into the formation of your opinion of the result?

A. It did; as well as also the first reports made in the papers as to the results of the election in those counties.

By Gen. Morgan—

Q. Were the certificates held by the members of the capitol assembly considered by you as having been fraudulently issued by the secretary of state?

A. I could not say he, himself, had been guilty of a fraud in their issuance, but that some one was guilty of a fraud in depriving the members from Barbour and Marengo of their certificates.

Q. Did you understand the supervisors of elections in Barbour and Marengo, had fraudulently issued certificates of election to the members from those counties in the capitol assembly?

A. I can't say I understood any one in particular had done it; nor that fraudulent certificates had been obtained.

Q. Was the fraud complained of the fraud of those who conducted the election or those who certified?

A. I can't say.

Q. In reference to the members from Marengo, both to the senate and house of representatives, did you not take the position that because you were assured they were elected,

·they were entitled to be seated in the respective bodies and participate in the organization thereof, notwithstanding they held no certificates of election?

A. My idea was that the right to a seat depended on the fact, whether a party received a majority of the legal votes and not upon certificates of election. If these members had received a majority of legal votes, that was the question we were to look at, and they should have their seats.

Q. With the view of the legal question just stated, if it is correct, what impediment was known to exist among the members assembled at the capitol to prevent a fair discussion and settlement of it between those assembled at that place and those assembled at the court house?

A. I don't know how others viewed the matter. My own opinion was, the state of political feeling was such that if the republicans had gone into the State house organization, giving the democrats the benefit of six members who had no right to seats in that body in reality, that we would not have been able to obtain a decision in season to prevent great changes we understood were in contemplation by the democratic party in our State government. Past experience tended to strengthen this view. When the convention of 1861 assembled, two members from Shelby county presented certificates of election to that body who were not entitled to seats therein, their opponents having received a majority of legal votes cast in that county; they were permitted to take their seats, and the delegates really elected instituted a contest, but were not able to obtain a decision upon that contest until the ordinance of secession was passed, on the 11th of January, 1861, nor was action had on that momentous question until those entitled to speak the voice of Shelby county could be heard in that convention. After the ordinance of secession was passed; after various military movements and preparations for others were on foot, counsel for contestants were informed that the investigation would result in no practical good; for, though they were entitled to their seats, the State had taken her stand, the ordinance of secession had been passed, and it was suggested that it would be best on the whole for them to take their mileage and go home, as what was done could not be undone.

Q. What great changes was it contemplated that the members at the capitol would work in the affairs of the State if they obtained control of the legislature in a joint meeting of the two bodies?

A. We understood they contemplated calling a constitutional convention to change the constitution, for one thing;

that they contemplated changing the election law, so as to
require every person to vote in his own precinct; that the
prepayment of a poll tax was to be one of the requisites of
voting; that an educational or property qualification, or both,
would be imposed as a requisite for voting; this was to be
done when the constitution was amended.

Q. Was the election of U. S. Senator one of the changes
contemplated?

A. Not that I know of.

Q. Did you think compelling a man to vote in his own
precinct injurious to the republican party?

A. We thought it aimed at colored voters of the republican party, more particularly.

Q. Did you think it necessary to secure the right of the
negro to vote, that he should go away from home to do so?

A. We thought it necessary for him to vote at precincts
where he had friends, who would see that he had the ticket
he wished to vote; and that the object of the democratic party in requiring him to vote in the precinct of his residence
was designed to defeat that.

Q. Did you not think it more necessary that he should be
allowed to vote according to the wish of his friends?

A. No, sir. I have never seen the time I wished a man
to vote a ticket other than he desired to vote.

Q. Did the friends of the negroes all reside in one place
in the county or in one precinct?

A. In different precincts, so far as I know.

Q. If they resided in different precincts, why did they
have to go abroad to find friends to protect them in voting?

A. Because in many instances they had been intimidated,
so that they were afraid to go to the polls and vote by themselves. They said they were.

Q. You have had large experience in political canvasses
in Alabama and elections, can you state one instance in your
own knowledge where such intimidation occurred?

A. I can not.

Q. When did you first become convinced the negro ought
to be entitled to vote?

A. When by the adoption of the 14th and 15th amendments to the constitution, his right to vote became a part of
the organic law of the United States and of Alabama.

Q. Then of course you voted for and advocated those
amendments?

A. I did neither. I was opposed to the adoption of both.

Q. Can the constitution of Alabama be amended except
by a vote of the people?

A. That is the only way.

Q. Was there any danger to the republican party if they were in the majority in the State, in submitting a constitution for their acceptance or rejection ?

A. We understood the democratic party contemplated changing the election law, so as to make that majority unavailable.

Q. Did not that majority become unavailing before last November, and was any change made in the election law before that time?

A. No change was made in the wording of the law, but in the practice I understood there was a very great change—especially along the line of the counties bordering on the State of Georgia.

Q. Do you really believe the State of Alabama gave a republican majority in the last election?

A. I think the republican party carried the election last November in a fair count of legal votes.

Q. How do you think it was in New York ?

A. I don't know any thing about the State of New York.

Q. Could the right of a man to vote depend upon his pre-payment of his poll tax without changing the constitution?

A. His right to vote could not be taken from him; but the mode of exercising it can be regulated by legislative enactment.

Q. Returning to the secession convention held in 1861, and to the fact that it rejected two members from Shelby, why is that considered by you a precedent upon which the capital legislature would act in 1872?

A. Many of the same men who were active in respect to matters in 1861 were active in 1872, and the importance of the questions involved in 1861 to the interest of the people of Alabama, were such as to lead me to suppose that the men who would disregard them in 1861, would disregard them in 1872.

Q. Were the men whom you assume to have disregarded those interests you mentioned, in 1861, members of the capitol legislature?

A. They were not; but some of them were active in advising.

Q. In advising what?

A. Advising the State house legislature.

Q. Was not Lt. Gov. McKinstry, who presided in the court house senate, a violent secessionist in 1861 ?

A. I don't know.

Q. Was not that his reputation in 1861 and during the war?

A. I don't know what his reputation was in 1861. His reputation during the war was that of a very moderate man.

By Mr. Price—

Q. You say "it was said" and "it was understood that certain great changes in the constitution were in contemplation by the Democratic party;" will you explain more specifically by whom it was so said and how so understood?

A. I don't think I could give the name of any individual, it was the general impression; it was thought that unless some great ideas were to be carried out they would not have taken such great risks; we were not in the councils of the Democratic party and could only judge of their purposes by such means as were within our reach, and the correctness of the opinion we then entertained is very much strengthened by what has transpired during the recent session of the legislature of this State.

By Gen. Morgan—

Q. What was the great risk you refer to as the Democratic party taking?

A. In taking those members from Marengo and Barbour into the senate and house; if the members from those counties had been allowed to take the seats to which they were entitled, who were really elected, there would not have been two organizations; the Democrats would have had a small majority in the senate and the Republicans a small majority in the house, but they acted differently and lost all.

Q. The risk you speak of was to the Democratic party and not to the country?

A. The Democratic party is a part of the country, and its action affects the country, as we have a painful experience in our recollection of 1861, and for some years thereafter.

Q. Then you regretted that by taking such risk it lost its influence?

A. I regret that any party should do anything essentially wrong.

Q. Were you the speaker of the court house assembly and afterwards of the consolidated body?

A. I was.

Q. Did the court house assembly continue its sessions after you were elected permanent speaker of the fusion legislature?

A. It did; the old organization was kept alive by meeting from day to day, until the new organization was perfected in both the house and senate.

Q. Did you preside as speaker in both organizations?

A. I did, so far as meeting and adjourning in the old organization.

Q. Was the fusion legislature and the court house legislature held at the same place?

A. They were held at the same place but not in the same room; the meetings of the court house assembly were in the office of the clerk of the house; they were held at different hours; no business was done other than to meet and adjourn.

Q. Were not two bills passed by the court house legislature after your election as speaker of the fusion legislature by the court house assembly?

A. I have understood two bills were passed of the nature indicated, at the court house, by the court house assembly; I was sick at the time and confined to my bed; I can't say whether this was after my election as permanent speaker of the two bodies.

Q. Was the house of the fusion legislature fully organized when you were elected permanent speaker?

A. That depended on whether the senate completed its organization.

Q. Was the senate organized with a Democratic majority?

A. My impression is that there was a Democratic majority of one, but I can't state with certainty.

Q. If there was a Democratic majority of one in the senate of the fusion legislature, how could there have been a quorum in the senate of the court house assembly?

A. I suppose that under the plan of the attorney general of reorganizing, a Democratic senator was admitted, who, upon a fair count of the legal votes may not have been elected, but I don't know this to be so.

Q. What senator do you refer to?

A. I have no one in my mind.

Q. Was it not understood by the Republicans, in both branches of the consolidated general assembly, that in order to sustain the action of the court house assembly in electing a United States Senator, it was necessary that Miller's contest for Martin's seat should be decided in favor of the contestant Miller?

A. I don't think I ever heard that question discussed at all; I may have heard the opinion expressed among members that it was, but my own opinion was the reverse; I thought the senate organized at the court house recognized by the house of representatives, which certainly contained a majority of members legally elected to that general assembly, and both senate and house being recognized as the general assembly of the State by the Governor, would render that body the senate *de facto*, and its public acts valid.

Q. Did you not advise that the senate and house should

pass a resolution recognizing the validity of the court house assembly, after the fusion?

A. I don't recollect anything about the Senate; I am confident I did not advise the senate anything about it, but such a resolution passed the house and I presume I voted for it, as it accorded with my views.

Q. Did any persons vote for it in the house except those who had been members of the court house assembly?

A. I do not remember.

Q. If the court house body was a legal body, why the necessity of the adoption of the resolution by the fusion legislature?

A. I think there was no necessity for it.

Q. Was it not agreed in caucus or consultation of the leaders of the Republican party that Judge McKinstry should rule, and an appeal should not be taken from his decision, in which he refused to put a motion to reconsider a vote to substitute the minority for the majority report in the Martin-Miller contest?

A. Not that I know of; I know of no consultation in regard to such a decision, and did not know that one was to be made until I heard it had been made in the senate.

Q. Do you consider the ruling of Lieutenant Governor McKinstry in refusing to put an appeal from his decision to a vote of the senate, deciding the motion to reconsider out of order, in accordance with parliamentary law and usage?

A. I do not; I thought then and think now, it was his duty to put the appeal.

Q. Did you consider the court house legislature a valid body before it received the recognition of Gov. Lewis?

A. I did not.

Q. Did it receive the recognition of Gov. Lindsay during his term of office?

A. Not that I know of.

Q. Did not a joint committee of the two houses of the court house assembly wait upon Gov. Lindsay asking his recognition?

A. I have an impression that the committee waited on him and he refused to recognize them.

Q. During the time of the remainder of Gov. Lindsay's term, after the assembling of the legislature at the capitol and its organization, did you regard that as the legislature of Alabama?

A. If there was a regular organized Senate or House at the capitol and each recognized the other, and the Governor recognized them both as the General Assembly of the State, any act passed by them would have the force of law. I think that that would be a General Assembly of the State.

Q. Would your opinion of the legality of such a body so recognized by the Governor, depend upon whether the members holding seats were actually elected or whether they held certificates issued in conformity with law?

A. The certificate of election, regular on its face, is only *prima facie* evidence of right to a seat and it is sufficient to authorize the Senate or House to seat a man, and, of course, to authorize the Governor to recognize a body so organized as the General Assembly; but fraud vitiates such evidence, as it does all other acts, even the most solemn acts of courts of justice, and when it is discovered such certificates have been fraudulently obtained the Governor is justified in withdrawing his recognition of a body when a majority is only secured by means of such fraud.

Q. Do you think the Governor can substitute one legislative body for another by his recognition?

A. I don't think he can; but it is his duty at all times, when communicating with the General Assembly, to decide, where there are two bodies, each claiming to be the General Assembly, which body he will recognize as such.

Q. Does his recognition of each body in succession make the body so recognized the General Assembly?

A. As a general proposition I think it does. There may be an exceptional case, as where a body composed of men a majority of whom hold fraudulent certificates.

Q. Do you not think such power as this would furnish a Governor with a convenience in avoiding impeachment?

A. It might do so.

Q. At the time the court house assembly convened, was not Mr. Hubbard, the speaker of the last House, in town?

A. I did not see him.

Q. Was any committee appointed to notify him the legislature was about to meet at the court house?

A. Not that I know of.

Q. After the fusion legislature was organized in both branches, and on the 2d Tuesday of such organization, did not the house of representatives, over which you presided, on motion of Mr. Afee of Talladega, vote to adjourn, and was not that motion put and carried immediately after the reading of the journal in the morning?

A. I can't say it was the 2d Tuesday after the reorganization of the two bodies. I remember Mr. McAfee made a motion to adjourn in the morning and it was carried. I do not

know whether it was immediately after the reading of the
journals or not.

Q. Was that not the day upon which an election for senator of the United States would have taken place according
to law, dating the commencement of the session of the legislature from the reorganization?

A. Yes, if that was the 2d Tuesday, on that assumption
that would have been the day.

Q. Did you not know or believe that motion would be
made before you went into the house that morning?

A. I had an idea a motion to adjourn soon after the house
assembled would be made.

Q. Was it not the purpose of that motion to prevent an
election for U. S. senator on that day?

A. If that was the purpose, it was not made known to me.

Q. What did you understand was the object of the motion?

A. It was understood that Mr. Hunter, acting in concert
with some others or under their advice, was to offer a resolution declaring the court house legislature an illegal and unauthorized body; and that such a resolution would produce a
long and acrimonious debate which would open up old wounds,
and it was to prevent this the motion was made.

Q. Don't you know Mr. Hunter voted for a resolution recognizing the legality of the court house assembly?

A. I do not know how he voted.

LEWIS E. PARSONS.

EX-GOV. W. H. SMITH

Being sworn says:

By General Coon—

Q. In what years were you Governor of Alabama?

A. In 1868-9-70.

Q. Was any requisition made for troops during your administration as Governor of Alabama?

A. There was.

Q. Who made it?

A. It was made by me and in connection with a committee
of the general assembly appointed to go to Washington and
solicit troops?

Q. What was the object in bringing troops?

At this point Mr. Price objected to the question, and to all
questions relative to the use of troops during Gov. Smith's
administration, as irrelevant. The committee sustained the
objection and the examination of Gov. Smith was resumed.

By Gen. Coon—

Q. Were you an active participant in the campaign of 1872?

A. I took some interest in it, but was not so active as some.

Q. Did you make any speeches in the interest of the republican party in the canvass of that year?

A. Yes; two or three, perhaps more.

Q. Do you know of any troops being brought to the State?

A. I saw troops in the State, but know nothing of my personal knowledge of how they came here. On reflection I remember I heard some one in Montgomery say that Spencer was in Washington to see about getting some troops to be brought into the State to procure a fair election, or to protect voters. My recollection is not distinct.

Q. Did you hear of any other purpose than to preserve the peace?

A. I did not.

Q. Had you any understanding the troops were to be used for political or personal purposes?

A. No; I never had any such understanding with any one, nor did I ever hear the matter discussed in that light.

Q. Were you here on the assembling of the court house legislature?

A. I was.

Q. Did you come here as the friend of Spencer?

A. I did not; but on the other hand I came to defeat him for the United States Senate, or doing what I could in that direction.

Q. Did you hear anything said in regard to any influences being used by Spencer to secure his election?

A. I was not on speaking terms with Spencer, and am not now. I have spoken to him once under peculiar circumstances.

Q. If you heard any conversation at your room at the Madison House in relation to the pairing off of Glass and Edwards, state it?

A. I can't say a conversation I heard in the hall of the Madison House, as I was passing through relative to the pairing off, but I heard a conversation between J. J. Hinds and some other parties; I think Moulton was of the number; it is an indistinct impression however as to Moulton. There was something said about Edwards going to North Alabama, and as to when he would return. I remember distinctly hearing Hinds say: "I have fixed him," and in that connection I heard the words "$500." This was all I heard.

Q. Was there any understanding among the leading republicans in the State that troops were to be brought here for political purposes?

A. There was not. I was opposed myself to the use of troops except in cases of absolute necessity to preserve law and order.

By Mr. Little—

Q. Might not Mr. Spencer have had troops used without your knowledge?

A. He might have done so; it is possible; I had no connection with the use of troops in that year.

Q. What were the relations between Spencer and Hinds?

A. Most intimate.

Q. What were the relations between Spencer and Robert Barber?

A. I only know what Barber told me at that time; he said he was working for Spencer's election.

By Mr. Price—

Q. What position did Barber hold in the party?

A. He was somewhat prominent; he had considerable local influence in Montgomery county, and was secretary of the republican State executive committee.

By Mr. Little—

Q. Do you know by what means Spencer secured his election to the Senate?

A. I myself was very much opposed to Spencer's election; I saw a good many were in favor of his election, and I said nothing much about it. I know Spencer had rooms at the Madison House, and that in one he had wines, cigars, &c., which were dealt out to the members of the court house assembly and others. I frequently saw white and colored members in there; Brainard stayed there; I saw Hinds about frequently.

Q. Do you know whether there were any disaffected members of the court house assembly that had to have inducements held out to them to remain?

A. I only heard there were some weak-kneed members.

Q. What part did Hinds seem to be taking in Spencer's election?

A. He was the most active man in the city of Montgomery in Spencer's behalf, according to my observation. He worked with members and those who were not members.

Q. Were you in the confidence of Spencer so as to know what means were used?

A. I was not, and when I fell out with Spencer, Hinds seemed cool towards me; before that he was cordial; I knew of no other cause than the difference with Spencer—the difference between myself and Spencer during the first investigation by congress into the conduct of Judge Busteed.

The witness was here handed the two letters, Exhibits E. and F., from Spencer to Barber.

By Gen. Morgan—

Q. Where did you live in 1872?

A. In Randolph county.

Q. Do you recollect whether any troops were stationed at Opelika in October, 1872?

A. I think I do.

Q. In a letter addressed by George E. Spencer to "My Dear Barber," dated Oct. 22, 1872, he says: "I wish Randolph, deputy U. S. marshal, would use the company at Opelika in making arrests in Tallapoosa, Randolph and Cleburne;" were any such arrangements made by the leading republicans of Alabama, within your knowledge or belief?

A. I never knew or heard of it before reading these letters.

Q. Look at the two letters shown you of October 16th and October 22d, 1872, from Spencer to Barber, and state whether, from your knowledge of Spencer's handwriting, they were written by him?

A. I am acquainted with Spencer's handwriting, and after examining them, I say they are in his handwriting.

W. H. SMITH.

W. W. GLASS

Being sworn, says:

I was elected Senator from Macon county in 1872; I am not a member of the Senate at this time; I resigned at the close of the last session of the legislature; I was in Montgomery on November 18th, 1872, the day fixed by law for the meeting of the general assembly; I held a regular certificate of election; I did not go to the capitol that day; I went to the court house; no legislature had ever met at the court house before that I know.

By Gen. Morgan—

Q. Why did you go to the court house?

A. Because my party was meeting there. I met Judge Pelham while I was on my way to the capitol, and he told me of the meeting at the court house.

Q. Did Pelham tell you the legislature or a caucus was going to meet at the court house?

A. He said the legislature, and that they were waiting for me to come up.

Q. Did you not know the capitol was the proper place to meet?

A. We had always met there before; I had been a member of the Senate four years before this.

Q. When you got there did you go into a caucus or into the general assembly?

A. In the general assembly as I thought; the roll was called in the Senate.

Q. Who was presiding?

A. I think Senator Pennington presided for a day or two.

Q. Where was Lt. Gov. Moren that day?

A. I did not see him.

Q. What was your object in meeting at the court house?

A. I don't know; I went there because my party did.

Q. When did you first see Mr. Spencer after you met at the court house?

A. Shortly after.

Q. Did he talk to you about being a candidate for the Senate?

A. He said he was a candidate.

Q. Was he your preference?

A. I can't say.

Q. Were not Messrs. Parsons, Pennington and White spoken of?

A. I think they were.

Q. Were you one of the thirteen known to be opposed to Spencer?

A. I don't know; I know there were other men I preferred to Spencer; I talked this to my friends, or mentioned it.

Q. Do you know J. J. Hinds?

A. I do; I sat side by side with him in the Senate for four years.

Q. Was Hinds a member of the court house senate?

A. He was a member of the legislature from 1868 to 1872, but was not a member in 1872.

Q. Was Hinds at the court house when that body met?

A. I think he was.

Q. Where did he live then?

A. I understood from him at Decatur.

Q. How long did he remain in Montgomery?

A. Until after the Miller-Martin contest was decided.

Q. Was he not here working more actively than any other man in Spencer's interest?

A. I think he was; I know of no other business he had.

Q. Did Hinds not talk to you about Spencer's election?

A. I think he did.

A. Was not W. H. Betts there working for Spencer's
election?

A. I should judge so from what I saw him doing.

Q. Did you vote for Spencer in the caucus that nominated
him?

A. I don't recollect, but I voted for him in the legislature.

Q. Before that election did you not know of a room where
Spencer entertained his friends?

A. I know he had a room where I went and got several
drinks of fine liquor. It was called Spencer's liquor, and was
a free thing. I saw many going in and out drinking. I went
in and drank frequently.

Q. Was this kept up until after Spencer's election?

A. I think it was.

Q. Did you draw any money for pay from the treasury up
to the time of Spencer's election?

A. I think I drew mileage. I think I did not draw any
per diem. I took my warrant home with me amounting to
$606. When I went home I had to send back $40 to pay my
board.

Q. How much money did you bring with you from home?

A. About $40 or $50, I can't say positively.

Q. How much was your mileage?

A. Thirty-six dollars.

Q. Do you recollect drawing any thing but your mileage
and the warrant for $606, while you were here?

A. I do not.

Q. How much was your board?

A. I boarded with Matt Blue at one dollar per day.

Q. Are you a man of wealth?

A. I live very savingly. We have in the family a store,
two plantations and a mill.

Q. Which of the plantations belong to you?

A. One belongs to my son, the other to my wife. The
store is under control of my son.

Q. How far do you live from Montgomery?

A. Forty-five miles.

Q. After you met in the fusion legislature a contest arose
concerning the seat of Martin by Miller. The journals show
that the vote was taken on that contest on the 30th January,
1873. On Tuesday the 28th, the journals show you got leave
of absence for three days. The journals show that on the
29th of January, 1873, Senator Edwards got leave of absence
for ten days. At the time you got leave of absence when
was it understood the Martin-Miller contest would come up?

A. There was no understanding with me when it would come up.

Q. What agreement did you have with Edwards about pairing off on the vote to be taken in settlement of the Martin-Miller contest?

A. My understanding was this: I told Edwards I had leave of absence for three days, and Edwards proposed to pair off with me for ten days on this contest. I told him if I got leave of absence for ten days (I had already leave for three days) I would not vote in the Martin-Miller contest. This is my recollection.

Q. What was then said?

A. Nothing more was said.

Q. Did you sign a written contract with Mr. Edwards in the presence of Senators Coleman and Carmichael, the purport of which was that you would pair off with Edwards for ten days.

A. If I did I don't recollect it.

Q. Was the agreement you made with Edwards made in the presence of Senators Coleman and Carmichael?

A. It was.

Q. Did not you agree that neither of you would vote during the three days leave of absence on that contest?

A. There was no such agreement as to the three days.

Q. Would you have left here without pairing off with somebody during the pendency of the Martin-Miller contest.

A. I did not care much about it. I would rather have got out of voting.

Q. Did not Edwards leave here with the understanding that he was paired off with you.

A. I do not know.

Q. Did you not go over to the depot at the same time Edwards went?

A. I did, and he saw me over there. I afterwards had a conversation with him in which he told me his friends had not treated him right in not granting me the ten days leave and in not telegraphing him that the leave had not been granted.

Q. Did the trains on which you and Edwards were to go leave at the same time?

A. About the same time, I don't know which left first.

Q. Were you to have gone on the same road?

A. No, I was to go on the Western road.

Q. Did you get on the train and how far did you go?

A. I got on the West Point train and went to the Fair grounds near this city, about 4 miles.

Q. Did you stop the train or was it stopped for you?

A. I suppose it was stopped by W. H. Betts. I did not have it stopped.

Q. Was W. H. Betts on the train?

A. He was at the time it stopped.

Q. Was he not on it when you started?

A. I don't know.

Q. Did you not have an understanding about it?

A. Not at that time.

Q. Did Betts ask you to get off the train at the Fair grounds?

A. He said, " Let's go back to the city ; you can go there and stay until the three days are out and vote in the Martin-Miller contest"—that I had a right to do so. I told him I would not do that.

Q. Did you object to getting off?

A. I did not.

Q. Was any other inducement held out to you save the mere statement of Betts?

A. None at all.

Q. Why had you got three days leave of absence?

A. It was my understanding I was to get three days leave of absence, and they would suppose I was gone, and would take up the Martin-Miller contest.

(After this answer was taken down the witness changed his answer, as follows :

It was my understanding that I was to get three days leave of absence, and that at *the expiration* of that time the Martin-Miller contest would be taken up, and that I would have the right to come back.)

Q. Was there any thing said about the Martin-Miller contest when you got the three days leave of absence?

A. Nothing that I recollect of.

Q. When you got out to the fair grounds how did you expect to get back to town?

A. W. H. Betts met up with me in the cars and got at me to come back, and said there would be a carriage there to carry me back, in a short time, which came. I got in the carriage and came back with W. H. Betts.

Q. Was it a close carriage?

A. Yes, sir, it was.

Q. What place did Betts take you to?

A. The Madison House.

Q. Did he not put you in a room there and tell you to remain concealed?

8

A. A room was furnished me; he did not tell me to remain concealed. No person knew I was there but my republican friends, that I know of. I saw a good many people; I did not know what or who they were.

Q. Was it not understood you were to remain concealed, and did you not take pains to conceal yourself from all but those who knew of the reasons for your being there?

A. I did not make myself very conspicuous. I did not wish everybody to see me. I was to remain concealed as much as possible and I did so. I had no conversation with any one I did not know were my republican friends. I remember conversing with Hinds, Baker, McKinstry and Dustan.

Q. If you went out at all in the day time were you careful to avoid being seen by any one who would be likely to disclose you were in Montgomery?

A. I was careful that the democrats did not see me.

Q. Did Hinds, Baker, Dustan and McKinstry know of the purpose to keep you in Montgomery. Did not they or some of them talk to you about it?

A. Yes, they talked of the purpose of keeping me in Montgomery. I don't know that I talked with each one of them, but with some of them I did.

Q. Did not McKinstry know that you were kept concealed in Montgomery with the intent that you should be notified when the vote was about to be taken on the Martin-Miller contest, and that at that moment you should appear and vote.

A. I do not know what McKinstry knew. He knew I was there.

Q. Who of the four men you have named did know what is stated in the foregoing question?

A. I think Hinds and Baker understood it; the others I could not say; I don't know.

Q. Do you not believe, and did you not then believe that all of them knew it?

A. Yes, I believe they all knew it. It is my opinion.

Q. Did not W. H. Betts know the purpose for which you were kept in Montgomery?

A. From what he said to me he must have known it.

Q. Were you not informed during your concealment in the Madison House, from time to time of the stage of the proceedings in the Senate on the Martin-Miller contest?

A. I was.

Q. Were you not told that you would be sent for at the proper moment to vote on that contest?

A. Yes, I was.

Q. Having a leave of absence for three days and not having used it to go home, why did you not return to the Senate chamber and take part in the proceedings.

A. Because I had leave of absence for three days and didn't intend to go back within the three days.

Q. Did you believe that you had the right to return to the Senate and vote on the Martin-Miller contest at any time within the three days covered by your leave of absence?

A. I did not think that I had; neither would I have done it. I understood my three days were out.

Q. The journals of the Senate show that your leave was granted on the 28th of January, and that you voted on this contest on the 30th of January. Can you count three days between those dates?

A. I can not.

Q. What time of day, on the 28th, did you leave the senate, and what time of day, on the 30th, did you return to it and vote in Martin-Miller contest?

A. I left on the morning of the 28th; I cannot say what time of day it was; it was about 12 or 1 o'clock, to the best of my recollection, when I returned on the day I voted.

Q. Were you not advised by Hinds, or Betts, or Baker, or McKinstry, or some other person, that you had the right to vote on the 30th?

A. I was; I think they all advised me, to the best of my recollection.

Q. Why did you believe that you did not have the right to vote on the Martin-Miller contest, during your three days leave of absence?

A. Because I said I would go away and stay for three days, and would not vote during that time.

Q. Did you not say this to Edwards?

A. I don't recollect whether I did or not.

Q. If you did not say it to some one with whom you agreed to pair off, what possible obligation did you conceive that you were under to keep the promise?

A. If I said I would not return and vote for three days to any one. I said it to Edwards; I reckon I told Edwards so.

Q. Don't you know you told Edwards so?

A. Yes.

Q. Did you buy any goods in Montgomery during the session of the legislature that winter?

A. I did not.

Q. How much was your board bill?

A. I paid a dollar a day.

Q. Did you get any money changed during that session of the legislature?

A. I did not.

Q. Did you borrow any money during that winter?

A. I did not.

Q. Did you pay your board bill for the time you were concealed at the Madison House?

A. I did not; I was going to pay it and somebody said they would pay it for me.

Q. Who was it?

A. I think it was Hinds, to the best of my recollection; I stayed there afterwards, and for that time paid it myself.

Q. While you were there concealed were you furnished with whisky?

A. I went to Spencer's bar, in his room, and got what whisky I wanted.

Q. Did you not hear McKinstry, Baker, Hinds, or Whiting, say that it was necessary in order to secure Spencer's seat in the senate that the Martin-Miller contest should be settled in favor of Miller?

A. I heard some conversation to that effect, but I can't say what was said.

Q. Who was the conversation with?

A. Some of these men.

Q. Did not some of these men say that this was the reason why it was necessary that your vote be recorded in favor of Miller in that contest?

A. I think there was something to that effect said, to the best of my recollection.

Q. Did you not agree to stay and vote for Miller?

A. It was understood I would vote for Miller.

By Mr. Little—

Q. Who went to the capitol with you when you went to vote?

A. W. H. Betts.

Q. How did you go?

A. In a close carriage.

Q. When you got into the capitol were there a large number of men in the lobby?

A. There was a crowd in the senate.

Q. When you went into the senate chamber was the vote being taken?

A. It was being taken or just had been taken, to the best of my knowledge; I called the attention of the president and recorded my vote.

By Mr. Price—

Q. You stated to the committee before the oath was administered, this morning, that you went home, forty-five miles, on the day you left Montgomery and returned the same day in a carriage; you have since sworn that you only went as far as the fair grounds; why did you make this statement?

A. I wanted to waive the thing; I was not under oath then.

Q. Why did you want to waive the thing?

A. I did not want to tell anything about this thing anyway.

Q. Why didn't you want to tell?

A. I didn't want to be persecuted.

Q. Do you think it would persecute you to tell the truth?

A. By certain persons it would.

By Mr. Brewer—

Q. Did you not desire to screen others?

A. I would if I could by talking a little, but I would not if I was put on my oath.

W. W. GLASS.

J. D. BEALE

Being sworn, says:

By Mr. Price—

Q. Where do you reside and where did you reside Nov. 1872?

A. I reside in Montgomery, and in 1872 was a clerk in the Exchange hotel.

Q. Do you know Wm. Stribling?

A. I do; he was a member of the legislature in 1872; was a member of the capitol and of the consolidated body.

Q. Where did he board in Dec. 1872?

A. At the Exchange hotel.

Q. Do you recollect the time when the election of United States Senator took place in the capitol legislature?

A. I recollect the time but not the date.

Q. Do you know where Wm. Stribling was at that time, and what do you know about him?

A. On the evening before the election for United States Senator was to take place by the legislature at the capitol, a boy came with a note for Mr. Stribling—he said he came from Mr. Beebe's—I told him Mr. Stribling was not in; shortly after Mr. Beebe came himself and asked if Mr. Stribling was in; I told him I did not know; he then asked for a servant and was shown to Mr. Stribling's room; Mr. Stribling did not stay in his room that night; the sergeant-at-arms came to me looking for Stribling next day; I went to his room and other rooms and did not find him; I did not see him for three days afterwards; he was very sick after that, and I sent for a doctor.

Q. About what time of day did Beebe come for Stribling?

A. Between 7 and 8 o'clock, P. M.

J. D. BEALE.

F. TITCOMB

Being sworn, says:

By Mr. Little—

Q. Where do you reside?

A. In the city of Montgomery.

Q. What connection did you have with the legislature of Alabama, assembled at the State House, known as the Capitol Legislature?

A. On the 21st day of November, 1872, I was elected sergeant-at-arms of the house of representatives.

Q. Do you know of any means used to prevent any member of the house of representatives from being present to prevent a quorum during the days when the two houses were attempting to elect a United States Senator; if so, please state in full what you know about the same?

A. On the 7th of December, the house met, and upon calling the roll no quorum was found present—fifty members only answering to their names. Mr. Speaker Stone called me to his seat and informed me that Mr. Stribling, a member of the house from Washington county, was in some part of the city, secreted and drunk, and ordered me to proceed and arrest him and bring him to the house, as the senate would come in at 12 M. for the purpose of electing a U. S. senator, and that if Mr. Stribling was present the house would have a quorum. I asked him if he could inform me at what place I could find Stribling. He referred me to Mr. Chapman, a member from Clarke county, who informed me that Stribling was secreted at the Rialto. This place is situated on Market street, having a bar-room below, and the rooms above have the reputation of being used as a gambling establishment. Mr. Chapman, of Clarke, Mr. McHugh, a member from Mobile, and myself, started for this place, and upon our arrival there, I asked the negro man who had charge of the rooms above, who was standing at the door, if Mr. Stribling was in any of the rooms. His answer was "No," but that he was there during the evening before. I then went up stairs and met Mr. Henshaw, one of the proprietors. and informed him of my official position, and the order I had to execute. He informed me Stribling was present last evening in company with Mr. Whiting, chairman of the radical State executive committee, Jake Farden and George Ellison, and that he had no objection to my "hunting him up." I then went into one of the back rooms and found Mr. Stribling on a sofa, in a fearful condition, in a state of unconsciousness. In a few moments he drew up his legs and arms and threw them out straight. I tried to get him up but found it impossible. I then left him in charge of responsible persons and went for Dr. Fremon, a physician, who came, and after examining Stribling, pronounced him drunk and drugged. This was about 11 o'clock A. M. The negro said the whisky they had did not come from the bar below, but was brought by those who came with Stribling, in a bottle, which was then on the side-board. I took the bottle and found it about half full, and remarked, if that was was all they drank, Stribling's condition could not be produced by the effects of the whisky. The negro then said they drank up the first bottle before 12 o'clock, and one of the party went out and brought it in again full. Three small glasses were on the side-board with cocktails in them. I asked the negro to take a drink with me from the bottle, and he said he would rather drink one of the cocktails, for they came from the bar below, and he knew they were good. A gentleman took up the cards from the table and remarked they were "marked" cards. Looking at them, I found this to be the fact, and put the three which I now have in my pocket. Dr. Fremon and myself made every exertion to awaken Mr. Stribling, but found it impossible. Dr. F. then gave me some medicine and I gave it to Stribling as he directed. In about one hour it had the effect the doctor said it would have. We worked upon him until about one or two o'clock, and succeeded in getting him up. We then took him in a coach to the Exchange Hotel, and had a strict watch kept of him until the election of senator took place.

I obtained a vial from the drug store of Wade McBryde, and filled it with whisky from the bottle I found in this room, and have it now in my possession. Mr. Stribling, with the assistance of friends, attended the sessions until the 10th day of December, at which time Mr. F. W. Sykes was elected senator by the house and senate, in the hall of the house— 51 members of the house and 18 members of the senate being present—Sykes receiving every vote. After which he was taken to the house of Mrs. Morse, in the vicinity of the capitol, and was confined by sickness for some weeks. He was not a well man during the balance of the session, and I believe he has never fully recovered from the effects of that night's debauch. The night before this occurrence, Mr. Whiting, one of the men who was present at the Rialto when he was drugged, offered to bet me one hundred dollars that the capitol legislature would not have a quorum on the next day. I declined the bet, but little thought that Spencer and his friends would resort to such tricks to prevent it. Upon the eighth day I found Mr. Mancill absent from roll call. I was directed to arrest him, and found he had left the city without the consent of the house, on the ground that his children were sick. I went to Covington county for him and learned from his wife he had started back to Montgomery. She also stated that the family were all well, and none of them had been sick. I had Mr. Mancill present in the house on the 10th.

It was the general conversation among the republicans at this time, that senator Spencer had plenty of money, and found the members of the court house body with as much as they wanted for their daily expenses, to keep them in that body, as they could not draw any pay from the State treasury.

F. TITCOMB.

### DR. JAMES A. FREMON

Being sworn, says :
I reside in the city of Montgomery, and resided here in 1872. I am a practicing physician and surgeon.
By Mr. Little—
Q. Were you at any time called to see Wm. Stribling, a member of the legislature?
A. I was, on December 7, 1872, as well as I can remember. It was on the day for the election for U. S. senator at the capitol.
Q. Who came for you?
A. Mr. Titcomb.
Q. Where did you find Mr. Stribling?
A. In a room over the Rialto saloon.
Q. State his condition when you found him, and for what you treated him?
A. I found him under the influence of an opiate, but evidently he had been drinking and had opiates mixed with his drink, or he had taken an opiate separately. I found him with all the symptoms of poisoning with opium, and considered him in a dangerous condition, and treated him accordingly.
Q. Did you inform him of his condition?

A. I informed him he was in a very dangerous condition and must be careful with himself, as soon as sufficiently re-suscitated to have his mental faculties under control.

Q. Did you see him afterwards?

A. I saw him the second day after this and discharged him on that day.

By Mr. Brewer—

Q. Who are the proprietors of the Rialto saloon?

A. Messrs. Beebe & Henshaw, as I understand.

By Mr. Price—

Q. Was he at all sensible of his condition when you were first called to him?

A. He was not.

Q. What kind of a room did you find him in, and how was it furnished?

A. It was an up-stairs room, the third room back, I think. The room was furnished with a lounge, a bureau, &c.

By Mr. Parks—

Q. Was his condition such as to incapacitate him for business for any length of time?

A. His condition was such as to prevent his properly attending to business, either of a mental or physical character, for at least two days.

J. A. FREMON, M. D.

M. D. BRAINARD

Being sworn, says:

By Gen. Morgan—

Q. Had you any official connection with the court house assembly that met in Montgomery in 1872?

A. I had not.

Q. State where you resided at that time, and whether you were an active member of the republican party?

A. I resided near the city of Montgomery, and was considered an active member of that party.

Q. Do you know George E. Spencer, and how long have you known him?

A. I do, and have known him for some years.

Q. Were your relations with him intimate when he was a candidate for the Senate?

A. They were friendly.

Q. Who were his most intimate and active friends when he was a candidate for the Senate?

A. J. J. Hinds, H. Ray Mayers, J. J. Moulton, P. G. Clarke, D. C. Whiting, Mr. Baker, at present marshal northern district of Alabama, Mr. Betts and others.

Q.   Was Mr. Baker at that time a member of the court house assembly?

A.   He claimed to be a senator from Morgan and the other counties in that senatorial district.

Q.   Did you take an active part is assisting in Spencer's election?

A.   I took a part in it.

Q.   What was the necessity for any activity in securing Spencer's election?

A.   There was an opposition that would have been very formidable if it had been allowed to develop itself, and it was thought best to crush it in its incipiency.   Mr. Reynolds and Mr. Parsons were thought to be formidable opponents, and were spoken of. as candidates.

Q.   Did you have any conversation with Spencer and Hinds on the subject?

A.   I don't remember consulting with them; I know I spoke to others.

Q.   Did not Gen. Spencer at that time have almost exclusive control of the federal patronage in this State?

A.   He controlled it to some degree, but not exclusively.

.  Q.   Name Gen. Spencer's most active friends in the court house assembly?

A.   Messrs. Parsons, White and P. G. Clarke were his most influential, if not most active friends.

Q.   Were you satisfied that Spencer had friends that he could have taken with him to the capitol?

A.   Beyond a doubt; he could have broken up the court house assembly in a half hour; seven-tenths of the members would have followed him.

Q.   Were you not equally certain that Messrs. White, Parsons and McKinstry favored Spencer's election to prevent him from taking off his friends to the capitol assembly?

A.   I do not know the motives governing those gentlemen.

Q.   Is it your opinion that they were controlled in their action for the reasons named in the last question?

A.   I considered Gen. Spencer master of the situation, because he had it in his power to break up the court house assembly at any time, and by collusion with the capitol legislature secure his election.   I had been informed overtures had been made to Buckley by the democrats, and I was satisfied they would not stickle on one man, their object being to get control of the legislature.

Q.   Could you have considered a collusion between the capitol legislature and Gen. Spencer's friends in the court house

assembly possible unless you believed Gen. Spencer would
have engaged in such a collusion?

A. I thought he would have engaged in such a plan; the
idea with me was that he was determined to be elected U. S.
Senator.

Q. Do you think he would have hesitated to form this collusion to secure that result?

A. If a sufficient opposition had developed in the court
house assembly to defeat Mr. Spencer, some combination with
the capitol assembly might have been formed. I heard at
that time Gen. Spencer had been present with some democrats and had made some invidious remarks against the republican party. This is one ground of my belief in the last
assertion made. I heard also the democrats had offered to
make Spencer senator if he would break up the court house
assembly. I give it as my personal belief, he would not have
hesitated if it had been the *dernier resort*.

Q. With whom did the idea originate of forming a separate assembly at the court house?

A. I mentioned it first in the republican State executive
committee rooms to Mr. Barber, the clerk. I afterwards mentioned it in the editorial room of the *State Journal* to Mr.
Bingham and others, as a good piece of political strategy,
which I conceived to be justified by the occasion. It was said
it was impossible to organize that way; that the legislature
must meet in the capitol. I examined the law and found it
required the legislature to meet "at" the capitol instead of
"in" the capitol. It was suggested there by those with whom
I conversed that the legislature meet at the capitol and organize with a rush and hurrah after the style of the Arkansas
legislature. I advised that it would be best to organize as a
seperate body, keep up the organization until the governor,
whose election was not questioned, was inaugurated and recognized the court house assembly by message. The governor was then to compel the dispersion of the capitol assembly, and if necessary call for troops to carry out his purpose.

Q. Was not this strategy adopted and advocated on your
part with a view to secure Spencer's election?

A. It was one of the motives that impelled me; I also desired to secure the fruits of a Republican victory.

Q. What other of Spencer's friends concurred with you
in that view?

A. They all finally concurred; some were conservative and
weak-kneed at first, but finally came in. The whole matter
was submitted to Messrs. White, Parsons and Ex-Gov. Smith;
they were considered the shining lights of the party.

Q. How long was it after this long consultation before the court house body assembled?

A. Several days.

Q. Was there any plan agreed upon to prevent the organization of the capitol legislature?

A. I suggested the arrest of the Marengo members and the sending of some one to Russell county to scare the county supervisors so as to cause them to make a fair return.

Q. To whom did you make these suggestions?

A. To Mr. White and Mr. Whiting and other republicans.

Q. What did Mr. White say?

A. He said, "that is smart."

Q. Was the plan suggested by you adopted?

A. The men were arrested, and Minnis, U. S. district attorney, went up to Russell.

Q. Was not the purpose of this plan to arrest the certificated members from Marengo county to prevent a quorum in the capitol assembly?

A. I thought they had violated the law and ought to be arrested, and I thought this a good opportunity to prevent a quorum at the capitol.

Q. How long was it before Calvin Goodloe joined the court house assembly after it first met?

A. I cannot say.

Q. Did you consider that Baker and Chisholm were elected?

A. If so, I thought it was a great stretch.

Q. Were they not induced to go into the Senate for the purpose of filling up the ranks of that body with the hope that they would get seats there?

A. They claimed to be elected.

Q. Upon what was their claim founded?

A. Upon their election.

Q. Were you not satisfied they were not elected?

A. I always looked with suspicion on contestants.

Q. Was not the introduction of Baker and Chisholm a part of the strategy adopted?

A. I give it as my opinion that it was.

By Gen. Coon—

Q. Did you hear Chisholm say anything about votes being thrown out in Limestone?

A. I heard him say they had thrown out a large number of his votes, and that he was elected.

By Gen. Morgan—

Q. Was it not your opinion at that time, notwithstanding

the claims set up by Baker and Chisholm to seats, that they were not elected or entitled to seats?

A. I think at that time I was of the opinion they were elected, and was influenced in that opinion by the action of the democratic party in Marengo and Barbour counties.

Q. Do you know what part Moulton took in Spencer's election?

A. He was very active; I saw him frequently in consultation with Hinds and Spencer.

Q. Do you know of any money being brought here by him and used in Spencer's election?

A. I know nothing of my own knowledge.

Q. Did you keep a room with refreshments at the Madison House, during the time Spencer's election was pending?

A. I did; I had champagne, liquor, cigars, &c., in room 10; I kept it red-hot; I kept it for Spencer and his friends; it was free to all. Spencer came to me several times and said he did not want me to be spending so much of my own money, and asked me if I did not want some money; I told him no, but finally took a hundred dollars; he gave no direction as to its use.

Q. Do you know whether Spencer promised any person office in consideration of his support of him?

A. I heard men talking and say they had a dead thing; I know men took advantage of the occasion to press their claims.

Q. Were you satisfied from the surroundings such promises were made?

A. I was morally certain such was the case.

Q. Do you know whether Hinds paid any money to any one in consideration of his support of Spencer?

A. I do not.

Q. State any influences you know were used to induce the Lowndes county members to keep away from the capitol assembly?

A. It was rumored Buckley had got these members, in consideration of $1,000 each, to go to the capitol assembly. A watch was put upon them, consisting of Rob't Barber, J. C. Hendrix and others; a professional pedestrian was procured to go to Hayneville and notify Bryant to come up to the city, as his presence was needed to influence the action of the Lowndes negroes; the pedestrian went that night, saw Bryant, who came to the city the next morning by 9 A. M.

Q. Do you know of any money having been used with any Democrats, or have you any information on the subject?

A. Pelham came to me one day and said he wanted to

get Peddy, an Independent from Lee county, out of town. I let him have some money, which he afterwards gave back to me saying, he had no need of it as he got him passes.

Q. From whom did you get the money?

A. I got $10 from Spencer; I did not tell him what I wanted with it; I furnished the balance.

Q. Did Peddy leave?

A. He did.

Q. State any instance of like kind you know of?

A. I was running room No. 10; a man introduced himself to me as a Democratic member from the capitol assembly, and inquired if Gen. Spencer was in; I invited him to take drinks, which he did, and I then took him across to Spencer's room and introduced him. There was some talk with me, in which he said he wanted to see Spencer about postoffice matters or mail contracts.

By Gen. Coon—

Q. Did you know anything about Goodloe?

A. It was rumored he was an applicant for the custom house at Mobile.

Q. Why was he so long getting down to the court house assembly?

A. I supposed he was waiting to be convinced.

Q. Was he acting as a spy for the court house assembly or for Spencer?

A. I thought he was trying to get the Democrats in deep water; I can't say he was acting as a spy.

Q. Do you know of any agreement that was made with Mr. Goodloe to induce him to come to the court house assembly?

A. I can't say that I do, more than the general agreement of party policy; it was understood Mr. Goodloe was the intimate friend and had great influence with Gov. Lewis; it was thought his co-operation with the court house assembly was of great importance; he seemed slow to come in, but I don't know his reasons for it; he acted with great alacrity when he did come in.

By Gen. Morgan—

Q. After the recommendation of the attorney general had been made, what was agreed upon by the managers of the court house movement as being the essential points to be made so as to sustain Spencer in his seat?

A. A resolution was to be passed by the reorganized legislature, declaring and affirming the legality of the court house assembly; this resolution passed the house but failed in the senate; that resolution having failed the same object was attained by a decision of the supreme court, in the case of Screws v. Ragland. Miller was to be seated if possible.

Q. Do you know anything of the circumstances connected with the appearance of Glass at the moment the vote was to be taken in the senate in the Martin-Miller contest, and with reference to his having been secreted in town to be dropped in on the senate at the proper moment?

A. It had been intimated to me Mr. Glass would arrive from *Macon* before the vote was taken in the Martin-Miller contest; I also had hints that Mr. Glass was about the capitol keeping out of the way; while the ayes and noes were being called, Mr. Glass dropped in, with a cotton umbrella under his arm, an old grey shawl over his shoulders, and a lean, lank carpet-bag in his hand, and asked to have his name called. He was dusty and had the appearance of having just come off of a journey.

Q. I suppose you were amused at Mr. Glass' sudden appearance as if he had come off of a journey?

A. I went to the capitol to enjoy the tableaux and was not disappointed.

By Mr. Brewer—

Q. Do you know how many of the court house assembly have received Federal appointments since Spencer's election, and who they are?

Mr. Calvin Goodloe, Collector of Customs, Mobile, Ala.; A. P. Wilson, Postmaster, Montgomery, Ala.; C. W. Dustan, Treasury Agent; N. S. McAfee, United States District Attorney; Geo. N. Duskin, United States District Attorney; P. G. Clarke, Special Agent Postoffice Department; Baker, Marshal Northern District Ala.; J. W. Dereen, Postmaster, Demopolis; J. N. Pennington, Governor Dakota; L. E. Parsons, United States District Judge, at present Assistant District Attorney; John Bruce, United States District Judge; Chisholm, Inspector Customs; Cochran, Postmaster Selma; Goldsby, Route Agent Postoffice Department. These are all I can remember at this time.

By Gen. Morgan—

Q. Do you consider the ruling of Lieutenant Governor McKinstry in the Martin-Miller contest in deciding the motion put by Senator Cobb to reconsider, and renewed by Senator Parks, out of order; and the refusal to put the appeal from his decision, as arbitrary and wrong, or correct.

A. In my opinion the ruling was highly improper and contrary to parliamentary law and usage.

M. D. BRAINARD.

## W. T. HATCHETT,

Being sworn, says:

I am the administrator of Francis Widmer, who died in October, 1873, in the city of Montgomery. Recently before his death he was revenue collector for the middle district of Alabama. I was informed by Louis Fritz, Jr., that at the time of Widmer's death he (Fritz) held two notes; one on George E. Spencer and one on J. J. Hinds. I do not remember that Fritz stated the amounts of these notes. I demanded them of Fritz as the property of Widmer. He said they were not the property of Widmer; that he had given them to his (Fritz's) wife and they belonged to her. I have the impression on my mind that the notes amounted to $3,000. Afterwards I instituted suit against Fritz for the notes and he denied having them, as I understood. The demand on Fritz for the notes and his response was in the presence of Judge Rice. Widmer at the time of his death was a heavy defaulter to the government. An account has been sent from the department at Washington against Widmer's estate, in which a deficit is charged of $40,000, to the best of my recollection. Widmer had no estate at the time of his death, except a few desks and two safes. He was a book-keeper at the time of his appointment as collector.

W. T. HATCHETT.

## R. H. KNOX,

Being sworn, says:

I am a member of the republican party. I am at present solicitor of this county, and was formerly a member of the legislature. I was in Montgomery at the organization of the court house assembly. I was a member, by proxy, of the republican State executive committee at the time.

By General Morgan:

Q. What was the leading object of the meeting of the court house assembly?

A. To secure republicans of the General Assembly and to elect a U. S. Senator to succeed Hon. George E. Spencer, whose term expired in the succeeding March.

Q. Were you actively engaged in politics here at the time, and were you familiar with the views of the leading men of the republican party.

A. I was, and was myself elected solicitor in the previous November election.

Q. Will you state the means by which Baker, Chisholm, Alfred English, or either of them, procured to be seated in the court house assembly and whether either of them were believed to be elected?

A.  I don't recollect any means by which they procured their seats, nor do I remember what was the opinion concerning their election.

Q.  Were Chisholm and Baker friends of Spencer?

A.  They were warm supporters and friends.  I have met Baker with Spencer at the house of Col. Hinds in Decatur.

Q.  Who was the most active supporter of Spencer—his most active friend and most fully authorized agent?

A.  J. J. Hinds was considered as Spencer's "managing man."  Capt. Whiting was very active; also Maj. Peter G. Clarke, special agent postoffice department.

Q.  What other members of the court house assembly were active supporters of Spencer?  Was George M. Duskin?

A.  I think he was.

Q.  How was Wilson of Montgomery?

A.  He was a strong supporter.

Q.  How was Gen. Dustan?

A.  He was a strong supporter.

Q.  Can you name any others?

A.  T. J. Clark (col'd) of Barbour, J. K. Green (col'd) of Greene, B. R. Thomas of Marengo, all of the Montgomery members, S. H. Murphy, since deceased, W. J. Gilmore and A. H. Curtis.

Q.  Did Spencer have any opposition in that legislature?

A.  It was feared there was opposition.  Hon. Alex. White and ex-Gov. Parsons were mentioned as candidates.

Q.  State whether Spencer and his friends conducted the canvass actively?

A.  They did.

Q.  State as far as you can what means were used?

A.  I remember on one occasion speaking to Spencer, telling him he ought to reward some of his supporters.  He spoke of promising a place.

Q.  Who did he promise?

A.  He told me that he promised Dr. Cloud, member from Montgomery county, a place for his son-in-law, C. H. May. Application had been made for a route agency on the South and North Railroad, and Spencer said he would get something better for him.

Q.  Did such information come to you, as solicitor, that you felt it to be your duty to ask for a special grand jury to investigate alleged briberies of members of the legislature?

A.  It did, and the grand jury was organized.

9

Q. Did you issue subpœnas for members of the legislature to come before the grand jury and testify?

A. I did. I offered as a part of my testimony a paper marked "G," which so far as it relates to the proceedings in the court and legislature, contain a true narrative of what occurred in reference to the matter mentioned in the question.

## "EXHIBIT G."

*Hon. M. Carpenter, Chairman Committee on Elections, U. S. Senate, Washington, D. C.:*

SIR: The subjoined statement is very respectfully presented to your consideration, to show that an effort was made by certain members of the general assembly of this State to proceed regularly and in the legal manner to the election of a United States senator, for the term of six years, to succeed the Hon. George E. Spencer, whose term expires March 3d, *proximo.*

Several persons were favorably mentioned as candidates for this high office, aside from the very distinguished gentlemen who are at present contesting for the position before your honorable committee.

It is claimed that there was no legally organized legislature at the time the certificates of these gentlemen bear date.

It is claimed that Tuesday, the 11th of February, inst., being the second Tuesday after the organization of the general assembly of Alabama, was the day indicated by the law of congress of 1866, for the election of a United States senator. An election for United States senator on that day was prevented by the friends of Mr. Spencer, in the wholly unauthorized and unwarranted arrest of a member of the legislature while presenting or attempting to present a resolution for this purpose.

The following extracts from the published proceedings of the legislature, are presented in evidence of the foregoing, and to sustain the positions assumed.

I have the honor to be

Your obedient servant,

WILLIAM H. HUNTER,

Member of the Alabama legislature from Lowndes county.

MEASURES OF COMPROMISE PROPOSED BY ATTORNEY GENERAL GEORGE H. WILLIAMS.

WASHINGTON, D. C., December 11, 1871.

*To David P. Lewis, Montgomery, Alabama:*

SIR—Two organizations at Montgomery, Ala., claiming to

be the general assembly of the State, have appealed to the President, and, with his approval, I submit as a plan of compromising the difficulty, the following :

First. Officers of each organization shall tender their resignations, to take effect upon the permanent organization of a house of representatives, as hereinafter provided.

Second. On the — instant, the hall of the house in the capitol shall be vacant, at 12 o'clock of that day ; all the persons holding certificates of election as representatives shall assemble therein; but the persons holding the certificates of secretary Ragland shall be the only representatives seated from Barbour county, and shall make, in the usual manner, the temporary organization.

Third. Two tellers, one republican and one democrat, shall be appointed by the speaker, *pro tem.*, who shall publicly, and in the presence of the house, count the votes cast for representatives in the county of Marengo, and for that purpose they shall take the returns of the precinct inspectors of said county, or in case they can not be procured, the evidence of said inspectors, so far as the same may be necessary, to ascertain the actual vote cast as aforesaid, and the persons found upon such count to have the highest number of votes for representatives shall be seated as such from said county ; but the persons now holding certificates of election as representatives from Marengo shall not vote upon or in said temporary organization. Nor shall any business, other than deciding the contest as to said county, be transacted during such organization.

Fourth. When such contest is determined, the house shall make a permanent organization in the usual way.

Fifth. On the said — instant, the senate chamber shall be vacant, and at 12 o'clock the persons holding certificates of election as senators shall assemble therein and organize, with the lieutenant governor presiding, with the person holding the certificate of secretary Ragland in his seat as the only senator from Barbour county; and the votes for senator in Marengo county shall be counted in the same way and upon the same kind of evidence as is hereinbefore provided for the house contest as to said county, and upon such count the person found to have the highest number of votes for senator from said county shall be seated as such, but the person now holding the certificate of election to the seat from said county shall not vote upon any question while the contest against his seat is pending. And then the contest, as to the district comprising the counties of Butler and Conecuh, shall be decided in the same way and upon the same kind of evidence, and the person now holding the certificate of election as senator from said district shall not vote upon any question before he is declared elected upon a count of the votes of the said district as aforesaid; nor shall the senate do any other business before these contests are settled.

No person not holding a certificate of election shall take a seat in the body until his right thereto is affirmed, as above provided. All those claiming to be members and seated in either organization shall be allowed mileage and per diem compensation prior to the temporary organization as hereinbefore provided for. After which persons holding certificates of election from secretary Parker, for Barbour county, shall cease to draw pay, and those contesting the seats for Marengo and the district of Butler and Conecuh, who are finally elected, shall be allowed per diem pay until said contests are respectively ended, and the officers and employees of each organization shall be paid the usual compensation.

GEORGE H. WILLIAMS,
Attorney General.

PROCEEDINGS IN THE HOUSE OF REPRESENTATIVES,

*On the morning of the 11th of February, 1873, and arrest of Mr. Hunter, of Lowndes county.*

There were exciting times in the house this morning. Without waiting to hear the journal read, Mr. McAfee, of Talladega, (known to the house by the euphonious epithet of Cock Robin,) moved an adjournment with a view to defeating the contemplated attempt of the disaffected republicans to bring on the senatorial election.

Mr. Hunter, of Lowndes, at once divining the intention of the mover, sprung to his feet and asked leave to make an explanation. He was proceeding to say that this was the day set apart for the election of a United States senator when the chair called him to order.

Mr. H. But I only ask to explain ——

The Chair. The gentleman from Lowndes will take his seat.

Mr. H. Does the chair refuse me the right ——

The Chair. The gentleman from Lowndes will take his seat.

Mr. H. Then I appeal to the house from the decision of the chair.

The Chair. The speaker has made no decision. The sergeant-at-arms will arrest the gentleman from Lowndes and bring him before the bar of the house.

Mr. H.   Does the speaker deny me my constitutional.
rights ?

The Chair.   The sergeant-at-arms will discharge his duty.

Mr. H.   I have constitutional rights upon this floor and.
am determined to maintain them if possible.

The Chair.   Officer, do your duty, sir !

Mr. H.   I come before the bar of the House.

The officer then took charge of Mr. Hunter and conducted
him down the aisle to the reporter's stand in front of the
Speaker's stand, where he stood facing the Chair.

The Chair.   What have you to say, sir, in justification of
your refusal to obey the mandate of the Speaker ?

Mr. H.   I appealed from the decision of the Chair, and—

The Chair.   The gentleman will come to order.

Mr. H.   Do I understand the Speaker to refuse me the
right to explain ?

The Chair.   The gentleman is out of order.

Mr. Boyd, interrupting, said the gentleman at the bar was
no longer subject to the rulings of the Speaker. He had been
arraigned at the bar of the House, and the House must now
dispose of his case.

By this time the confusion had increased and the excite-
ment had become fevered to a degree that was decidedly in-
teresting.   Motions flowed in thick and fast upon the House;
*first*, to allow the gentleman to explain; *second*, to excuse him;
*third*, to send him back to his seat without further action;
and *fourth*, to postpone his case a day or two in order to allow him time to prepare his defense.   These motions were
merely dilatory, with one exception, perhaps, introduced to
allow Radical members to speak against time.   The rule for
which Mr. Hunter was arraigned for breaking was Rule
No. 7 :

**"If the Speaker calls to order the member shall immedi-
ately sit down *unless* permitted to explain, and the House *shall*,
if appealed to, decide without debate."

The argument in behalf of Hunter was, first, that he was
compelled to obey the mandate of the Speaker *subject to the
condition* of a refusal, *not* by the *Speaker*, but by the *House*, to
hear and determine his appeal ; second, that the condition
not having been complied with by the Speaker, it relieved
Hunter of his obligation to render that obedience which would
have otherwise been due; and third, that the Speaker can only
order an arrest after the House shall have convicted the
offending member of contempt; fourth, that the law of congress requiring on that day the legislature of the State to
proceed to elect a United States Senator, there could be no.

violation of any rule of the House in calling attention to the law of congress.

COPY OF RESOLUTION

*In the hands of Mr. Hunter, the Member from Lowndes, and which he desired read and acted upon when arrested by order of Speaker Parsons :*

*Resolved,* That pursuant and in obedience to the requirements of an act of the Congress of the United States, entitled "An act to regulate the times and manner of holding elections for Senators in Congress, approved July 25th, 1866, this House proceed to-day, the same being the second Tuesday after the meeting and organization of the General Assembly of this State, to elect a Senator in Congress in place of the Hon. George E. Spencer, whose term of office expires on the fourth day of March, 1873.

REPLY OF MR. HUNTER, MEMBER FROM LOWNDES.

HOUSE OF REPRESENTATIVES, Thursday, Feb. 13.

The House met pursuant to adjournment.

Prayer by Rev. Mr. Kinzer.

The journal of yesterday was read and approved.

Mr. Howell moved a suspension of the rules in order that the House bill to authorize the negotiation of a loan by the Governor might be taken up for concurrence in the Senate amendment thereto.

Mr. Hunter asked the gentleman from Cleburne to be kind enough to withdraw his motion in order that he might be permitted to submit the explanation required at his hands by the former action of the House.

Mr. Howell withdrew his motion with the understanding that he should be allowed to renew it.

Mr. Hunter then submitted a written explanation in words and figures as follows, to-wit :

*To the House of Representatives of the General Assembly of Alabama and the Speaker of the House:*

In obedience to a resolution passed by this honorable body on the 11th day of this month, directing the undersigned to make a statement in writing explaining my conduct in this House on the morning of the 11th day of February, 1873, which led to my arrest by order of the Speaker, I have the honor to submit the following :

The undersigned, a member of the House from the county of Lowndes, respectfully states that on yesterday morning he had reason to believe that some members of the House were determined, if in their power, to prevent any and every member of the House from voting on the question for a United States Senator from the State of Alabama as the successor of the Hon. George E. Spencer, whose term will expire on the 4th day of March next; that when he entered the House on yesterday morning, he had, and still has, the clear conviction, that it was the duty of the House, imposed by the supreme law of the land, to-wit: the act of Congress of July 25th, 1866, "to regulate the times and manner of holding elections for Senators in Congress;" to proceed on yesterday to vote for a successor to the said Spencer; that under the aforesaid belief and conviction he entered the House on yesterday with the determination to offer for the adoption of the House, a resolution then in his possession, in the following words and figures :

*Resolved*, That pursuant and in obedience to the requirements of an act of the Congress of the United States, entitled "an act to regulate the time and manner of holding elections for Senators in Congress, approved July 25th, 1866," this House proceed to-day, the same being the second Tuesday after the meeting and organization of the General Assembly of this State, to elect a Senator in Congress, in place of the Hon. George E. Spencer, whose term of office expires on the 4th day of March, 1873.

The undersigned further states that the journal of the proceedings of the House on the preceding day was not read on yesterday morning; that the roll was called and without any other business being done, a member from Talladega (Mr. McAfee) moved to adjourn until the succeeding day; that under the belief that such adjournment would be an abandonment by the House of a plain duty, imposed by the supreme law of the land, and a deprivation of each member of the House, who desired to vote for a United States Senator on yesterday of his plain right to do so, and being determined to do all in his power to present the foregoing resolution for the consideration of the House, the undersigned addressed the Speaker of the House (who is also a member from Talladega county) and was recognized by him, and was proceeding to state a point of order he desired to raise against said motion to adjourn. The point of order he thus desired to raise was, that as the supreme law of the land (said act of congress) imposed upon the House the duty of voting for a United States Senator on yesterday, no rule of the House or other State author-

ity could overrule this supreme law or constitute a sufficient
excuse for avoiding this duty ; that the motion to adjourn
was, in effect, a motion to avoid indirectly a compliance with
the supreme law, and was therefore out of order under that
supreme law. The Speaker pronounced the undersigned out
of order, and the undersigned appealed to the House from said
ruling of the Speaker ; the Speaker did not entertain said appeal or give the House any opportunity to express its sense
or judgment on the appeal, or allow the undersigned an opportunity to explain his point of order or his motion or reasons, but, without taking the sense of the House, or obtaining
any authority from the House, caused the undersigned to be
arrested and brought before the bar of the House. In this
mode, the undersigned was deprived of his right to explain,
of his right to state his point of order, of his liberty as a citizen and member, and the House itself of its right to allow explanation, its right to determine the point of order, and its right
to determine the appeal. The undersigned, in his entire conduct on yesterday, had no intention or idea of contempt of the
house or its speaker, and is guilty of no such contempt, unless the honest belief that the house and each of its members
are bound to obey the supreme law of the land which they are
sworn to support and defend, coupled with an honest effort to
induce them to do so, amounts to such. But the undersigned
having as he hopes, fully excused himself for the supposed
contempt, begs now, further to say that while he is willing to
believe that the speaker did not from any personal motive,
abridge the right of the undersigned, yet in view of his own
character and rights, he is bound to protest against the action
of the speaker in causing him to be arrested and placed in
custody as was done on yesterday.

He is advised and fully believes that neither the rules of
the House nor the usage of parliamentary bodies, nor any
power inherent in the speaker's office, gives that officer the
right to order any member into custody for words spoken in
debate, nor for any violation of the rules of orders as the
speaker may interpret them.

The right of the speaker to call a member to order, does
not carry with it the right to punish if the member disobeys.
The House alone has the power to imprison or expel, or repri-
mand a member, and in carrying out the order of the House
in inflicting such punishment, the speaker is the mere mouth-
piece and servant of the House, as in all other of its acts and
doings. In this case the speaker did not ask the House what
course it would take, or wait for the action of the House in
the premises, but assumed the authority as the presiding offi-

cer to put the undersigned protestant into custody and order him brought before the bar of the House as a criminal, and in so doing the speaker was guilty of a gross and dangerous violation of the authority vested in him, at once taking away the exclusive and constitutional rights of the House, and of the member to a trial and adjudication by his peers and according to the prescribed rules. The constitution provides "that each house may determine the rules of its own proceedings, punish members for disorderly conduct, and with the consent of two-thirds of the house expel a member, and shall have all other powers necessary for a branch of the legislature of a free and independent State." It is evident from this clause of the constitution that the power to punish for disorderly conduct and to prescribe rules of proceeding rests with the house alone; it is a power which has never in this, or any other State, been delegated to the presiding officers and which cannot be delegated. By the exercise of such a power the speaker of the house at his option can destroy the freedom of debate, and instead of being the servant may become the master of the house; and the undersigned confidently asserts that no instance can be cited from British or American parliamentary history where the presiding officer of a deliberative assembly ever before put a member into custody or claimed a right so to do, because the member failed or refused to obey his call to order. It is not in the power of the speaker to punish for disorderly conduct, even in the lobby or gallery, but only to repress it for the time being with the aid of the sergeant-at-arms.

The undersigned, therefore, enters this his solemn protest, for by his confinement on yesterday at the bar of the house, he suffered wrongs and indignity in his person and character by an order without authority of law, and destructive of the freedom and independence of the house. While he freely admits his own error in violating one of the rules of the house, and repeats his apology for the apparent but not willful breach of order, yet he asks that his constitutional right to protest against the action of the speaker on yesterday, as injurious to himself and the public, be respected, and that this his protest and apology may be spread on the journal of this house.

W. H. HUNTER,
Member from Lowndes.

Montgomery, Feb. 12, 1873.

## ARREST OF STROBACH, SHERIFF, AND KNOX, SOLICITOR, OF MONTGOMERY COUNTY.

Mr. Hunter stated that Paul Strobach, sheriff, and R. H·

Knox, solicitor, for Montgomery county, were before the bar of the House, in obedience to a mandate of the House made on yesterday, and moved to suspend the regular order of business for the purpose of considering the cases of said gentlemen. Agreed to.

The clerk then read the following warrant:

STATE OF ALABAMA, HALL OF HOUSE OF REPRESENTATIVES }
     OF THE GENERAL ASSEMBLY OF ALABAMA. }

*To S. D. Oliver, Sergeant-at-arms*
     *of said House of Representatives:*

It having been made to appear to this House that Paul Strobach, as sheriff of Montgomery county, Ala., has this day and during the session of this House, served a summons on one member of this house, which said summons purports on its face to have been issued by Robert Knox, as solicitor, etc., by which said member is required to appear before the grand jury of Montgomery county, at the December term, A. D. 1872, of the circuit court, on the 12th day of February, and from day to day thereof until duly discharged, to give evidence before said grand jury in certain matters pending before them, which summons bears date the 11th day of February, 1873, and the said House of Representatives having duly considered the said foregoing facts, it was therefore

*Resolved*, That the sergeant-at-arms be and he is hereby directed and ordered to arrest and bring to the bar of this house the said Robert Knox and the said Paul Strobach, and that the proper warrant therefor be issued.

These are, therefore, to command you, the said S. D. Oliver, as sergeant-at-arms of the House of Representatives of the General Assembly of Alabama, forthwith to arrest the said Robert Knox and the said Paul Strobach, and bring them to the bar of the House.

Herein fail not, and have you then and there this warrant with your endorsement thereon showing how you have executed the same.

             LEWIS E. PARSONS, Speaker
       of House Rep. of Gen. Assembly of Ala.

Witness: ROBERT BARBER, clerk of House of Representatives of the General Assembly of Alabama, this the 12th day of February, A. D, 1873.

With the following endorsement thereon:

Executed the within warrant by arrest and bringing Paul Strobach, sheriff, and R. H. Knox, solicitor, of Montgomery county, before the bar of the House of Representatives, February 13, 1873.      SAMUEL D. OLIVER, Sergeant-at-arms.

cxxxix.

Mr. Clark, of Perry, then offered the following resolution:

*Resolved,* That R. H. Knox and Paul Strobach, now under arrest by order of this house, be each permitted to address this house for ten minutes, in explanation of their conduct in serving or causing to be served, civil process on the speaker and other members of this house in violation of section eleven of article four of the constitution of Alabama.

Mr. Anderson moved to amend the resolution by allowing Messrs. Knox and Strobach until 10 o'clock to-morrow, and that they be directed to explain in writing. Agreed to.

REPLY OF R. H. KNOX, ESQ., SOLICITOR OF MONTGOMERY COUNTY.

*Mr. Speaker and Gentlemen of the House of Representatives:*

I am here in obedience to your summons, served upon me by the sergeant-at-arms, to answer for an alleged breach of the privileges of this honorable body.

This breach, as I gather it from the resolution which orders my arrest, consists in the service by the sheriff of Montgomery county on Lewis E. Parsons, a member of this body, and during the sessions of this house, of a summons issued by the authority of a grand jury empanneled in the circuit court for the county of Montgomery, and bearing my name with the addition of the title of my office, namely, solicitor for Montgomery county.

It is not claimed in the resolution that the service of this subpœna was directed by me to be made upon the said Lewis E. Parsons while he was upon the floor of this house, or during its session, or while going to attend any of its sessions, or that I gave any directions whatever in relation to its service, or that I had any other connection with it besides the fact that it bore upon its face my name with the designation of my office, nor unless this honorable house takes legislative notice of the authenticity of my handwriting, does it appear that the signature is in my own proper hand.

I suggest these things to show that this honorable body, when it passed the resolution by virtue of which I now appear here, did not have before it any fact showing or tending to show that the act of the sheriff, if it were a breach of the privileges of this house, was participated in or in any manner sanctioned by me. I do not suggest them by way of evasion, or by way of answer to the charge embraced in the resolution of this house, so far as it concerns me.

I deny, Mr. Speaker and gentlemen of the house of representatives, the right of this honorable body thus to arraign me, and I deny that, intentionally or otherwise, I have committed any contempt of the lawful authority of this honorable body or any breach of its legislative immunities. In aid of this denial, I invoke the constitution of the State of Alabama, which this honorable body, any more than the humblest citizen may and shall not invade. I invoke in aid of this my denial the instrument of authority under whose sanction alone this honorable body can exist. Nor do I think I assume too much when I say that I will make it clear to this house that the act which is complained of as an offense against its proper dignity is not lawfully entitled to be so considered. Section 17 of article vi of the constitution of this State provides that "a solicitor shall be elected, in each county in this State, by the qualified electors of such county, who *shall* reside in the county for which he is elected and *perform such duties as may be required of him by law.*"

Certain acts passed by the general assembly of the State of Alabama, and which constitute a part of the body of its written law, provides for the organization and meeting of grand juries within and for the several counties of the State. I presume I need not refer to or designate these laws with particularity.

Section 11 of article iv of the constitution of the State of Alabama declares, that "members of the general assembly shall, in all cases, except treason, *felony*, or breach of the peace, be privileged from arrest," etc.

On the 10th day of February instant, in the circuit court for Montgomery county, the Hon. James Q. Smith presiding, I made a motion in these words:

May it please your honor, certain facts have come to my knowledge within the last few days in relation to alleged offenses against some of the public laws, which make it my duty as prosecutor of the criminal pleas for this county to ask that your honor issue an order for a special grand jury to investigate these representations.

I would not ask this for a case that depended merely upon public rumor, however extensive. The information conveyed to me is, however, from responsible sources, and appears to be well supported by circumstances of great apparent force.

To fail in making this application would be to fail in the discharge of a plain duty, while at the same time I hope that persons who stand in suspicious connection with the facts to which I have alluded will be exonerated upon and after a free investigation by the grand jury.

The presiding judge thereupon granted an order, by virtue of which a grand jury convened on the 11th day of February instant. I did not then care to give any unnecessary publicity to the matters which were to be laid before this grand jury. These matters related to the honor and the integrity and the virtue of the general assembly of the State of Alabama, nor except in vindication of my oath of office and of myself, which the resolution of this honorable body compels, would I now state that this grand jury was asked for by me, because representations which I believed to be well founded had been made to me, that in the matter of the election of a United States Senator by the present general assembly of this State, certain members of this honorable body were guilty of the high crime of bribery. This crime, Mr. Speaker and gentlemen of the general assembly, is declared by law to be a felony, and is within the exceptions of the 11th section of article iv of the constitution, privileging members of the general assembly from arrest. That it is a felony, I take it, will not be disputed in the face of section 3560 of the Revised Code, which declares:

*Section* 3560. *Bribery of Executive, Legislative or Executive Officer.*—Any person who corruptly offers, promises, or gives to any executive, legislative, or judicial officer, after his election or appointment, either before or after he has been qualified, any gift, gratuity, or thing of value, with intent to influence his act, vote, opinion, decision or judgment, on any cause, matter, or proceeding, which may be then pending, or which may be by law brought before him in his official capacity, must, on conviction, be imprisoned in the penitentiary, or sentenced to hard labor for the county, for not less than two nor more than ten years.

In pursuance of the duties cast upon me by the laws of the land and my oath of office, I attended before the grand jury as aforesaid convened, and in further pursuance of the same duty I caused to be issued and to be delivered to the sheriff, to be served, the subpoena for Lewis E. Parsons, named in the resolution of this honorable body.

Its delivery was unaccompanied by any instructions to the sheriff as to the time, place, or manner of serving it. On reference to it, it will be found to have been dated the 11th day of February, 1872, and returnable on the following day, and the actual facts, as to the time of its issue and the time for its return conform to the statements of the process. I did not suppose that the discharge of a plain official duty, the non-performance of which would make me perjured, would be construed or could be tortured into an offense against the legislative department of the government or into a breach of the privileges of either of the houses of the general assembly of the State, and standing at the bar of this honorable body, and with all becoming deference and respect, I deny that for

the acts I have thus set forth, and which constitute the whole
of my conduct in connection with this alleged contempt, I am
liable to be here arraigned, challenged or punished, and I
deny these acts, or any of them, constitute in law or in fact,
expressly or by implication, any breach of the privileges of
this honorable body, or any contempt of its proper dignity or
lawful authority, and I insist that the mere issuance and
service of the process of subpœna to appear and testify before a grand jury is not, and cannot be construed to be an
arrest of the person, and is not within the true and legal
meaning of the words "civil process," as those words are
used in the 11th section of the 4th article of the constitution.

And now, Mr. Speaker and gentlemen of the house of representatives, standing upon the constitution and the laws of
the State, and within the ægis of their protection, I demand
that I be released from the imprisonment and the restraint
which you have imposed upon me, and that I be allowed to
depart hence to attend to my official duties, which are most
pressing.

Mr. Anderson then presented the following resolution :

*Resolved*, That the answer of Robert Knox to the resolution of this house, permitting him to show cause why he
should not be proceeded against for a breach of privileges of
this house, be and the same is hereby referred to a committee
of seven, to be appointed by Hon. Lewis M. Stone as speaker
*pro tem.*, who shall consider said answer and report to this
house as soon as practicable the course proper to be taken in
the premises, and that the sergeant-at-arms may permit the
prisoner to go at large on his word of honor that he will appear when called for by order of the house.

SOLICITOR R. H. KNOX'S APPLICATION FOR A SPECIAL GRAND JURY.

May it please your honor, certain facts have come to my
knowledge within the last few days in relation to alleged
offenses against some of the public laws, which make it my
duty as prosecutor of the criminal pleas for this county to
ask that your honor issue an order for a special grand jury
to investigate these representations.

I would not ask this for a case that depended merely upon
public rumor, however extensive. The information conveyed
to me is, however, from responsible sources, and appears to
be well supported by circumstances of great apparent force.

To fail in making this application, would be to fail in the
discharge of a plain duty, while at the same time I hope that
persons who stand in suspicious connection with the facts to
which I have alluded, will be exonerated upon and after a
free investigation of the grand jury.

### FEBRUARY 10TH, A. D. 1873.

#### ORDER FOR SPECIAL GRAND JURY.

No grand jury having been drawn and summoned for this term of the circuit court, and it appearing to the presiding judge that there is occasion for a grand jury at this term of the court, on motion of the solicitor,

It is therefore ordered by said judge, that the sheriff of Montgomery county forthwith summons eighteen persons, qualified to serve as grand jurors, to be empanneled at this term as a grand jury for said county.

### FEBRUARY 11TH, 1873.

#### ORGANIZATION OF THE GRAND JURY.

The following named persons, being either freeholders or householders, and registered voters of the county, and possessing the other qualifications required by law, were duly empanneled, charged, and sworn, according to law, as follows, to-wit:

Benjamin Trimble was appointed foreman of the grand jury, and the statutory oath was administered to him by the clerk, in the presence of the court and the other grand jurors, and the statutory oath was also administered by the clerk to each of the following named persons, to-wit: G. B. Holmes, D. H. Lewis, Henry Jones, J. R. Warren, E. G. Carew, W. G. Wharton, A. H. Gillett, Jacob Griel, Holland Thompson, Harry Martin, James Foster, Samuel Phillips, John T. McDonald, and J. R. Dillard, in the presence of the foreman and the court, to serve as a grand jury at the present term of this court. The said grand jury, being now complete, retired to the discharge of their duties.

### FEBRUARY 13TH, 1873.

#### SOLICITOR'S MOTION TO DISCHARGE THE GRAND JURY.

If the court please, a few days ago I submitted a motion to empannel a special grand jury, for the purpose of investigating certain charges affecting the character of members of the general assembly in connection with allegations of bribery and corruption. That grand jury was granted by your honor, but as the members of the general assembly whom I had summoned as witnesses in the matter have seen proper to shield themselves from the process of the court, behind their plea of their constitutional privilege from arrest and exemption from civil process, the grand jury is powerless in the premises, and therefore unnecessary. I therefore move the court to dismiss it.

### DISCHARGE OF GRAND JURY.

This day came the special grand jury, and in open court presented to the judge an indictment which was ordered to be filed.

Robert H. Knox, Esq., solicitor, read to the court a sub-pœna, and endorsement thereon, in the words and figures following, to-wit:

"The State of Alabama.

"To any lawful officer of said State—Greeting:

"You are hereby commanded to summon Lewis E. Parsons, Alexander White, P. G. Clark, Ransom L. Johnson, January Maull, W. H. Hunter, Napoleon B. Abercrombie, to appear before the grand jury of Montgomery county, at the December term, A. D. 1872, of the circuit court, on the 12th day of February, and from day to day thereof until duly discharged, to give evidence before said grand jury, in certain matters pending before them.

"This 11th day of February, 1873.

"ROBERT H. KNOX,
"Solicitor for Montgomery county.

"Received in office, February 12th, 1873.

"PAUL STROBACH, Sheriff."

Executed on P. G. Clark, R. L. Johnson, and January Maull, who claim their constitutional exemption as members of the general assembly. Executed on Lewis E. Parsons, who positively refuses to obey the mandate of the court, being a member of the general assembly, and on his motion a resolution was adopted in the house of representatives ordering the arrest of the solicitor and sheriff of Montgomery county. Not found as to Alex. White, W. H. Hunter, and Napoleon Abercrombie. February 12th, 1873.

PAUL STROBACH, Sheriff.

Filed February 13th, 1873, in open court.

M. D. BRAINARD, Clerk.

The solicitor then moved for the discharge of the grand jury on account of the persons subpœnaed, members of the legislature, refusing to obey the request to appear and testify, and on account of the arrest of himself and the sheriff by the sergeant-at-arms of the house of representatives for a contempt in performing the duties prescribed by law.

The Judge then read the following notice and resolution, served on him by the sergeant-at-arms of the house on his way to the court-room, which is as follows:

"Whereas, Paul Strobach, as sheriff of Montgomery county,

Alabama, has this day and during the session of this house, sent a summons on Lewis E. Parsons, one of the members of this house, which said summons purports on its face to be issued by Robert Knox as solicitor, &c, by which said Parsons is required to appear before the grand jury of Montgomery county, of the December term, A. D. 1872, of the circuit court, on the 12th day of February, and from day to day until duly discharged, to give evidence before said grand jury in certain matters pending before them, which summons bears date the 11th day of February, 1873—therefore, be it resolved:

"1st. That the said Parsons be and he is hereby declared not subject to the said process during the session of this house and for fifteen days before and fifteen days thereafter.

" 2d. That a copy of this preamble and resolution be served upon the judge of the circuit court now in session in the county of Montgomery, and upon Robert Knox as solicitor and Paul Strobach as sheriff."

This copy of notice was handed to me by sergeant-at-arms Oliver, February 13, 1873, at 9½ a. m., half hour before the hour of opening the court.

J. Q. SMITH, Judge.

HALL OF HOUSE OF REPRESENTATIFES }
OF GENERAL ASSEMBLY OF ALABAMA. }

I certify that the within resolution is a true copy of the same, adopted by the house this day.

ROBERT BARBER, clerk.

The Judge, then, addressing the grand jury, said:

*Mr. Foreman and Gentlemen of the Grand Jury:*

You have been organized for the special purpose of enquiring into the alleged bribery and undue influence used on members of the house of representatives. To this end the subpœna read by the solicitor was issued, and with the result in the return made thereon by the sheriff.

The members claiming exemption from appearing before the jury, hold they are so exempt under article four, section eleven of the constitution, which reads as follows:

" Members of the General Assembly shall in all cases, except treason, felony or breach of the peace, be privileged from arrest, and they shall not be subject to any civil process during the session of the general assembly."

I do not hold with the members claiming exemption that a subpœna to appear in court is such " civil process " as is covered by the section of the constitution just read.

10

This holding, however, would at once bring about a conflict between the judicial and legislative department of the State government.

This conflict can alone be settled by force.

I am not prepared to resort to the force necessary, but will leave the matter to the public to judge whether, even if the privilege set up exists in law, such privilege ought to be waived in favor of the furtherance of the administration of justice.

Your investigation into the special matter given you in charge, is of course rendered impossible in consequence of the exemption claimed, and you are therefore discharged.

THE STATE OF ALABAMA, }
    Montgomery county. }

I hereby certify the foregoing is a true and correct copy of the proceedings in the organization of a special grand jury for Montgomery county, at the December term, A. D. 1872, of the circuit court of said county, as the same appears of record in said court.

Witness my hand, this 1st day of March, A. D. 1873.

MARK D. BRAINARD, Clerk.

By Gen. Morgan—

Q. State whether in consequence of the proceedings taken in the house of representatives against you, as set forth in the foregoing paper, you were compelled to desist from a further prosecution of the alleged offenses, and ask for the discharge of the grand jury?

A. I was.

Q. In the paper which your have presented, it appears that you stated to the court that facts had come to your knowledge within the last few days in relation to offenses against some of the public laws, made it your duty as prosecutor of the criminal pleas of the county to ask a special grand jury to investigate these representations, to what offense did you refer?

A. Specially to corrupt influences of members of the legislature to secure the election of Hon. George E. Spencer to the Senate of the United States.

Q. State whether the matters to which you referred were freely spoken of in the community?

A. They were.

Q. Had you proceeded to examine other witnesses than members of the legislature?

A. I had; and subpœnas were issued for others.

Q. So far as you were permitted to examine witnesses

state whether the evidence tended strongly to show corrupt influences had been used ?

A.   I so regarded it.

Q.   Were the offenses in reference to which you were examining and in reference to which you had summoned members of the legislature, felonies ?

A.   They were.

Q.   Is it your opinion as a lawyer that the constitution of Alabama shelters a member of the legislature from attending as a witness before a grand jury in the county in which the capitol is situated, to prove the commission of a felony by any one ?

A.   I don't think the term "civil process" used in the constitution applies to subpœnas issued by grand juries.

ROBT. H. KNOX.

FREDERICK WOLFFE .

Being sworn, says :

I knew Francis Widmer, and was one of his bondsmen as collector of internal revenue for the middle district of Alabama.   He died in October, 1873.   He left at his death personal property of trifling value that could be found.   I went on his bond in May, 1873.   This was an additional bond with a penalty of about $25,000.   After he had been arrested in September, 1873, I saw him and asked for some explanation of his arrest and state of his accounts.   He said that his accounts were not short and that Beach was in arrears, he was afraid, $16,000, for which he was responsible; that his own accounts were short only about $3,000 or $4,000; that the amount he was short was due him by very influential parties, who would be able to pay as soon as he called upon them ; if the government would give him time to do so, he could make up his own accounts ; he refused at that time to give me the names of the parties who owed him; I offered him my assistance in attending to some business in Selma in Beach's matters and went to Selma and garnisheed several parties who were bondsmen for Beach ; upon my return from Selma, or a short time thereafter, Widmer showed me three notes on parties who were owing him money ; he stated that with those three notes and the amounts for which parties in Selma were garnisheed, he could make good his accounts.

Q.   Describe the notes as to amounts and names of makers and dates ?

A.   To the best of my recollection, there was one note of J. J. Hinds for $2,500 with a credit on the back of it for $900 ; there was another note made by Hinds and Spencer, either payable to Hinds and endorsed by Spencer or payable to Spencer and endorsed by Hinds, for $1,800, I think; I am not certain of the amount. The third note I think was Strass-burger's.

Q. State what he said concerning the money loaned these parties?

A. He said they owed him for money loaned; that occu-pying his position he was compelled to do more for them than other persons; I saw the notes and have no doubts about their being genuine documents; I know Hinds' signature and am satisfied the note was signed by him; he said he had called upon the parties for the money and at that time he had no response but expected to get the money.

Q. Shortly after this did not yellow fever break out in this city?

A. It broke out about the 22d of September and continued until the middle of November, and was a fearful epidemic. About the 7th of October Widmer took the yellow fever and died; he had intimated he would turn these papers over to me, but I took yellow fever at the same time; Widmer said Faber and another of his bondsmen had called upon him after his arrest for an explanation, and that he made one and also showed him the notes or told him he had them, I am not cer-tain which; he said he was anxious to convince his bondsmen that he was not a willful defaulter, and made the statements and exhibits of these papers for that purpose. The U. S. government is asserting demands against Widmer's securities for alleged defaults, and at that time had been arrested as a defaulter and was on bail, I being one of his bondsmen. Wid-mer was born in Switzerland in the same country with myself. He was an honest, liberal, confiding man, easily influenced by his friends.

F. WOLFFE.

JOSEPH GOETTER

Being sworn, states on oath that the annexed copy of an examination taken before James F. Dresser, contains a full and correct statement of what he knows in respect to the mat-ters therein spoken of.

JOS. GOETTER.

"Joseph Goetter called and sworn for the U. S.

I reside in Montgomery, Ala.; sustain toward the late Mr. Widmer, as collector of internal revenue, the relation of bonds-man; Mr. Widmer is dead; Mr. Fritz (the defendant) came at the request of myself and Mr. Faber, to see Mr. Faber and myself at the office of Munter & Faber; Mr. Fritz there stated the last conversation between himself and Mr. Widmer, in which he stated Mr. Widmer placed in his hands certain notes which Mr. Widmer had taken for his security, naming them as Mr. Strassburger for $2,000, Senator Spencer for $2,500, Senator Hinds $2,000; I think Mr. Fritz named Mr. Warner and Mr. Buckley, but am not sure; he also stated that Mr. Widmer said that he held enough paper on high parties to secure his bondsmen against any charges that Mr. Lotz could bring; I never saw those papers; Mr. Fritz stated further that Mr. Widmer said when he was alive that this money was taken from public funds; Mr. Fritz has stated to me several times that he would give up these notes as he proposed to keep them to clear up Widmer's name.

Cross-examination—

Mr. Fritz stated that this money was spent for political uses; that Mr. Widmer so stated to him; Mr. Fritz, to the best of my belief, said that this money was government money; the money referred to as loaned to parties named and others was told to me by Fritz to be government money; we claimed those papers as belonging to the administrator, Mr. Hatchett; after the statement made to me that the money was government property, we claimed the notes of Fritz for the administrator of Mr. Widmer.

Re-direct.

Mr. Widmer's means outside his position (as collector) from my knowledge of him were not much; he had scarcely anything of his own; he was carrying on a little groggery establishment—think the business was closed before his appointment as collector; he told me he had made nothing in the business.

E. R. MITCHELL

Being sworn, says :
By Gen. Morgan—

Q. Look at the accounts (Exhibits "H") which are shown you and state whether during the period covered by these accounts you were cashier of the First National Bank of Montgomery?

A. I was.

Q. How long before this had you been cashier. (From Nov. 1872 to Feb. 8, 1873.)

A. From the time of the organization of the bank in 1871, I continued to be cashier until about March 1873.

Q. State whether Geo. E. Spencer had any account with that bank before Nov. 19, 1872?

A. Not to my knowledge or recollection.

Q. State whether J. J. Hinds had any account with that bank prior to Nov. 19, 1872?

A. Not to my recollection.

Q. State whether D. C. Whiting had any account with that bank prior to Oct. 26, 1872?

A. Not that I recollect.

Q. Were either Spencer or Hinds engaged in any commercial business in the city of Montgomery, between Nov. 19, 1872 and Feb. 1873?

A. Not that I know of or ever heard of.

Q. State whether Hinds knew of the state of Spencer's account, both as to deposits and checks?

A. He knew as to the condition of Spencer's accounts as shown by the books from time to time as well as Spencer did.

Q. Why did you permit Hinds to become acquainted with the condition of Spencer's account.

A. Because I regarded their interests as identical; they came in together and made their first deposits and opened their accounts at the same time, and frequently conversed with each other in my presence as to the condition of their accounts.

Q. Do you know, from information received from Spencer, Hinds or Whiting, that any of the money used was in the interest of Spencer's election?

A. To my knowledge, I do not know; as a bank officer I avoided knowing what they did with their money.

Q, If Hinds at any time made a request of you to advance money for him, state when it was, the amount he wanted and all the circumstances attending the request, and state what was done by you and by Hinds to carry his wishes into effect?

A. Some time about the middle of January, 1873, Hinds stated to me that he would need a thousand or more dollars, could not tell exactly when he would need it, it might be the next day or during the week, but when he did want it he must have it, and as he did not have that amount of money on deposit asked if the bank would advance him what he needed, to the extent of $1,000; I replied the bank could not advance him any money, but that he might prepare himself by drawing drafts and the bank would collect and place to his credit when paid; and if he needed money in the meantime, and was compelled to have it as he said, that I would assist him in getting the money until the drafts were paid. To this arrangement he consented and drew two drafts for $1,000 each upon parties in Washington or New York, I do not know but am inclined to think they were in Washington, and requested me, in my individual name, to forward the drafts for collection, as he did not wish the record of the drafts to be placed upon the bank books so as to let any one know where he got his money from. In due course of mail I received advices that one of the drafts was paid, and after waiting two or three days, not hearing from the other draft and knowing if it was not paid that I would have received a notice of protest, I, therefore, concluded that both drafts were paid and so entered them to Hind's credit upon the books of the bank, and he checked the same out as he required it. Sometime after I left the bank I was informed that the draft which I supposed had been paid was not paid, and no trace could be found of where the draft was; I then, by correspondence with Hinds, while he was at Washington, obtained a duplicate draft and the bank collected the same. When Hinds gave me these drafts he, at my request, sent telegrams to the parties notifying them of his having drawn upon them, and to see that they were promptly paid. These telegrams he sent up the railroad by hand to some point upon the road that was in telegraphic communication, in place of having them go through the Montgomery office. He remarked to me at the time that his object was to prevent any person obtaining any knowledge of the draft.

Q. State whether Spencer and Hinds drew their balances on the 4th of Dec., whether they came together and if they spoke of leaving the city?

A. Sometime in the early part of December, from the bank account it appears it was the 4th of December, they both came into the bank and requested to know their balances, and drew the same as they were going to leave on that evening or the next day.

Q. What was the real balance Spencer drew on that day?

A. It was $10,785.00, paid by the bank as follows: One check on New York for $5,085.00, another for $3,385.00 on New York, another for $2,250.00 on Mobile, and $115.00 in currency. All the drafts were drawn in his own favor. The next day, owing to an error in stating the balance, he returned $650, which had been overpaid him the day previous.

Q. State any conversation you have heard between Hinds and Spencer, or between Hinds and any other persons, in reference to the bestowal of offices by Spencer or through his influence, to secure his election to the senate, or any other arrangements which were made by the managers for Spencer to secure that result, and state when the conversations occurred?

A. I have heard no conversation between Hinds and

Spencer, but Hinds told me that he had everything arranged, and that they would win if they succeeded in fixing one thing that night, and that was to get a democratic senator to be absent at home at the time the vote was to be taken; that they had fixed more democratic senators than the democrats could possibly take away of republican senators. This was in reference to the Martin-Miller contest. In another conversation in Hinds' room, when five or six persons were present, the suggestion of getting a democratic senator to be absent was made, and Hinds remarked "we have fixed him." Several persons told me Spencer had promised them federal offices, but I can't now recollect the persons or offices that were promised, but there were at least five or six or more persons who stated that Spencer had promised them office for their influence and services in his behalf. Sometime after Mr. Spencer's election, about a month, Mr. Rob't Barber told me he had done a heap of work for Spencer, had worked night and day and that Spencer had promised him to have him appointed U. S. Marshal as soon as Gen. Healey's term expired which was either to be that fall or the next spring; that he, had received several letters from Spencer, in which Spencer stated that there was no doubt about his getting the office and to rest easy. During the next year, Barber, not having received the appointment, and from certain actions of Spencer which led him to believe that he would not fulfill his promises and was acting treacherously, he became angry with Spencer and wrote him some very harsh letters, in which, he stated to me, he told Spencer he knew better than to go back on him entirely. In reply to these letters Spencer sent him an appointment to an office in the Mobile custom house, by which he was to draw his pay as an officer of the custom house and still remain at Montgomery, and render no service. Spencer stated that this pay would help him to provide for his family until something better should turn up. Barber then remarked to me that Spencer expected to keep him quiet by throwing this little crumb of an office into his hands; but he would find himself mistaken in the man he was dealing with. I saw a letter from Goodloe, the collector of the port of Mobile, after Barber said he had written Spencer, in which he enclosed the form of an application upon which he was to make his application for the appointment, with the usual stipulations, which application was to appear as an original from Barber without any suggestion from Goodloe, and when made out, sent to him, and he would arrange the balance; that there was no necessity for him (Barber) to come to Mo-

bile; but that when the month expired he would send him
the blanks for him to sign and he would send him his pay.

When Reynolds received the appointment of collector of
the port of Mobile, it was stated to me by several of Spencer's
friends, that he would never be confirmed if it was in the
power of Spencer to prevent it, as he had promised and
pledged Goodloe to get him that place as a reward for his
services in his behalf in the legislature.

Some time during the year 1874, Patrick Robinson told me
that Wilson, P. M., was indebted to him for the appointment,
as Spencer was greatly indebted to him for the work done in
his behalf as senator, and in acknowledgment of the same
Spencer promised and agreed to have any one appointed
postmaster at Montgomery that Robinson wished, and as
Wilson had been clerking for him, he told Spencer to make
Wilson postmaster; that Spencer and his friends had used
his rooms for their meetings with the negro members, and
that he had furnished lights and whisky for the crowd.

Whiting also told me he had got an appointment in the
custom house at Mobile in consideration of his services for
Spencer. Ben DeLemos, of Lowndes county, also told me
that Spencer had also procured his appointment in the custom house. I knew he had done a great deal of work for
Spencer's election. There are others who secured appointments from Spencer, who had worked for Spencer's election,
that I do not now remember.

E. R. MITCHELL.

In accordance with the request of the committee made at
the close of my examination I have examined my letter book,
and from the information it contains. I state further that the
sum of $1,990, which was placed to the credit of J. J. Hinds'
account in the First National Bank of Montgomery, on the
27th day of January, 1873, was the proceeds of the two drafts
or bills mentioned in my testimony as being drawn on parties
in New York or Washington on January 22, 1873. One of
these drafts was drawn on George E. Spencer and the other
on John H. Semmes, as I read the name on my letter book.
The draft on Spencer was first paid, and both were payable
at Washington, D. C.

E. R. MITCHELL.

JACKSON MORGAN, (COL'D)

Being sworn, says:

I knew Mr. Widmer, late revenue collector of the middle
district of this State. I was a messenger in the office. I had
his personal effects in charge. I knew more about his per-

sonal matters than any man in town.  I was with him at his death.  I had charge of his things.  I took his keys out of his pocket when he died.  Mr. Farden had the outside key to his safe.  The key to the inside, or private drawer in which Mr. Widmer kept his private papers, was in his pantaloon's pocket and was taken out by me and after his death, in the presence of Mr. Olcott and Mr. Crenshaw, I turned the key to this drawer over to Mr. Fritz as soon as I had shrouded Mr. Widmer.

By General Morgan:

Q.  State what you know of any dealings between Mr. Spencer or Mr. Hinds with Mr. Widmer?

A.  During Mr. Widmer's sickness I stayed with him.  He talked with me a great deal and confided in me as much as in any one.  I nursed him and stayed with him until he died.  One morning after he was arrested, he was confined in his room instead of being taken to jail.  While there I had a conversation with him.  The first word he said to me, he hated to tell me, was "Well, Morgan, I am arrested; if they would untie my hands and let me write, I have more than enough to pay my default."  I remember distinctly his saying "Spencer owes me more than enough to pay my default."  He said he had a note on Mr. Hinds, the amount I disremember, and also a note on Warner for either five hundred or five thousand dollars.  My best recollection is five thousand.  He said he had a note on Spencer, I don't remember the amount.  I have seen these notes and also a note on Strassberger upon which there was a payment.  After Widmer's arrest he went to his safe and took some papers out of a lower drawer and put them in his private drawer.  I know the notes were in his drawer when he died.  Mr. Widmer was not an extravagant man—the most of the money he spent was in treating his friends after supper.

By Mr. Price:

Q.  How long after Mr. Widmer's arrest before he was taken sick with the fever with which he died?

A.  Either ten or eleven days.

By General Morgan:

Q.  Did you hear Mr. Widmer say he had written to Mr. Spencer?

A.  I did, and I know he wrote to Mr. Spencer at least three times, for I mailed the letters, and know he got no answer from Spencer.  He said he did not know what to think of Mr. Spencer.

JACKSON MORGAN.

### HENRY E. FABER,

Being sworn, says:

I knew Francis Widmer. I was one of the sureties on his bond as collector of internal revenue for the middle district of Alabama.

By Mr. Little:

Q. Was he a defaulter?

A. He was so declared.

Q. Did he assign any cause for his default?

A. He told me he had loaned money to Hinds for Spencer, and that he had either Hinds' or Hinds and Spencer's, or Spencer's notes, as well as those of other persons. That the notes he held of these persons would more than cover his deficiency.

Q. What became of those notes?

A. Mr. Widmer always told us he had them in his private box in his safe. After his death, the box and contents disappeared, and we could never get possession of it.

Q. Did you ever have any conversation with Lewis Fritz about those notes or the private box?

A. I did, repeatedly. He told me on the cars, between Montgomery and Deatsville, while the yellow fever was prevailing in Montgomery, and shortly after Widmer's death, that the box was in his possession, and that notes of value were therein, and that he would surrender the box and contents, which would be sufficient to make good any deficiency of Widmer's and keep his bondsmen from being in any way troubled. He afterwards failed to comply with his promise and one of the bondsmen, during my absence, instituted suit against him before a U. S. commissioner, and he was bound over to appear to answer any action the grand jury might take. This is the present condition of the matter.

Q. In the conversation, did he mention the Hinds and Spencer note?

A. He did. Widmer stated to the chief of the settlement bureau of the revenue department, who discovered a deficiency in his accounts of about $10,000 here and about $9,000 in Selma, that he (Widmer) had notes on Hinds, Spencer, Buckley and Strassburger, that would cover all of his alleged deficiencies. He also stated this money was furnished for party and political purposes to Hinds, Spencer and Buckley.

Q. When was the deficiency definitely ascertained?

A. In the fall of 1873.

Q. Was there any political campaign that year?

A. There was not.

Q. When was the last political campaign previous to the ascertainment of this deficiency?

A. The campaign of 1872.

Q. Did Hinds and Spencer take an interest in the campaign of 1872?

A. They did. Spencer was re-elected to the U. S. senate.-
By Mr. Price—

Q. Do you hold any office?

A. I am mayor of the city of Montgomery, and have been for three terms.

HENRY E. FABER.

C. J. CAMPBELL

Being sworn, says:

I am cashier of the First National Bank of Montgomery. The accounts of Geo. E. Spencer, J. J. Hinds, and D. C. Whiting, chairman, marked Exhibit " H, 1, 2," are true statements as shown by the books of the bank.

Q. Have they ever had any accounts before or since that time with your bank?

A. Not that I know of.

Q. Do you know of any commercial or other business engaged in by Hinds, Spencer or Whiting?

A. I do not.

C. J. CAMHBELL.

EXHIBIT H—I.

Geo. E. Spencer, in account with First National Bank of Montgomery.

| Dr. | | | | Cr. | | |
|---|---|---|---|---|---|---|
| 1872. | | | | 1872. | | |
| Nov. 20. | To check.... | $ | 200 00 | Nov. 19. | By deposit....$ | 7,000 00 |
| " 23. | " " (2) | | 450 00 | " 21. | " " | 800 00 |
| " 25. | " " | | 200 00 | Dec. 2. | " " | 4,487 00 |
| " 26. | " " | | 200 00 | " 5. | " " | 650 00 |
| " 27. | " " | | 100 00 | " 5. | " " | 497 50 |
| " 28. | " " | | 100 00 | | | |
| " 30. | " " | | 150 00 | | | $ 13,435 00 |
| Dec. 2. | " " | | 100 00 | | | |
| " 3. | " " | | 500 00 | | | |
| " 4. | " " (3) | | 11,435 00 | | | |
| | | | $13,435 00 | | | |

D. C. Whiting, Chairman, in account with First National Bank of Montgomery.

| Dr. | | | | Cr. | | |
|---|---|---|---|---|---|---|
| 1872. | | | | 1872. | | |
| Oct. 26. | To check (2) | $ 1,000 00 | | Oct. 26. | By deposit....$ | 2,493 75 |
| " 23. | " " | 500 00 | | Dec. 5. | " " | 1,000 00 |
| Nov. 2. | " " (2) | 993 75 | | | | |
| Dec. 5. | " " | 1,000 00 | | | | $ 3,493 75 |
| | | $ 3,493 75 | | | | |

## EXHIBIT H—H.

J. J. Hinds, in account with First National Bank of Montgomery.

| Dr. | | | | Cr. |
|---|---|---|---|---|
| 1872. | | | 1872. | |
| Nov. 21. | To check....$ 50 00 | | Nov. 19. | By deposit....$ 1,300 00 |
| " 22. | " " 50 00 | | " 22. | " " 983 83 |
| Dec. 4. | " " 2,650 34 | | Dec. 5. | " " 466 51 |
| " 10. | " " 500 00 | | " 10. | " " 2,985 00 |
| " 11. | " " 2,485 00 | | " 19. | " " 2,000 00 |
| " 20. | " " 200 00 | | " 21. | " " 1,480 00 |
| " 23. | " " 3,280 00 | | 1873. | |
| 1873. | | | Jan. 17. | " " 1,990 00 |
| Jan. 27. | " " 1,000 00 | | Feb. 8. | " " 995 00 |
| " 31. | " " 100 00 | | | |
| Feb. 3. | " " (2) 200 00 | | | $ 12,200 34 |
| " 4. | " " 100 00 | | | |
| " 8. | " " (3) 800 00 | | | |
| " 11. | " " 426 00 | | | |
| " 12. | " " 250 00 | | | |
| " 14. | " " 109 00 | | | |
| | $ 12,200 34 | | | |

### R. W. HEALY

Being sworn, says :

I came to Alabama in March, 1865; since that time I have been prominently and actively connected with the Republican party ; I was chairman of the republican State executive committee from 1870 to 1872, and was succeeded by D. C. Whiting ; I have held the office of U. S. marshal for the southern and middle districts of Alabama for eight years, and have held that office continuously up to the present time, except during a short time it was held by J. J. Hinds, from April 1st to the 22d of that month of the present year.

By Gen. Morgan—

Q. Do you think you were acquainted with the opinions of the republican party in this State in 1872?

A. I think I was.

Q. Do you believe Gen. Spencer at the time of his re-election was the choice of that party for U. S. Senator?

A. I don't think he was the choice of the best men of the party, but he may have been the choice of a majority of the party ; I don't think he would have been re-elected in 1872, but for certain circumstances.

Q. Please to state fully the circumstances to which you refer?

A. It was the desire of the leading men of the party, the ablest and best, to retain control of the legislative branch of the State government, which they firmly believed they had won by the election. The certificates of election were given to the democratic candidates for the legislature from Barbour and Marengo, both of which counties gave a republican majority. This would have given the democrats control of both houses at the organization; the republicans believing they would not get justice in the matter of a contest for the seats for those counties, determined to go into a separate organization, which they did. Gen. Spencer was not here at the organization and was not one of the advisers. In that organization there was a minority opposed to his election, but after his arrival it appeared to be understood among many of the republicans that he had gone into negotiations with the democrats with the view of their electing him to the senate on condition that he broke up the court house assembly and brought his friends to the capitol. This forced them into a unanimous support of himself, as they preferred the success of the party to the defeat of an individual to the senate.

Q. Did you and other gentlemen in the lead of the minority of which you speak, believe that Spencer was capable of colluding with the democrats in the manner you allude to, to secure his election?

A. Yes, sir, I think several believed it. It became a party necessity to elect him to save the organization at the court house and preserve it afterwards at the capitol, as the great desire of the leaders was to have the legislature in harmony with the executive.

Q. Who were Spencer's most active personal friends in Montgomery at that time in procuring his election and afterwards providing for his retaining his seat?

A. Jerome J. Hinds was very active; also D. C. Whiting, Robert Barber, and several members of the legislature, amongst whom were P. G. Clarke, Gen. Dustan, J. C. Goodloe, and some other members from north Alabama.

Q. Did you at that time enjoy the confidence of the gentlemen you have named, notwithstanding you were an advocate of the court house assembly?

A. I did not.

Q. Why not?

A. I presume it was because I was believed not to be heartily supporting Mr. Spencer.

Q. Were you apprised at the time by rumors among the knowing members of the legislature, or by any facts that come to your knowledge, of any promises of official patronage made by Spencer or his immediate friends, to cause men to adhere to him in procuring his election. If so, please state all you know on that subject?

A. I don't know personally of any such promises, but rumors were prevailing among the knowing men of the assembly that such promises were made promiscuously.

Q. State whether the rumors of which you speak as prevailing at the time connected the names of certain individuals with certain offices to be afterwards conferred?

A. Yes, sir.

Q. As far as you can, please state what individuals were thus rumored as having office promised who afterwards received appointments?

A. Two thus received appointment, but they are now associated with me in the service and I prefer not to give their names.

Q. Do you know of any understanding among the Republicans to prevent an election by the fusion legislature of a U. S. Senator?

A. I know of nothing except by public rumor.

Q. Do you know whether J. J. Moulton was here assisting in Spencer's election?

A. I think he was.

Q. Was he taking an active part in that matter?

A. I so understood.

Q. Where did J. J. Hinds live at the time of Spencer's election?

A. It was said, at Decatur.

Q. Do you know of any business at or about the city of Montgomery he or Spencer had of mercantile or commercial character, which would require the use of ten or twelve thousand dollars ($10,000 or $12,000) between the 19th of November, 1872, and the 14th of February, 1873?

A. I do not.

Q. Did either of them have any business not connected with politics?

A. Not that I know of, except that Hinds was a mail contractor; but if he had any contracts about here I do not know of them.

Q. Did Mr. Hinds or Mr. Spencer have the reputation of being wealthy?

A. They did not.

Q. Did you know Francis Widmer in Nov., 1872?

A. I did; he was collector of internal revenue for the second Alabama district.

Q. What was his apparent condition as to property and wealth?

A. He was not a man of property or wealth.

Q. Please examine these letters (Exhibits E. and F., Spencer's letters to "My dear Barber,") and state whether there was a deputy U. S. marshal acting under you at the time mentioned in these letters?

A. There was.

Q. Did he have any authority from you to make arrests in Tallapoosa, Randolph and Cleburne counties?

A. He had authority to make arrests upon capiases issued by legal authority, and he had only such authority.

Q. Did you demand the assistance of federal troops in the counties named to aid in the execution of any process that came to your hands?

A. A large number of indictments for violations of the enforcement act were had at the November term, 1871. The capiases on those indictments were returnable to the May term, 1872. Anticipating difficulty in making arrests under them, I applied for military aid early in the year 1872, in January or February. In compliance with that application, a company of cavalry was ordered by the secretary of war to Opelika which I designated as the station. After its arrival, which was some time early in March, they used it pretty actively in making arrests up to the commencement of the spring court, which was the 4th Monday in May. After that I do not recollect an instance in which they were used for the purposes required.

Q. After the May term of the court in 1872, were you aware of any attempts to resist the process of the U. S. courts, by the people of the counties of Randolph, Cleburne and Tallapoosa, or of that part of the State?

A. I was not.

Q. Did Gen. Spencer have any authority to control your deputies?

A. He had not. If that (Spencer's letter to Barber, telling him, "I wish Randolph, deputy U. S. marshal, would use the company at Opelika in making arrests in Tallapoosa, Randolph and Cleburne, as ——— suggests,") was ever communicated to Mr. Randolph, I have no knowledge of it.

Q. Did you know anything of this proposition of Spencer as set forth in his letter of October 22, 1872?

A. I have seen the letter and am aware of the proposition for the first time to-day.

Q. Are you acquainted with the handwriting of Geo. E. Spencer, and if so, do the letters marked Exhibits "E." and "F." bear his signature?

A. I am. They bear his signature.

Q. Was Squires or Perrin either deputy marshals under you at any time?

A. Mr. Squires never was. Perrin held a temporary appointment in 1874.

Q. Did Squires ever hold any office in the revenue deparment?

A. I think he did.

By Gen. Coon—

Q. Do you know of troops ever having been used by your authority for any other purpose than the enforcement of the laws and the protection of voters in the State?

A. They were never otherwise used by my authority.

Q. Is it your opinion that the proposition made by senator Spencer in his letter of October 22, 1872, in reference to the illegitimate use of troops, would have been approved by the party generally in the State, had it been made known to them?

A. I don't believe they would have approved the measure except for the purpose only of keeping the peace and offer-ing protection to the people generally without regard to politics. R. W. HEALY.

### WADE A. M'BRYDE

Being sworn, says:

I knew Francis Widmer from the winter of 1865 up to the time of his death, which occurred Oct. 14, 1873. He had no visible property that I know of except his furniture. I had a conversation with him shortly before his death, at the foot of the steps going up into his room. He said he had been badly treated, and, to use his own language, " that my head has been cut off; but mine is not the last one that is going to come off. These damned thieves have got money from me, and at the proper time I will expose them all, from senator down." Widmer was a republican.

WADE A. McBRYDE.

### LOUIS FRITZ, JR.,

Being sworn, says:

I knew Francis Widmer. I was in business with him. He went out of business in 1869, when he was appointed revenue collector. He had no property or money when he went out of business. I think he got his appointment through Mr. Buckley. He was an honest man and was con-sidered a good business man.

Q. When he was in office, was he an extravagant man?

A. I can't say that he was. He was a generous, liberal man. He did not gamble, that I know of. I was very sel-dom with him after office hours.

11

Q. Do you know any transactions he had with Hinds or Spencer?

A. I do not.

Q. Did you ever see any notes taken by him from Hinds or Spencer?

A. I did not.

Q. Do you remember a conversation had with Mr. Hatchett when Judge Rice was present?

A. I do. They called on me and stated they wanted all notes and other evidences of indebtedness, and all other papers I had belonging to Mr. Widmer. They asked me for Spencer's note. They also asked for notes of Warner, Buckley and Hinds. I told them I had none. I think they referred to conversations I had with Messrs. Faber and Goetter, in which I said I had notes. I told them I had notes I would tell them of if they would not tell any living soul. They promised, and I told them I had notes on Strassburger, and nothing was said concerning any notes of Hinds or Spencer. At that interview their names were not mentioned.

Q. Did you see Hinds here just about the time of Widmer's death?

A. It may have been a week or less, or more; he was here and I saw him on the street, but I did not see him in my office or at Widmer's.

Q. What did you do with Strassburger's notes?

A. I turned them over to the sheriff.

Q. Where did you get these notes?

A. He gave them to me before his death three or four days; he gave me a package and told me not to part with it, not to open it, and not to let it go out of my hands; I took the papers and locked them up in my trunk; I took them out after his death and found two notes for $1,000 each; I kept them until the sheriff called on me for them.

Q. Did you give them to the sheriff before you saw Hinds here?

A. It was after; it may have been three or four weeks afterwards.

Q. Was there any interview in which Messrs. Faber or Goetter, or Wolffe, asked you concerning any notes of Hinds or Spencer?

A. No, sir.

Q. Did you know before Widmer's death what the package contained?

A. No, sir.

Q. What injunction of secrecy did Widmer impose?

A. None but what I have stated.

Q. Then why was it when you spoke to Goetter and Faber about it you made them promise they would never tell it to any human being.

A. As they were given to me that way I did not care to have the matter, exposed as Mr. Strassburger was in business here.

Q. Did you know the consideration of the notes?

A. I did not.

Q. What exposure did you think would be involved of an improper character by the mere fact that a dead man's estate was found to possess two notes against a man for $1,000 each?

A. I thought it might injure him as a business man here.

Q. Did you not know he would have to pay the notes to Widmer's estate if he owed them?

A. I did.

Q. Were the notes on Strassburger & Co., or H. Strassburger?

A. On H. Strassburger.

Q. Was Strassburger not able to pay them at that time?

A. I don't know; I should judge from appearances he was.

Q. Did you consider it would be any injury to a man to pay a debt?

A. Of course not.

Q. Did you not have some better and stronger reason for the solemn promise you exacted of Faber and Goetter not to tell a living soul of the notes?

A. I did not.

Q. Did you not have some reason to believe the money obtained by those notes was public funds?

A. I did not, I told them only of the Strassburger notes.

Q. Did you and Hinds not eat together while he was here?

A. I never eat or drank with him in my life.

Q. Did you, or your wife, get a letter from Hinds or Spencer about that time or afterwards?

A. I did not, nor did my wife.

Q. Did you ever speak to Faber about a box containing notes belonging to Widmer?

A. I did not.

Q. Did you have a key to one of the inner drawers or doors of Widmer's safe, or to some place where he kept his private papers?

A. No, sir.

Q. Was the safe unlocked with a key?

A. It was; Farden had both keys to the safe; I never, at the time of Widmer's death or afterwards, had any key to the safe.

Q. Did not Jackson Morgan take the inside key from Widmer's pocket, that belonged to the safe, and give it to you?

A. No, sir; he gave me the keys to his desk and the furniture that belonged to me—the wardrobe and bureau drawers.

Q. Did Widmer have any private papers in his bureau drawers?

A. Not that I know of.

Q. When Widmer's safe was examined were any notes or evidences of debt found?

A. I was not there when it was opened.

Q. How long before Widmer's death before Hinds was here?

A. I don't remember; they were together in Widmer's office when I saw them; this was before the yellow fever broke out.

Q. Was that a severe epidemic?

A. It was, and was very fatal; there were a number of deaths.

Q. Did you do more than to speak to Hinds when he was here?

A. I did not. I had no conversation with him.

Q. Where was Hinds stopping when in Montgomery?

A. At the Madison House.

Q. Where did he stop when he came that time?

A. I don't know.

Q. Do you know of Mr. Widmer's lending any one large sums of money before his death?

A. I do not of my own knowledge. Widmer told me once, after an interview with Faber, that Faber had insulted him, and remarked that if he darkened his door again he would shoot him down like a dog; that that was the thanks he got for favors shown that man.

Q. How long after Widmer's death before you told Faber and Gœtter of these notes?

A. It was the day after his burial. I telegraphed my wife of Widmer's death; she was at Deatsville. Mr. Faber sent me word he was going up, and Mrs. Fritz wanted me to come up and unless I came she would come down. I went up, and as I came back the next day I told Mr. Faber to tell Mr. Gœtter I intended to do all in my humble power to vindicate Widmer; that I had some papers in my possession.

I was sent for as soon as I got to town by Messrs Faber and Gœtter, at Faber's store. Gœtter told me I had some papers and they wanted to know what I had. I told them I would tell them if they would tell no living soul what papers I had. They promised and I told them I had the notes of Strassburger. They said they wanted an administrator and would have me appointed. I told them there was no use of an administrator, there was nothing to administer upon. We then separated.

Q. At this time had you seen the notes?

A. I had just glanced at them as I came from the train. I didn't take in the amount. I did not know whether they were for five cents, or five thousand or fifty thousand dollars.

Q. How did you know they were promissory notes?

A. I saw they commenced to read "I promise to pay Francis Widmer," and could see they were signed by Strassburger.

Q. If these were notes, what made you think there was no use to administer?

A. I did not know what the amounts were. He had no real estate or other property, and I knew of nothing to administer upon except the notes.

Q. What did you expect to do with the notes?

A. I expected to hold them according to my instructions.

Q. What were your instructions?

A. Not to allow them to go out of my hands until he called for them.

Q. Did you intend to hold on to them?

A. I did until I delivered them to the sheriff on his demand.

Q. You did not then hold them till Widmer called for them?

A. Nor, sir, he died.

Q. If you intended to hold them till Widmer called for them according to your instructions, after his death, you would have been likely to have held them until the resurrection?

A. Possibly, sir.

Q. Did you not intend to keep them and collect the money on them?

A. Nor, sir. I intended to vindicate Widmer as far as laid in my humble power.

Q. If that was your intention, why did you not turn the notes over to the securities?

A. I thought them as good in my hands as theirs.

Q. Did not Mr. Hinds, when he came here, buy those notes from you?

A. He did not.

Q. How long after Widmer's death before the sheriff demanded the notes?

A. About three weeks.

Q. Under what process?

A. A writ of seizure issued at the suit of W. T. Hatchett, administrator. I delivered the notes immediately the call was made.

Q. Did not Hatchett demand the notes before the writ of seizure issued?

A. They first requested all papers I had, afterwards they demanded the Spencer and Hinds notes—they may have said all other papers of indebtedness.

Q. Why did you not deliver them when demanded?

A. I thought them as safe in my hands as the administrators.

Q. Did you not conceal from them that you had the notes of Strassburger?

A. I did not?

Q. What inducement had you for withholding from the lawful administrator of Widmer, the notes of Strassburger you held at the time this demand was made?

A. None at all, except the request of Mr. Widmer that I should not allow them to go out of my hands.

Q. Did you claim no interest in these notes as being in any way your property?

A. No, sir.

Q. Did you not refuse to give them up because you believed they would be the basis of a criminal prosecution against Strassburger for having converted money belonging to the United States?

A. No, sir.

(Signed,)                    LOUIS FRITZ, Jr.

MOBILE, June 12, 1875.

The committee met pursuant to notice this day at 12 M., at the Court-house of Mobile county. Members of the committee present—Messrs. Brewer, Coon and Price. Wm. Stribling being duly sworn, upon his oath testifies as follows:

By Mr. Price—

Q. Were you a member of the general assembly of Alabama in the year 1872, if so, of what branch?

A. I was a member of the general assembly in 1872, was a member of the lower house of what is known as the capitol legislature.

Q. Was there any other organization in Montgomery in the winter of 1872, claiming to be a general assembly?

A. There was what was called a court-house legislature.

Q. Of whom or what political party was that court-house legislature composed?

A. It was called the legislature of the republican or radical party.

Q. Were you in Montgomery at the time, or before the day set by law for the election of U. S. Senator?

A. I was.

Q. Do you know where the leading republicans kept their headquarters in Montgomery while the senatorial election was pending?

A. I think at the Madison house.

Q. Do you know of any effort being made to secure the election of Gen. Spencer to the U. S. Senate?

A. I know that Gen. Spencer was there and a candidate for U. S. Senator, and that his friends Pelham, Brainard, W. Jones, Whitney and others were actually working in his interests, and they were generally about the Madison house.

Q. Just before the day of the senatorial election, was there any effort made by Gen. Spencer or his friends to influence your action favorable to Gen. Spencer's election to the Senate?

A. One Sunday shortly before the day of the election, perhaps a day or so, I was in company with some gentlemen walking, we had started to take a short walk to the country. I think the company was composed of myself, Nick Stallworth, and perhaps John Chapman, and Jim Slater. We were passing the Madison house, and in front of the Madison house, we saw a group of Spencer's friends, and among them was Bill Jones of Marengo county. As we were passing Jones spoke to me, and stopped me, saying he wanted to see me. He asked me if I did not want to make some money? I told him, "yes, I did," and asked him "how?" He said "if

I would quit the capitol legislature and come down to the
court house body, that he would show me a man that would
give me eight or ten thousand dollars for doing so. I then
told him the capitol was the proper place for the legislature
to meet at, and that before I would quit that legislature, and
come down to the court house, I would lay down on the
pavement of the sidewalk where I stood and suffer my arms
beat off with a maul." He remarked that I was a fool, or to
that effect. I am not positive as to his exact words. I then
left him, and went on with my company, who were all members of the capitol legislature, and I told them about it at the
time, and we talked about it a good deal on our walk, they
approving my conduct.

Q. Do you know J. S. Perrin, and if so, state whether you
saw him at Montgomery at the time you have been speaking of?

A. I know him, I played poker with him and others at my
room at the Exchange hotel.

Q. Did you play with him and McHue at your room at
the Exchange before the conversation you had with Bill
Jones, of which you have spoken, and if so, did he quit the
game loser or winner?

A. I did play with him before the time I had the conversation and he quit the game loser, and he quit owing me
money which I had won from him in that game, and which
he has never paid me.

Q. About how long was this before the senatorial election?

A. I can't exactly say how long before; but it was only a
few days—a short time before.

Q. Do you remember any special thing that transpired in
which you participated the evening and night before the election for senator was to take place? If so, state it as fully and
particularly as you can remember.

A. If I am not mistaken, and I am partly certain that I
am not, George Ellison and myself were together a good deal
during the day before the election, and I think we walked in
the drinking saloon owned by Beebe, called the Rialto, the
evening or night of the day before the election. When we
got in, I saw Whitney and Whiting (republicans), and George
said to me, "yonder is two radicals who have plenty of money,
and they love to play poker," (referring to Whitney and
Whiting.) I said to George, "All right; if they want to play,
let's have a game;" and as we went down towards them, they
came up meeting us, and some one proposed to drink when
we met; and while we were drinking the game was proposed,

and we all agreed to play. Some one inquired where we
should go to play, and if I am not mistaken, I proposed to
get a room from Beebe, and I probably spoke to him about
it, and then I asked Mr. Beebe if he had any cards; he said
he did not. I then went off and got the cards and give them
to Beebe, and he gave them to a boy, who he said would wait
on us at the room. Then we went up stairs to the room. As
we were going up the steps, some one of them proposed that
we should send off some where and get some whisky to drink,
saying that Beebe's was not good; and to this we all agreed,
and they did send off somewhere and get some whisky in
bottles. I don't know where they sent to, but I think something was said about a "drug store." We remained in this
room over the Rialto, playing pretty much all night. They
made me banker of the game, and along about two or three
o'clock in the morning they proposed to send off and get some
cock-tails to drink. I agreed to this, and the cock-tails were
sent for. I took one of them, and very soon I became very
stupid and sleepy—so much so I could not keep awake, and
the last thing I remember was, that I was so sleepy I could
not play any more; and I told George Ellison that I must
quit and go to sleep, and got upon a lounge that was near,
and told George to be sure to wake me up at 9 o'clock in the
morning, without fail, and he promised upon the honor of a
gentleman to do so. I left my check on the table where we were
playing; and I must have lost consciousness by the time I got
on the lounge, for I do not remember anything from that time
until I was aroused by the Sergeant-at-arms (Mr. Titcomb)
and some other persons. One of them was a doctor, and I
believe one of the party was Mr. John Chapman. I think the
doctor gave me some medicine before I was taken from the
room to my room at the Exchange Hotel. My recollection is
that it was late in the evening of the day following the night
we played the game.

Q. Had you been in the habit of drinking to excess before
that time?

A. I have been drinking whisky for twenty-five years, and
have often drank to excess before; but I have never been ef-
fected by any manner of drink before as I was this time. The
effect was very serious upon me, and I don't think I have ever,
to this day, fully recovered from it. I had a long spell of
sickness after it, which I feel certain was brought on by that
night's work.

Q. Do you remember that any one aroused you while you

12

were on the lounge, before you were aroused by Mr. Titcomb
and the doctor and others?

A. I have no recollection of anything of the sort. I am
not conscious of anything from the time I went to sleep until
I was aroused by Mr. Titcomb in the evening, and even then
my mind was by no means clear. I know I was finally taken
out and carried to my room at the hotel late that evening.

Q. Did Mr. Beebe call to see you at any time during the
day you were in the room where you played?

A. If he did, I have no recollection of it in the world. I
am not conscious of anything of the kind.

Q. Do you have any recollection of taking breakfast or
anything to eat while you were in that room?

A. I have no recollection of any breakfast, or anything of
the sort; don't think I took anything to eat that day—certainly did not in that room, that I know of; and have no
knowledge of any one else eating in that room that day.

Q. How long after that night's work was it before you
were able again to take your seat in the house?

A. I was able to take my seat in a day or two after, in
time to vote for Sykes for senator, and did not vote for him.

WM. C. STRIBLING.

And the committee adjourned to meet again on Monday,
14th inst., at 1 o'clock P. M., at the office of the circuit clerk,
in the court house of Mobile county.

The committee met pursuant to adjournment at the court
house of Mobile county, this 14th June, 1875. Present—Hon.
Leroy Brewer and D. E. Coon of the committee, and Harry
Pillans, Esq.

### JOHN T. FOSTER.

Being called and sworn, deposeth and saith as follows:
Examined by H. Pillans—

Q. Please state where your residence was in the 1872;
your age and your occupation or business at that time?

A. I was living in the city of Mobile, was collector of U.
S. internal revenue for the first district of Alabama, having
an office in the custom house at Mobile; was about fifty-five
years of age.

Q. To what political party did you at that time belong?

A. To the republican party, and still belong to it.

Q. Was it known to you, and was it generally known to
the members of the republican party in and about Mobile at
that time, that George E. Spencer would be a candidate be-

fore the general assembly of Alabama for re-election to the United States Senate?

A. That was the understanding. The matter was talked about, and that was the general understanding.

Q. Do you know of any means that were taken during the fall campaign preceding the elections that year, to secure a general assembly which would be certain to re-elect Mr. Spencer? If yea, please state fully in what they consisted?

A. I don't think that I do, except so far as to make the republican party successful.

Q. Do you know the fact that there were troops sent to any part of Alabama previous to the election? .

A. I am satisfied that such was the case, as I got such information from a variety of sources.

Q. Did you ever hear any of your associates, U. S. revenue officers or others about the custom house, advocate the use of troops at that election? State fully, and what was the occasion, and who so advocated their use?

A. The most pointed conversation I had on the subject was with Lou H. Mayer (at that time assessor, but now collector of internal revenue for this district,) he requested me to assist him and others in causing troops to be sent into portions of the first collective district, to secure a fair election as he said. Several other republicans about the custom house were in favor of the use of troops at the then coming election.

Q. Into what counties in the first collective district did Mr. Mayer express a desire that troops should be sent?

A. Into Monroe, Clark, Washington, Choctaw and Marengo counties.

Q. Into what other counties (if any) out of this district did he say he wished troops to be sent?

A. Into Sumter and Pickens counties.

Q. Did you assent to Mr. Mayer's proposition to send out troops, and if not why did you assent?

A. I did not. I objected to aiding him in getting the troops sent, upon the ground that in my judgment it was not the best way to secure the largest republican vote.

Q. Was, or was not Lou H. Mayer's plan carried out?

A. Yes! There were squads of troops sent into some of the counties named, into which, however, I cannot say, but think into all.

Q. Do you know who were Spencer's warmest and leading friends, who were working for his re-election during the campaign of 1872?

A.  Yes—there were P. G. Clarke, Jacob Black, Lou H. Mayer, and Charles E. Mayer, Meyer Goldsmith, Jerome J. Hinds, DeWitt C. Whiting, Henry Cochran, P. D. Barker, Wm. R. Chisholm, Charles W. Dustan, Baker of Morgan county, Isaac Heyman of Lee county, Charles Pelham, A. W. McCullough.  These were all strong adherents of Spencer.

Q.  Do you know of any means used for raising money to carry on that campaign—if so, what were they?

A.  I do not know of any, except the means used by the assessor, Lou H. Mayer, who demanded of his assistants ten dollars a month (it might have been twenty a month) for three months, for "political purposes," (that was the way they generally phrased it).  Some of the money was paid by some of the assistant assessors.  One of them, F. M. Hill, paid it, and complained to me of it, saying that contributions ought to be voluntary, not forced.  As I have stated, it was an assessment levied on each employee.

Q.  Have you any recollection of any money being raised by Messrs. Lou H. Mayer, J. J. Moulton, and others, out of Foster's bank?

A.  I do not know.

Q.  Do you know of any effort being made by either Spencer or by his friends to influence any votes or support for Mr. Spencer, by the promise of office, or by getting office for any person or persons?

A.  I do not, so far as Spencer personally is concerned. As to Spencer's friends, I will say I was approached by J. J. Hinds and Phillip King.  This was during the session of the court house legislature, shortly previous to Spencer's election. King came alone to me, said to me that he controlled six votes in that legislature, which would not be cast for Spencer unless he (King) got some office or appointment—as he said, "something,"—and asked for an appointment from me as deputy collector.  J. J. Hinds seconded his appeal at a later time, and insisted strenuously that King should have what he wanted—that appointment of deputy collector—so that it appeared clearly that they understood one another.  I was in Montgomery at the time as member of the board of education.  King was an ex-State Senator.  There was another instance somewhat similar to this.  It was as follows:

M. G. Candee came to me and said he wanted the appointment of deputy collector for the Wilcox division, where there was a vacancy.  He did not mention Spencer's name, but he said to me that "he intended to help those who helped him, and he wanted that appointment."  Afterwards, say a half a day or a day, J. J. Hinds came to me alone, and said that

Candee wanted that appointment in the Wilcox division, and he *must* have it; and added, it is necessary for him to have it right now.

Q. When was this?

A. It was some few days (within a week) before Spencer's election.

Q. Did Candee get the appointment?

A. Yes, I made the appointment.

Q. Did you often see Spencer in Montgomery during the session of the court·house legislature, previous to Spencer's election in 1872? If so, who appeared to be his most intimate supporters—his right-hand men?

A. Yes, I saw him frequently. The ones who seemed most energetic and devoted were J. J. Hinds and M. D. Brainard. I could not say which was leader, as both seemed to do all they possibly could for Spencer.

Q. Did Phillip King get the appointment he sought from you—and if not, why? Did he get any other appointment under government about that time—and what was it—to or by whom made?

A. He did not get it, because I could not make the number of divisions necessary to give him the place without detriment to the public service. This all occurred in November and December, 1872. Lou H. Mayer succeeded me on 19th of May, 1873, and after a month or two he appointed King his deputy collector in the division which he had sought from me.

Q. Had you any knowledge or information that Spencer, or any of his friends for him, had promised the office of internal revenue collector, then held by you, to Lou H. Mayer, in the event of Spencer's re-election to the United States Senate? Answer fully.

A. I was informed before the general election repeatedly that there was such a pledge given by Spencer to Lou H. Mayer that he should be appointed collector in my stead. I heard, also, that Mayer had said that he preferred this collectorship of the port of Mobile, and I was surprised, inasmuch as the collectorship of the port of Mobile is legitimately worth nearly double the internal revenue collectorship. Mr. Mayer did get the internal revenue collectorship after Spencer's election.

Q. What friends of Spencer's actually received offices by federal appointment after Spencer's election?

A. P. D. Barker, internal revenue collector for 2d district of Alabama; Henry Cochran, postmaster at Selma; P. G. Clarke, special agent P. O. department, Selma; A. P. Wilson,

postmaster at Montgomery, Alabama; Lou H. Mayer, interna
revenue collector for 1st district of Alabama; Chas. W. Dustan, special treasury agent; Baker from Morgan county, U.
S. marshal, northern district Alabama; W. R. Chisholm, inspector of customs, Mobile; Meyer Goldsmith, re-appointed
auditor and deputy collector under J. C. Goodloe; J. C. Goodloe, collector of customs, Mobile; D. C. Whiting, appraiser of
merchandise; James Somerville, receiver in the land office,
Mobile; Peyton Finley, receiver in the land office, Montgomery; Nick S. McAfee, U. S. attorney northern and middle districts of Alabama; J. J. Hinds, U. S. marshal, mid. and so.
districts; J. J. Osburn, deputy collector, 1st district; H. A.
Candee, deputy collector, 1st district; H. J. Europe, deputy
collector, 1st district; Phillip King, deputy collector, 1st district; M. G. Candee, deputy collector, 1st district; Ben. H.
Thomas, deputy collector, 2d district, reappointed and afterwards revenue agent; M. C. Osburn, special clerk for the supervisor; R. A. Mosely, postmaster at Talladega; Gov. L. E.
Parsons, U. S. district judge for Alabama; J. L. Pennington,
governor of Dakota territory; R. M. Reynolds, collector of
the port at Mobile.

These are all the appointments which occur to me at this
time.

JOHN T. FOSTER.

And the committee adjourned to meet again at 10 o'clock
on to-morrow, at the office of the circuit clerk in the court
house of Mobile county.

MOBILE, June 15th, 1875.

The committee met pursuant to adjournment, at 10 o'clock
A. M., at the office of the circuit clerk.
Present—Messrs. L. Brewer and D. E. Coon.

### W. J. SQUIRES,

Being duly sworn, upon his oath testifies as follows:
By Mr. Brewer—
Q. Please state where you lived in 1872, and what was
your occupation?
A. I resided in Mobile, Ala., in the year 1872, and was
deputy U. S. marshal during a portion of the summer and
fall of that year.
Q. Did you participate actively in the campaign of that
year?
A. I did.
Q. Was it understood at the commencement, and during

the campaign, that Spencer would be a candidate for re-election to the U. S. Senate?

A. It was, as a matter of fact; the republican state convention was organized, and run with that object in view, and the whole campaign was conducted for the purpose of securing a majority of Spencer's friends in the ensuing legislature.

Q. Were you a friend of Gen. Spencer's in that campaign, and did you have ample opportunity to know the plans and schemes of Spencer and his friends?

A. I was his friend and had the opportunity to know what was going on.

Q. Do you know of the U. S. troops being used for the purpose of securing the election of Spencer to the United States Senate?

A. I know of troops being used for political purposes on at least three different occasions. One squad of infantry, under control of J. S. Perrin, deputy assessor U. S. revenue, was sent up through Washington county, and intended also to operate in Clark county for the purpose of encouraging negroes, and intimidating the whites. Their ostensible purpose was to prosecute a search for illicit distilleries—the real object being what I have already stated.

Another squad of infantry was sent by boat to report to J. S. Perrin at Camden, Wilcox, Monroe and Conecuh counties.

A squad of cavalry was sent up the Alabama river under the control of Geo. Turner and W. H. Holly; said Holly was deputy assessor of U. S. internal revenue. They proceeded to Monroeville, Monroe county, where a republican mass meeting was held, and addressed by said Turner. The cavalry returned by the same route.

One other squad of cavalry, under command of Lt. Nave, reported to Mr. Perrin, at Evergreen, Conecuh county, and proceeded from that place to Monroeville, Monroe county, stopping at intermediate points; from thence to Claiborne, Monroe county, thence to Mount Pleasant, Monroe county; thence to Gainestown, Clarke county; thence to Point Jackson, Clarke county; thence to Grove Hill, Clarke county; thence to Bell's Landing, Monroe county; thence to Camden, Wilcox county, returning via Bridgeport and steamboat to Mobile, Ala.

That trip occupied about two weeks of time. Meetings were held at all the places mentioned, and the national guard was organized.

Q. Were the people intimidated by these expeditions in

the sections they operated in, either by arrests being made, or blank U. S. warrants exhibited for the purpose of frightening, and running voters out of those sections.

A. Yes, the white people were intimidated. The simple presence of the U. S. troops at those times and places, accompanied by parties acting as U. S. officials, was a source of great alarm to the whites.

Some genuine warrants were issued. Mr. Perrin frequently made inquiries as to the location of numerous citizens, intimating that they were likely to be arrested. The color of probability was given of this statement by the exhibition of genuine warrants for parties, and of a large number of blank warrants which were not allowed to be examined ; but were nevertheless exhibited to convey the impression that all the white men in each neighborhood were to be arrested. This programme did result in frightening many from the country, and from the election. I will state a case in point, when we arrived at Monroeville, county seat of Monroe county, it was nearly dark ; the next morning there were scarcely any white men to be found in the place. Upon inquiry we found many had left very early that morning, fearing arrest, as they had no doubt heard that there were warrants out for their arrest; but as a matter of fact there was no warrant out for the arrest of any party in that town.

Q. Did Lou H. Mayer, U. S. assessor, and now collector of internal revenue, know of these military expeditions, and their intent?

A. He did. The troops were granted upon his requisition, and all the plans were formed by him, or submitted for his approval before they were executed.

In order to mislead the public, orders were issued that the troops should not be used for political purposes, and it was officially stated by Mr. Mayer that they were asked for simply for revenue purposes, while the real object was political, as there was no occasion for the use of troops in the collection of revenue, which Mr. Mayer well knew.

Q. Was Spencer aware that troops were being used for the purposes above mentioned?

A. He was. The plan was approved by him before it was executed. I have seen letters from him stating that it was through his efforts and representations that troops were brought to this State for political purposes.

Q. Did Spencer have any conversation with you during the campaign, if so, did he make you any promises of office, or position, or other promises as a reward for your services in his behalf in the campaign.

A. He did. He promised that he would give me a position which would bring me a living salary until the election was over, which he did, and after the election a better position.

Q. What position did he give you during the campaign?

A. I was offered the position of inspector in the custom house about the 1st of July, but having declined it, I acted as deputy U. S. Marshal during the campaign, and my name was put on the roll of the custom house officers, at the instance of Spencer, about the 15th September of that year. I was not, however, required to do any duty in the custom house; but drew my pay regularly except a considerable portion, which was retained for political purposes.

These were the only positions I received at the hands of Spencer during the campaign.

After Spencer's election, I did not get the position promised me, and did accept that of inspector in the custom house.

Q. Were you present at the time J. S. Perrin shot the hole in his hat?

A. I saw him shoot the hole in his hat. It was his proposition for getting up a sensation, in order that he could keep the troops at his disposal.

Q. Who were Spencer's most confidential friends during this campaign?

A. In Mobile, L. H. Mayer, J. J. Moulton and H. Ray Myers. In Montgomery, J. J. Hinds, D. C. Whiting, and Robt. Barber.

Q. Which of these parties named do you think was his most confidential friend and adviser?

A. It was understood that J. J. Hinds was Spencer's manager, organ and mouth-piece.

Q. Were you at Montgomery during the court house legislature and pending Spencer's election?

A. I was for a short time, but know nothing of my own knowledge of what transpired.

Q. Do you know of your own knowledge, or otherwise, of any promises of office, or, of money, made to any person for his support to secure the election of Spencer to the U. S. senate other than you have already mentioned.

A. Of my own knowledge, I know nothing more than I have already stated.

W. J. SQUIRES.

And the committee adjourned to meet again upon the call of the chairman.

MONTGOMERY, Sept. 26th, 1875.

The committee met at the call of the chairman.
Present—Messrs. Little, Price and Brewer.

### JAMES D. HARDIN

Being sworn, testifies as follows:
By Mr. Price—
Q. Where were you living, and what was your occupation in November, 1872?
A. I was living in this city, was bar-keeper for John Cashin, who kept a drinking saloon on Perry street.
Q. Do you know any facts tending to show that Geo. E. Spencer was using, or had used any money to secure his election as U. S. Senator by the court house assembly?
A. Parties came to the saloon and requested that members of the court house assembly coming there for liquor should get it, and it should be charged to Mr. Spencer, which was done.
Q. Name the parties who made this arrangement for Spencer?
A. W. V. Turner, Jones of Lowndes county, J. K. Greene of Hale, Green Lewis of Perry, Phillip Joseph, and W. E. Cruzan.
Q. Were these accounts opened?
A. They were, and were charged to them, and afterwards taken to Spencer, who paid one account of $45.00.

JAMES D. HARDIN.

### W. V. TURNER

Being sworn, testifies as follows:
By Gen. Morgan—
Q. How long have you known Geo. E. Spencer.
A. Since 1868. I met him here as a candidate for the U. S. senate in that year.
Q. Were you one of his friends and supporters in that race?
A. I was not. I was in the legislature from the county of Elmore, and voted for Mr. Warner, and Mr. Glascock for U. S. Senators.
Q. Had you any correspondence with Senator Spencer between 1868 and 1872.
A. I had, and corresponded with him frequently. Some of the letters I now have, and some I did not preserve.
Q. During the canvass in 1872, were you in the employment of Mr. Spencer as a canvasser?

A. He never employed me to canvass for him at that time, but I was employed by the executive committee. Mr. Spencer was very influential with the committee.

Q. Who was the chairman of the committee at that time?

A. D. C. Whiting.

Q. State what you know in regard to the purpose or aim of the committee regarding the election of Mr. Spencer to the U. S. Senate?

A. At that time, during the canvass of 1872, the republican party was divided into two factions—the Warner and Spencer factions.

The committee desired me to secure the votes of the ten counties of the third district for Spencer for U. S. senator; that was the object in sending me to the 3d district. Major Norris was an influential man with the negroes in the third district, but some how they had more confidence in me than Norris. I followed up Norris, and in the conventions, secured the nomination of Spencer men. I met him, and beat him at every point; Norris was a Warner man.

Q. State whether Mr. Spencer made you any promises for the services you had rendered him?

A. He promised me any position I wanted in the U. S. service that could be secured by his influence, for the services I had performed in securing for him the votes for U. S. senator.

Q. Did you secure votes for him for U. S. senator?

A. I did. I secured the votes of J. R. Treadwell, G. R. Millen, both of Russell, Henry St. Clair and Patterson of Macon, and other members of the legislature.

Q. Did you require pledges of these members to go for Spencer?

A. I did. I procured their nomination on condition that they would vote for him.

Q. State whether Spencer furnished you any money in in conducting this canvass?

A. He did. He furnished me money at any time and place I wanted it.

Q. State whether he authorized you to make any promises of office or preferment to members of the legislature in consideration of their support of him.

A. I told members, according to his instructions, that he would give them office if they would support him for the U. S. Senate.

Q. State whether or not Senator Spencer paid your expenses while you were a delegate to the National Republican Convention in June, 1872, at Philadelphia.

A.   He paid my expenses while I was there.

Q.   Were you at Montgomery at the meeting of the General Assembly in November, 1872?

A.   I was.

Q.   At what time did Senator Spencer arrive in Montgomery?

A.   Very soon after the legislature assembled.

Q.   When he arrived, did you have any conversation with him about his election for U. S. Senate?

A.   I did.   It was at his instance I was here.   I had frequent conversations with him.

Q.   Who were his chief agents or assistants in his efforts to secure his election to the U. S. Senate?

A.   J. J. Hinds, D. C. Whiting, and Calvin Goodloe.

Q.   State whether or not Spencer, in order to secure his election to the U. S. Senate, did authorize you to make any promises to members that he would secure them positions, in consideration of their support of him.

A.   He did.   He said he would secure them positions in the custom house, and other places.

Q.   Do you know of any pecuniary considerations that passed between Spencer, or any of his agents, and members of the court house legislature, in order to secure his support of him for the U. S. Senate, or anything tending to show that there was such consideration?   If so, state it.

A.   I did not see any member receive any money; but it was generally understood that Hinds was Spencer's cashier, and any member that needed money, could get it from him. I told several to go to Hinds and get money.   They had none before they went to him, and when they came back they had money—ten and twenty dollar bills.   I saw Calvin Goodloe on one occasion bring a thousand dollars into the room of Mr. Spencer while I was there, and hand it to Spencer.   Mr. Spencer seemed disappointed that it was not two thousand, and stated as much.   Spencer said he had spent two or three thousand dollars already.   Goodloe said he would get another thousand for him.   This was while the election of Spencer was pending in the court house assembly.

Q.   What use did you understand had been made by Spencer of the two or three thousand dollars?

A.   I inferred from what was said, and what I know of the correct history of the campaign, that the money was used for securing Spencer's election to the U. S. Senate.

Q.   Do you know John Cashin?

A.   I do.

Q.   What was his occupation in November, 1872?

clxxxi.

A. He was keeping a bar and billiard saloon on Perry st., near the U. S. court room.

Q. State any arrangement Mr. Spencer made with you to procure liquors for members of the court house assembly.

A. He authorized me to contract for liquor and cigars for them wherever I could—to have an open bar. I went to Cashin and made the arrangement with him.

Q. State whether the colored members of the court house assembly were supplied according to this arrangement.

A. They were liberally supplied.

Q. State whether Spencer paid the bill.

A. The day before his election he paid forty-five dollars. He told Cashin in my presence to let the colored members have anything they wanted—to spare nothing—he would be responsible.

Q. What did the bill amount to?

A. The night of the day he was elected, Cashin threw open everything—the bill was heavy—we had a jubilee—the bill was $160 or more.

Q. Has this bill ever been paid?

A. It has not. Spencer refused to pay it. Cashin went to him for it. He told Cashin to come to me for it, and if I did not pay it, to have me indicted for obtaining goods under false pretenses.

Q. During Spencer's canvass for the Senate of the U. S. did he secure to you any position? If so, what was the position, what services did you perform, and what pay did you receive?

A. He secured for me the position of inspector of customs at the port of Mobile. I performed no services; my commission was special inspector of customs; I was in the canvass; I received four dollars a day; I signed my vouchers and sent them to Mobile; I was not there during my term of office, except when I was sworn in.

Q. Why was this office bestowed upon you by Senator Spencer?

A. It was to support me in the canvass, and to secure my support of him for the Senate of the United States.

Q. By Mr. Little. How long did you hold the office?

A. Until after Spencer's election. I received $248, two months pay.

Q. Did Goodloe receive any office?

A. He was appointed collector of customs of Mobile.

WM. V. TURNER.

MONTGOMERY, December 29, 1875.
The committee met at room 31 Exchange Hotel, and

J. J. ROBINSON

Being duly sworn, testifies as follows:

I was a member of the State Senate from the 11th senatorial district during the session of '72–3, and am still a member.

I have examined the protest, signed by myself and fifteen other senators, introduced into the Senate on the 23d April, 1873, and printed in the journals of the Senate for that session on pages 640 to 644 inclusive, and the statements of facts in said protest touching the action of the Senate, and the presiding officer thereof, in the Miller-Martin contest, are true as set forth, and a full and correct account of said proceedings.

(Signed)      J. J. ROBINSON.

www.ingramcontent.com/pod-product-compliance
Lightning Source LLC
Chambersburg PA
CBHW030733280326
41926CB00086B/1303